UPLIFT

UPLIFT: How to Harness the Hidden Engine
of Continuous Renewal
Copyright © 2022 by Bruce Miller

For information contact;

Miller eMedia
www.milleremedia.com

Bruce Miller
www.ithou.com

Book and Cover design by Bruce Miller

ISBN: 978-0-9983138-6-3

First Edition: February 2022

UPLIFT

How to Harness the Hidden Engine
of Continuous Renewal

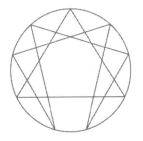

BRUCE MILLER

CONTENTS

Foreward

*"When you're new to something, you bring an ignorance
that can be highly innovative."* ~ *Rick Rubin*

WRITING BOOKS IS A LOT OF WORK. For that reason, I resisted writing this one – also because book-writing is a luxury. The endless hours take away from more productive activities like earning a living or engaging with other humans.

It was only after watching the Showtime docu-series, "Shangri-La," that I stepped off the cliff to write another book. In the series, legendary music producer, Rick Rubin explores the creative process while pushing his young recording performers to the edge that looms in every creative endeavor. His central lesson: Be willing to fail.

Rick's unorthodox style of producing inspired me to step off that cliff, so I signed up for a blind date with Hazard, and without a fixed plan for the chapters. I apologize if my storytelling appears to be all over the map (blame Rick); to my surprise, a deeper structure guides the story.

The central idea, derived from the original Enneagram, explains how the human lifetime serves as a creative engine for continuous renewal. Welcome or not, the angst and drama of daily life carry an intelligent design to build an eternal soul.

The book uses personal stories, ancient knowledge, and current events to demonstrate how natural laws and creative risk fuel the engine for perpetual self-renewal.

My wife Karen and I are now at the age where we have faced all manner of fortune and misfortune – including the basic package of marital, financial, medical, parental, and spiritual calamities. But our lifetime of spiritual work has also revealed the hidden currents and sources of buoyancy that bring meaning and Uplift to our lives. I admit to pushing Karen to appear in these pages. It's out of love, and not preference, that she graciously shares the wisdom from her journey.

Several of the scenes in *Uplift* appeared in my first book, *Fortune*. I wrote that book under the dual duress of my wife's life-threatening illness and the loss of my business. Seven years ago, when I wrote it, I had no idea what I was doing writing a book other than trying to outrun fate. In this book, I have chosen to revisit scenes from *Fortune* to show Uplift in action.

Many of the ideas in *Uplift* derive from the Fourth Way philosophies of G.I. Gurdjieff and J.G. Bennett, to whom I feel profound respect and deep gratitude. The term "continuous renewal" came from *The Intelligent Enneagram* by Anthony Blake. Thank you.

My crazy-quilt personal story shouldn't trivialize their contributions to Western thought. If I lean toward heresy, it's because I'm reporting on the life I've lived and not the one I hoped for. Plus, my Chicago sense of humor inevitably infects everything I do.

Finally, from whatever rabbit hole you may have fallen into – may it be temporary. All rollercoasters hit bottom before the mysterious chain of life pulls you up to coast again.

Wishing you Uplift,
Bruce Miller
February, 2022

Introduction
THE GIANT WOODEN HAMMER

"It is the hero, on who fall three blows of fate,
the last of which fells him as a tree is felled."
~ *Gustav Mahler*

WHERE'S THE UPLIFT?" I pleaded.

Karen's news hit like an asteroid — a medical monkey wrench thrown from the heavens. "We're supposed to be the experts," I complained.

"Just give me a moment to take this in," Karen replied, feeling fragile.

Life likes to deal a wild card – not a joker or a deuce, but an UNO card falling from the poker deck. One moment you're playing poker, the next UNO.

Seven years ago, while riding up a creaky elevator, my beloved wife collapsed in my arms. In sequence: the aging mechanism clunked to a stop, I glanced at the elevator certificate, I studied a stunning woman riding with us, and finally, the door opened with a slow screech. And then, the wild card — the one card I wasn't expecting: Karen collapsed, full weight, into my arms. I braced my legs and held her with a desperate grasp.

"Is she alright? Can I do something?" The stunning and suddenly helpful woman asked.

"Get the doctor, Doctor Jacobs, down the hall," I implored.

The scene morphed into freeze frames — an *ER* episode — until Karen murmured tenderly, "I'm not feeling well."

That's how it works. The wild card messes with time. In a symphony, the kettle drums signal the change. But here in the elevator, one moment, it was Bee Gees and the next, Shostakovich.

Dr. Jacobs sent us racing to Piedmont Hospital, where they found stage-four lung cancer metastasized to Karen's brain. Over the next three months, she endured brain surgery, chemo, radiation — the whole Megillah. We learned later, Karen had seven months to live.

Did I mention it was New Year's Eve?

By now, you're thinking, "Poor Karen," but there's more. The deck tossed me a wild card too. I'm a marketing guy, so let me run with this —

> Introducing Wild Card™ Like a wild animal, a wildfire, and the Wild West, but all in a card!

"Yes, officer," handing him my card, "I was going 90 mph, but, touché, I have a Wild Card!"

Here's how my wild card dropped. Forty minutes before the elevator, I was at the bank, inserting a death dagger into my collapsed business. In short, my business partner of 15 years left the business, took the clients, and left me with four mortgages and no income at an unemployable age. I moved money to pay the business loan, closed the accounts, then raced home to take Karen to the doctor.

I don't play chess, but I understand enough of the game to know that a single move can incapacitate two pieces simultaneously. One deft move from the Almighty short-circuited Karen's brain and checkmated my business with brutal timing.

My life capsized from a double dose of *deus ex machina* (literally, "God by machine," but better known as a movie term for a contrived plot device that pushes the story forward). Robert McKee, my screenwriting teacher, warned us budding writers:

> "*Deus ex machina* not only erases all meaning and emotion, but it's an insult to the audience. We must choose and act, for better or worse, to determine the meaning of our lives... *Deus ex machina* is an insult because it is a lie."

Was this *Deus* or *machina*? My thoughts at that moment: "THIS IS REALLY HAPPENING!!!"

My friend Brigitte, who lost a child and two marriages, wisely explained the fortune of double misfortune. "It's better this way," she counseled. "Since Karen was going through hell and needed your full-time attention, double misfortune relieves you of having to focus solely on your own private misery."

Say what?

Karen and I awaited the diagnosis in the ER as one friend after another appeared in the tiny room with New Years' food and drinks. Amid the commotion outside our door, I clutched my wild card. It screamed at me like a flashing red sign: "Don't you get it? It's a set-up, a double-dose, a double whammy — a boom-boom!"

If we were discussing music (say, Mahler's Sixth Symphony) where – boom-boom — a Giant Wooden Hammer blow at the end of the fourth movement shatters complacency, we would marvel at the composition. The Allegro shifts into Scherzo, then Andante, until — boom-boom — the finale. It's a lovely piece of music as long as the Giant Wooden Hammer isn't aimed at you.

Mahler originally wrote three hammer-blows into the piece, re-portedly for the three blows of fate in his life: the death of his eldest daughter, his fatal heart diagnosis, and his forced resignation from the Vienna Opera.

You can't reason with a hammer blow. After our guests left the ER at midnight, a stream of revelers staggered into the hospital on what was now a frigid star-crossed night. And Bruce, that's me, the golden child, the new age man, and the expert navigator of life suddenly joined their ill-starred ranks. I didn't see it then, but now know that my double hammer blow sent an unsubtle signal to my clever mind — that to penetrate my wall of despair, I would need to submit to the hand moving the pieces.

Without recounting each dip on the roller coaster, Karen wriggled free from her terminal diagnosis by latching onto an inner sense of buoyancy and doggedly following her intuition. Parting with a portion of my brain would have sent me into a tailspin, but as Karen prepared for surgery, she became calm, even serene, as she entered a new realm – what we affectionately called "Karen 2.0." Weeks later, as we snuggled pillow-to-pillow, she recounted:

"Yes, it was scary to have brain surgery," Karen whispered. "It was also necessary. I didn't know what might happen; it was just the journey that I was on. I was just going with it. I was completely going with it. It was like being on the whitewater rapids. I was in the boat, and I knew that if I became all emotional and upset about it, that could turn the boat over and cause a lot more problems. So, I chose to surrender and relax. I knew that by being relaxed, it would all go better."

I remember taking Karen's hand moments before the surgery while Dr. Solomon, a snappy Jewish anesthesiologist, waited patiently in the hall. My words gushed out in a river of feeling:

"Karen, this is crazy, but I just have to say it, whoa, I just feel so in love…."

"Isn't it funny," Karen confided, wired to the gills, "I feel myself entering a space I long dreamed of when I was young. I imagined what it would be like to surrender into love without any shame — a kind of freedom, to be myself without inhibition or fear."

Dave and Joey, Dr. Solomon's assistants, unplugged the tubes and cables and started to wheel Karen away.

"Wait," I called out. "One more goodbye." I held both of Karen's hands and whispered, "I won't miss a breath. I will hold you and be with you.

We won't be apart for a second."

"I love you, Honey," Karen whispered.

And with that, Dave and Joey wheeled Karen away. The three of them continued to kibbitz.

"I've never had anesthesia before," Karen confided.

"It's just like tequila," Joey explained. "But stronger."

The next morning in recovery, I didn't know what to expect, but a new version of Karen appeared — not the result of the expert tumor removal, but she seemed to have released a weight — a karmic load of her past. A more substantive person emerged, one settled into self — Karen 2.0.

After the surgery, Karen and I settled on *buoyancy* as our magic word. According to Archimedes, buoyancy describes the upward force that opposes an immersed object's weight. We stumbled onto buoyancy on our own. We hadn't read the 1989 landmark study that found cancer patients with a positive mental attitude (from meditation and self-hypnosis) survived twice as long as the control group.[1] Nor had we read the subsequent studies that concluded that there was no evidence that meditation or support groups increased survival rates.[2]

After Karen's daily chemo sessions, we hiked downtown in the evenings. Pausing at each light, I would send a spark of eye-sex her way– *bzzt* – a quick shot of non-researched buoyancy to empty the emotional bilge. We even joked about how when the Bible said Jesus walked on water, the scholars must have mistranslated the Aramaic word for buoyancy.

When people asked, "How did you get through it?" we couldn't share the truth that Karen and I learned to walk on water. So, we told people whatever they wanted to hear.

Buoyancy may not be the ancient secret you expected when you bought this book, but it served as our secret code for Uplift— a bit of love shorthand we winked from one to the other when the going got rough.

---

1   https://www.thelancet.com/journals/lancet/article/PIIS0140-6736(89)91551-1/fulltext

2   https://med.stanford.edu/news/all-news/2007/07/support-groups-dont-extend-survival-of-metastatic-breast-cancer-patients-stanford-study-finds.html

We found a deep trust that the universe would hold us aloft (because we had no other option).

It took me some years to deal with my wild card – my financial plight – not because the process was complicated, but because I was slow to follow Karen's lead – to relax in the tiny boat and surrender.

I drew deeply from my inner resources — one being my memory as a kid watching the plate-spinner on The Ed Sullivan Show. I was fascinated as the spinner spun five glass bowls on four-foot-long sticks while spinning eight plates on tables. He instinctively darted to keep it aloft whenever an errant plate began to wobble. His gestures seemed frantic, but I could see how calm he was on the inside. Expert plate spinning – learning to become calm on the inside while my world wobbled – is the only explanation I have for being solvent today.

I have a keen memory of Karen's plate-spinning moves. She remained ever vigilant, living in the metaphorical question, "Which plate needs a spin." If someone said, "Coffee enema," coffee would course through her colon the next day. If another friend warned, "A coffee enema is the worst possible thing you could do," that would end that. We called it "following the breadcrumbs."

As part of her regimen, Karen walked two miles a day, took a zillion supplements prescribed by an integrative oncologist in Chicago, and worked with a California cancer researcher. She also practiced yoga, swam regularly across the lake at our cabin, and took spiritual retreats — all while losing her hair and starting her long-awaited new career two weeks after surgery as the director of a chaplain training program.

Years later, I asked Dr. Bhagwan Awatramani, my meditation teacher of 25 years and a former doctor, to explain Karen's miraculous recovery:

"Karen had seven months to live but survived? What is that? Was it her healing regimen?"

"No, not at all," Bhagwan casually replied. We were at an Indian buffet.

"Not at all?" I blurted in disbelief. "Karen never missed a beat!"

"It's all about the will to live," Bhagwan answered while tearing off a piece of naan.

Bhagwan was no ordinary meditation teacher or doctor. He had first-hand experience with who lives and who dies. He shared his story:

"I practiced in a poor area of Bombay, a slum area, where anyone could just walk in without appointments. They lined up like in a refugee camp. I charged one rupee per person, approximately two cents in today's value, or about 25 cents back then. So, I had to see a large number of people, on average, over one hundred patients per day. The maximum was 160 patients in one day. So, you could hardly spend two minutes per person.

"In those two minutes, I would ask the person's name, what they were suffering from, examine the person, diagnose the person, give an injection, and give instructions for follow up — all in two minutes.

"To do that, patient after patient, I needed tremendous focus, an inner silence. If I was in a state of meditation, I could grasp what the patient was experiencing, what he was suffering from, and the treatment. This way, I could use meditation to diagnose and treat a large number of people."

"Is that how you knew to text me during surgery, 'Everything is going to be okay?'" I asked.

"Did I say that?" Bhagwan replied, dumbfounded.

Bhagwan had no memory of emailing me from India while Karen was undergoing brain surgery. But, he seemed pleased with his prescience.

The will to live tugged at me — like a koan. I imagined Bhagwan facing a stream of human misery. Over time, I saw the will to live as a timeless force, an inner filament that glows with sufficient voltage to keep us here. Will is the expression of who we are. This voltage may wane with illness or despair and resurface in a crisis as Uplift.

For decades, I wanted to write a book about the Octave and the Enneagram — "Fourth Way" ideas that describe this *will*. It is a *will* that is not willful and an inner resolve that renews itself. As Bhagwan explained, "To be able to do that, patient after patient, you need tremendous focus."

No matter how hard you crank the blowtorch of focus, *willfulness* will not penetrate the walls of despair. Like riding a mechanical bull, the rock and roll of emotions inevitably throw you off your game. The Octave and Enneagram chart this emotional maze and show how effort and effortlessness must fuse into one to navigate it.

It's a tricky maze to navigate. If you set off on a journey with a leaking radiator, these laws predict that a Good Samaritan with duct tape will show up to patch your hose. These laws also explain why you shouldn't count on it. (Google: "Tether your camel.")

Just an hour ago (as I edit this copy), Karen and I were hiking in the Tennessee hills with our friends Roger and Zora when a dirt-poor couple with a bouncy black Labrador walked toward us.

"You wouldn't happen to have any motor oil, would you?" the Lab guy asked.

"Uh no," Roger replied. "You got any, Bruce?"

I wanted to reply, "Let me check my canteen," but I politely replied, "Nope."

"Our car is at least two quarts down – smoking under the cap."

"Hey, we're heading out," Roger offered. "I'll get a couple of quarts in Ducktown and bring it back."

"Wow. We don't have any cash," the black Lab guy apologized. "Can I give you my card?"

"Nah, no problem; don't worry about it," Roger replied. "I'll leave it by your car."

As I watched this scene unfold, I thought, what is the chance of this encounter? Nobody else on the trail; it's getting dark and cold. Maybe, the Lab guy has one of those Wild Cards™.

The Law of the Octave explains when and why you bump into someone on the trail. The Octave was famously discovered almost 2,500 years ago by Pythagoras when he plucked a taut string. He plucked again at half the length and one-third the length to decipher the ratios that form the musical scale. He extended his discovery to heavenly bodies and how their relative distances were concordant with musical intervals. Astrologers and mystics know about this. The part we miss is how the ebb and flow of our daily lives sing to the same notes.

In 1916, George Ivanovich Gurdjieff, the Russian philosopher, mystic, spiritual teacher, and composer, gathered students in St. Petersburg,

Russia, to pass on esoteric knowledge from his travels. Gurdjieff explained how the Octave and the Enneagram govern dramatic shifts in human affairs, but without giving many details. Gurdjieff's teaching was timely as the Russian Revolution raged in the streets.

A century later, I gave a six-month Zoom course on the Enneagram using the Trumpian chaos, violence in the streets, and the pandemic as my learning lab for this book. I wanted to help people discover the "energetic gear shift" at the heart of transformation and change. Mahler called it "transitions;" I am choosing to call it Uplift.

After my Zoom course, my close friend Sarah confessed, "I enjoyed your class, but I don't know what to do with it." Karen poured more water on my creative embers with the wifely warning, "Don't go writing about the Enneagram." When I asked her why, Karen replied with a rim-shot only spouses can deliver: "The world doesn't need another intellectual, spiritual book."

That takes me back to my original plaint: "Where is the Uplift?"

I wish I had challenged Sarah, "Whadya mean, 'Don't know what to do with it?' The Octave and the Enneagram form the compass of life! They explain how this world, despite its darkness and despair, functions as an engine of continuous renewal – a veritable fountain of youth!"

The fountain would certainly perk Sarah's interest as she continues to court men in her seventies with the determination of a young lass. I wish I had answered, "Imagine if Ponce de Leon had a map. The Enneagram is also a map – like you'd get from the gas station. It charts the trap doors, jujitsu moves, and the inner Houdini one must follow to escape the gravitational grip of living in this world."

Bob Dylan described it best:

> May you build a ladder to the stars
> And climb on every rung
> May you stay forever young

I didn't say any of that because I took Karen's admonitions to heart and realized she was right. If I handed you sheet music for *Bohemian*

Rhapsody and you didn't read music, it wouldn't spark your soul. But drop the needle, and Freddie Mercury surges in your heart. The Octave and Enneagram announce the moment of Uplift at 2:22 when Freddie Mercury cries, *"Mama, ooh, I don't want to die. I sometimes wish I'd never been born at all."* At that precise moment, the bass guitar roars, the Stratocaster screams and the whole song suddenly flips — like an UNO card — into a Gilbert and Sullivan riff.

So, where is the Uplift?

This morning, as Karen and I rode the elevator to the Emory Winship Cancer Center Phase One Clinical Trial, I grinned while the female sound-chip voice intoned, *"GOING…UP…."*

"Karen, that's our girl."

The same sultry sound chip — *"Going up"* — cued our trips seven years earlier as we rode the elevator to Piedmont oncology. Being a hopeless romantic, I would open my arms toward Karen and make my trademark elevator move. But this time, like with all things, COVID, our matching KN95 face masks — the pointy ones that look like beaks — killed our moment of intimacy. Yes, a perfect Seinfeld moment.

Seven years ago, illicit kissing in the Piedmont oncology elevators had become our buoyant statement: *This disease will not define us.*

If I post a Yelp review of the Piedmont Cancer Institute, it should read, *"Great elevator (with mirrors!) for making out on the way to chemo."*

Uplift demands effort and effortlessness — and timing is everything. Case in point: the Piedmont Cancer Institute was on the 7th floor, whereas the Emory Clinical Trial, on the fourth floor, only offers elevator time for a quickie.

Joking aside, when the Giant Wooden Hammer comes down, finding Uplift is no laughing matter. In April 2020, the nightly news unnerved us night after night — patients dying in NYC hospital corridors, doctors and nurses slammed, no tests or PPE, a dearth of ventilators, morgues full, mass graves, sirens into the night, and over 20,000 ill-prepared New York City residents dead in eight weeks.

Like everyone in America, Karen and I hunkered down, watching

Rachel Maddow in lockdown horror. I turned to Karen: "Could you imagine facing a cancer diagnosis during a pandemic? Poor souls."

"My God, could you imagine?" Karen gasped.

Two weeks after Rachel Maddow, we fiddled with our laptop to launch a telehealth session with Dr. Tran, Karen's oncology doctor.

"Can you adjust your camera; we can't see your face," Karen asked. Like all of us, Dr. Tran was a newbie in the brave new world of Zoom.

"Oh, sorry," Dr. Tran replied. Her droopy mask matched the burnt-out look in her eyes.

Dr. Tran studied the scan report. Even she expected a routine hi-and-goodbye, but the smile we knew from seven years of routine visits wasn't there. I wondered if she was experiencing pandemic burn-out like so many doctors.

"The scan shows a growth on your retroperitoneal lymph nodes, also an adrenal gland," she announced without any bedside preamble.

"Is it cancer?" Karen asked.

"Most likely. I'll order a biopsy."

And just like that, after seven years of remission, the Giant Wooden Hammer slammed us back into the medical-industrial complex during the lockdown days of COVID. Yes, poor souls.

Three weeks later, we telehealthed to get the biopsy results.

"It's cancer, same cancer as before," Tran announced. "There's nothing more we can do at Piedmont other than full chemo. Emory has a clinical trial that's being run by Dr. Ramaligam, the doctor who trained me. I've already reached out. You'll be in good hands."

And boom, or maybe boom-boom if you count COVID, that was the gear change we were not expecting. With the Octave, that's the giveaway: the shock arrives from left field.

The wheels of medicine grind slowly, especially when joining a clinical trial. Karen studied and signed 75 pages of warnings and disclaimers, endured another biopsy and another round of MRI and CT. Finally, after four months hanging in limbo while the thingy was presumably growing, Karen received her first dose of the new medication.

During these same months, I felt paralyzed to start this book. Karen's admonition, the negative financial returns from writing, and the specter of adding more bloat to the canon of spiritual literature tied my hands.

That takes me to today, three months into the clinical trial. While beak-to-beak in the elevator and deprived of my oncology kiss, I felt frozen whether to write this thing. After a passenger left the elevator, my literary miscreant said, "Fuck it. Just write the damn thing." Pedantic, poignant, pure, or puerile — the artist in me suddenly didn't give a flying "f" whether a market existed for a book on the Octave, Uplift, or continuous renewal. Gurdjieff proclaimed, "Nobody could make any practical use" of this thing. Probably not much practical use for *Bohemian Rhapsody* either. But here in the elevator, my sultry digital muse ignited my artistic fire:

"*Going... up...*"

After a routine blood draw, an EKG, anti-nausea medication, and the phase I clinical trial drug known as U31402-A-U102, Karen zonked out in the big chemo chair. Stealing the luxury of a quiet space, I pulled out my laptop, waited for the pixels to glow, and typed:

WHERE'S THE UPLIFT #@!!!?

Three hours later, Dr. Ramalingam arrived.

"How's it going? The upbeat doctor asked.

"Oh hi, Dr. Ramalingam," Karen mumbled, waking from a drug-induced dream.

"The scans look very good," Ramalingam continued.

"Are they shrinking?" I piped in.

"Yes, 25 percent shrinkage."

"I thought they were 25 percent last time," I countered.

"Thirteen percent," Dr. Ram explained. "We track some markers."

I must have looked disappointed, so Ramalingam added a sweetener, "Yes, very, very good. We're very excited. We expect the drug to be approved next year."

I wanted to say, "Give my best to big pharma," but I didn't.

Ramalingam left, and Mashunte, a former touring modern dancer and now PhD clinical trial coordinator, entered. Time for another EKG.

"Hi, Mashunte," I greeted. "We heard that the scans show improvement."

"Yes, they look very good," Mashunte replied, attaching electrodes.

"So, tell me how this works," I asked. "Is it a straight-line process? Does everyone show similar shrinkage from week to week?"

"Oh, no," Mashunte explained.

"How so?"

"Most people are stable; the drug basically stops the progression. We've never seen results like Karen's – not once in the entire trial."

Instead of a round of cheers, I felt disoriented. Mashunte left, so I prodded Karen, "Did you hear that?"

"What?" Karen's eyes opened. "Yeah, it's still sinking in…."

"You're number one!" I leaned in to kiss Karen, but ugh, those beaks. "Remember when you got that scan before the trial? I asked.

"Yes..."

"And they said the tumor was already shrinking before you even started the medication?"

"Yeah…so?"

"Maybe, it's not the medication."

"What? That's ridiculous."

"Maybe… Just maybe, IT'S THE UPLIFT!"

CHAPTER1
A DRAMATIC UNIVERSE

`"Don't underlook the Sixties...We did a lot of good stuff.*
But it shouldn't shut you down from the moment."
~Wavy Gravy

"TURN AROUND," the radio warned. "The New York Thruway is closed! If you're heading to the Woodstock Festival, turn back. Now."

I fiddled with the dial to find a scratchy station in Poughkeepsie.

"What should we do?" I asked my high school buddies, Rob and Joel. "What a mess."

Our boyhood adventure lurched slowly toward "Three Days of Peace & Music," but we now discovered that half of the nation's youth were following the same lark.

The organizers expected 50,000 aquarian concert-goers to commune near Wallkill, New York, but after the locals blocked the permit, the Woodstock Music and Art Fair made a last-minute move to a 300-acre alfalfa field near Bethel, NY. The idyllic weekend of music and art suddenly hemorrhaged into a half million people heading to a dairy farm

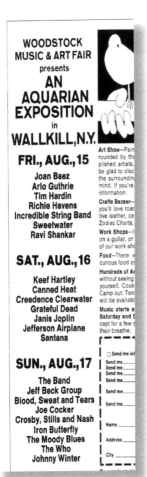

owned by Max Yasgur, a Jewish Republican.

We had just graduated high school — our magical last summer of childhood — and while reading comics, spinning records, and snarking about life in general, Rob spotted a small ad in the back of *Rolling Stone*. Every great band short of The Beatles was in the line-up.

"We're going," Rob announced.

"Yes!" I seconded.

Our certitude was stunning — no deliberations, no considerations, no asking for permission. Somewhere in our Boomer firmware, the Woodstock subroutine had activated.

We borrowed Rob's mom's brand new Meadow-Green Olds Cutlass, swapped the back seat for a crib mattress, cranked up Crosby Stills & Nash, and embarked on a 13-hour road trip. As Chicago guys driving across the mid-section of New York state, we had the back-route advantage over the kids driving up from NY, Philly, and DC. Our fates merged on State Route 17 — a four-lane, 70 mph divided highway that hemmoraged into a bumper-to-bumper crawl of Beetles, hippie busses, and long-haired lemmings. Even the grassy shoulder and median had become a miles-long campsite. No planning could anticipate that a half-million kids would act on the same tribal impulse — and this was before the Internet.

"Let's just turn around," I moaned.

"We came all this way," Joel urged.

We crept off the highway and devised a plan: As long as we could keep the car moving, we were good. Side roads, back roads, cow paths — our goal was to maintain forward motion. Finally, we hit a final impenetrable wall, pulled over, and walked. Granola bars hadn't been invented yet, so like everyone else, we packed our oranges, filled our Boy Scout canteens, and walked.

A ten-mile stream of humanity swept us along like a biblical migration — iron filings pulled toward a lodestone of love. We cast our lot with the river of freaks, flower children, hippies, and wannabes — mile after mile of kids who had spent the last five years absorbing every riff of Hendrix, Who, Stills, and Nash, all longing to baptize their souls in the collective impulse. The *dramatic universe* was not yet an idea for me, but my being was quickly steeped in its epochal power and scale

Finally, the muck and mess of Woodstock emerged over the hill. Seeing the mud-soaked, sleep-deprived crowd camped under precarious light towers was unnerving. Every battle needs fresh troops, so we took our positions.

I won't bore you with the performances, but the production values were rough. As the world's first mega rock festival, The Who, Sly, and Santana still live in Rob and Joel's memories. My pole star awoke when Wavy Gravy, the event's announcer and clown impresario, took the stage:

"The Governor has just declared this a disaster area," Wavy Gravy grinned with his goofy hoarseness.

Governor Rockefeller's official proclamation set the dire tone for every story coming off the wire:

WHITE LAKE, UPI, August 16, 1969 — Tens of thousands of young music fans today began abandoning the muddy chaos of the Woodstock Music and Art Fair.

Advertised as three days of "peace and music," the fair in this Catskill community has turned into a massive traffic jam in a giant mud puddle that has resulted in the death of one youth and the hospitalization of scores of others, many of them suffering adverse drug reactions.

Early today, promoters of the rock and folk music extravaganza, which had drawn an estimated 300,000 youths from throughout the United States, issued an emergency appeal for volunteer doctors and medical supplies to cope with the large number of sick.

Wavy Gravy took a dramatic pause, then giggled the sagacious punchline: "You know what I always say? There's always a little bit of heaven in a disaster area."

I didn't know it then but know now: Wavy Gravy nailed it. The secret of Uplift lay hidden in the gumbo of mud, urine, and orange peels. A little bit of heaven held us together like a yin dot in a mud pit of yang. We shared our oranges, and the kids next to us shared theirs. This was my first taste of Uplift and its ability to distill a pint of heaven from a bucket of mud.

Fifty years later, I still wonder how 500,000 like-minded souls found their way to this improbable patch of land — home on any other weekend to Jersey, Guernsey, and Holstein cows.

For you social media geniuses, here's your marketing assignment: Next August, attract half a million kids to an obscure farm in Sullivan County, NY. Make it happen without email, Twitter, SMS, radio, TV, Web, Facebook, or even fax. For difficulty, throw in a last-minute venue change, and for extra points, three days before the event, you must choose between erecting ticket stands and fences — or building a stage!

My Woodstock right of passage pales compared to what my parent's generation faced on Omaha Beach, but each generational wave is different. Each is tasked to navigate the dramatic universe it encounters. Today's kids face cyber wars, fake news, the end of democracy, and climate collapse — no small thing.

The universe is constantly in flux, but the drama continues its spiraling story. My dad's World War II experience reminds me how the basic themes in the dramatic universe keep re-emerging:

While working at GE as a Naval officer, Ed Miller helped develop the first sonar-guidance systems for torpedoes, a technology that sank 37 Axis submarines. One day, near the end of the war, my dad's superior took him aside. "Ed, I'm going to show you the work we are conducting in a top-secret lab, but I need you sworn to absolute secrecy."

My dad, expecting to see a death-ray in development, nodded yes. The supervisor unlocked the passage to a closed-off lab where, in direct violation of Roosevelt's Defense Production Act, GE engineers were busy developing color television for the anticipated post-war consumer boom.

Yes, the Big Boom. I'm a product of that Boom, and from it, my peeps were charged to rip up the canvas and paint something new. I imagine *every other* generation gets a Boom inoculation during childhood. Gen X'ers were inoculated with Reagan (sorry) and Millennials with Obama. The Post-War Boom shot us out of the cannon into a Land of Plenty, and as a result, I grew up with Uplift hard-wired into my being.

Woodstock left an indelible impression that a cosmic pendulum swings from one generation to the next — from bust to boom to bust, and from Bob Hope to George Carlin to Sarah Cooper. The mysterious forces that summoned half a million hippies up State Route 17 are the same pendulum forces that move the planets. I can't prove this in a lab because self-awareness is the only instrument that can penetrate the impenetrable.

After Woodstock, I spent the next half-century exploring self-awareness and the hard-wiring it rubs against in its search for inner freedom. Self-awareness can't be activated like a light switch. It must be fermented and aged from crushed dreams. And like good wine, it elevates the experience of whatever tawdry menu your generation serves up.

J.G. Bennett, my philosophic mentor, described this awareness as the creative imagination – the ability to raise your vantage point above the world at hand and joyfully create the new. Music, art, poetry, architecture, and scientific breakthroughs all come from somewhere — but where?

J.G. Bennett explained:

> There is this power of creative imagination that has all these properties: making doing possible, rejoicing before the Lord, giving the power to see through the inner eye, and working in all nature."[1]

Bennett makes it clear that the creative imagination is not God, but rather, a holy force that can become part of us. Were it not for our resistance, the creative imagination seeks to animate an inner freedom – what we experience as the creative act.

For artists and creatives, the creative imagination is the basic tool in the toolkit. For the student of Uplift who seeks to distill a pint of heaven from a bucket of life, the creative imagination opens the inner eye. It paints a road map to a better place.

Henry Corbin (1903 - 1978) takes this power of the inner eye further in his exploration of *The Creative Imagination of Ibn' Arabi:*

> Between the universe that can be apprehended by pure intellectual perception and the universe perceptible to the senses, there is an intermediate world, the world of Idea-Images, of archetypal figures, of subtle substances, of 'immaterial matter.' This world is as real and objective, as consistent and subsistent as the intelligible and sensible worlds; it is an intermediate universe where the spiritual takes body and the body becomes spiritual... The organ of this universe is the active imagination.[2]

When I think of the creative imagination – the archetypal world that lives between intellect and sense perception – one name comes to mind: Doug Engelbart, the father of desktop computing. Doug had an epiphany in 1950 that changed the world. In a single creative flash, a complete vision of the information age appeared to him. This vision became the basis for the Internet and the modern personal computer, including, in 1968, the handheld mouse.

Doug Engelbart demonstrated how the future comes into the present, not step-by-step, but like a birth from a higher world and through game-changing leaps from the creative imagination. From *The Guardian*:

Doug Engelbart

Next time you drag a document across your desktop and put it in a folder, spare a thought for acid. Organizing your files might not seem like a psychedelic experience now, but in 1968, when Douglas Engelbart first demonstrated a futuristic world of windows, hypertext links, and video conferencing to a rapt audience in San Francisco, they must have thought they were tripping. Especially because he was summoning this dark magic onto a big screen using a strange rounded controller on the end of a wire, which he called his *mouse*. Like many California tech visionaries of the time, Engelbart was an enthusiastic advocate for the mind-expanding benefits of LSD. As head of the Augmented Human Intellect Research Center at the Stanford Research Institute, he and his team would drop acid under test conditions in the hope of inspiring new breakthroughs.[3]

Unlike the computer engineers at Stanford, I didn't drop acid at Woodstock. But, one month after sensing myself as a yin dot in a sea of mud, my creative imagination awakened again — this time as a freshman at the University of Illinois, 1969.

College life thrust me into a potent brew of political chaos. I grew up in a leafy suburb, so watching the geopolitical forces erupt on my campus came as a shock. A few weeks after unpacking my suitcases, we chartered busses to the Vietnam Moratorium in Washington, DC, to be hazed with tear gas. Upon return, the school was disrupted by a convulsive series of events — a student strike, fire bombings of the police station, recruiting station, ROTC, and Lincoln Hall, followed by the inaugural Earth Day, and a speech by Dr. Benjamin Spock reminding us that the Declaration of Independence entitles people to a revolution. Next came the disheartening discovery that our school's namesake Illiac IV — the fastest computer in the world — was secretly funded by the Department of Defense. Topping it off, the National Guard fired 67 rounds in 13 seconds into a crowd of fellow Midwestern students at Kent State.

There was more. As a harbinger of Black Lives Matter, on the morning of April 29, 1970, a local cop fatally shot 23-year-old Edgar Hoults near his home. Hoults, a security guard at Follett's, our campus bookstore, had been unable to sleep one night, so he went to the store to help his co-workers while his 21-year-old pregnant wife, Alice, slept with their two small children. Hearing commotion, Alice looked out her front window and saw nothing. Suddenly, she heard a gunshot at the rear. She opened her back door to see her husband face down, bleeding in the grass. Her neighbors had to restrain Alice, shaking and crying as her husband was lifted into an ambulance. Alice never saw Edgar again until his body was presented at the funeral home. No police officers or city officials explained to her what happened.

At the trial, cops claimed that Edgar had been pulled over behind the bookstore, fled by car, crashed, and was chased to the field behind his apartment. They did not offer a reason why Edgar fled. The officer said his service weapon went off accidentally when he slipped on wet grass (while scoring a perfect bullseye to the back of Edgar's head). Adding to the terrible, horrible irony, Edgar was working late at Follett's to clean up firebomb damage from the students.

Pumping up the crazy, the school trustees, in their infinite wisdom, disinvited Chicago Seven defense attorney William Kunstler from speaking on campus. I was in the crowd of 2000 students waiting to hear Kunstler speak, and — crowds doing what crowds do — we "decided" to march toward the President's mansion, but we first made a strategic detour through Dormitory Row to gather troops.

Imagine hanging in your dorm, spinning records, and suddenly hear-

ing a raucous protest from the street below. One after another, stereo speakers popped out of dorm windows, blasting the Rolling Stones. The crowd's roar of angry epithets mixed with Jagger's lyrics to paint a dark, dystopian scene. "Hey!" Jagger yelled, his voice ricocheting off multiple buildings, "Think the time is right for a palace revolution!"

Instantly, the march grew to 4500 students. As we neared the President's mansion, the cops formed a barrier — not campus cops — but the fearsome, sadistic State cops with their four-foot clubs. A row of meek National Guardsmen stood to the side with their military jeeps lined for battle. Who were these Guard guys, 18 and 19 years old? They looked like the guys in my high school locker room, but now with different helmets, different uniforms, and loaded M1 rifles. One guy even had a double-tank flame thrower strapped to his back in case a rice paddy needed immolation on the campus quad. "Sorry guys," I snarked, "All we got are cornfields."

And me, I just wanted to hear Kunstler.

The frolic of protest quickly morphed into menace, ratcheting up the anger and fear. Wavy Gravy could have diffused the "seriousness of it all," but he wasn't there. I was there. And then, my active imagination took hold. Maybe I was Arjuna, taking Krishna's counsel on the battlefield. I became very still inside – a yin dot in the sea of anger. Hippies and cops, cops and hippies — each performing a desperate kabuki, one side creating the other. The universe had a score to settle that night — maybe Mars got too close to Jupiter, and this cosmic slight rippled to Earth in performative response — like an imagined opera, "The Fight of the Illini." Strangely, Bruce's Arjuna-feeling body didn't know how to respond.

"I don't feel anger. Shouldn't I be angry?"

Without Krishna telling me what to do, I felt confused. "Everyone else is angry. Does a protester have to feel anger? Does a falling tree have to make a sound? Am I just the witness? The yin dot in a sea of violence? Does a point of stillness pen the script for the dramatic universe?

The escalating threat of cop violence became too much, thinning the crowd. Some hardcore comrades continued toward Follett's Bookstore to break more windows — oblivious to the fate of Edgar Hoults. I retreated from this modern-day *Mahabharata* and stumbled back to my dorm room. I couldn't read the Sanskrit of confrontation, but my inner eye saw how bigger forces enlarged my present moment:

From JFK to LBJ, Gulf of Tonkin, Dien Bien Phu, Ho Chi Minh, Ngo Dinh Diem, Nguyen Cao Kỳ, to Nixon, Kent State, and even to Edgar Hoults. Each player hit their marks and performed their scene. But like the kids breaking windows, no one had the full script in hand. That's the thing with extras. Hitchcock would have calmly directed, "Take your rocks. Now throw! Cut! Thank you. You can leave."

Nguyen Cao Kỳ was more than a bit player in this story. As the leader of the Republic of Vietnam, he had a bigger role. When Shakespeare penned "All the world's a stage," the Bard would have anticipated the flamboyant Nguyen Cao Kỳ, with his dashing flyboy charm, tailored suits, glamorous wife, and silky corruption.

Sudden reversals of fortune signal the plot points of the dramatic universe. After nineteen years of conflict, the Vietnam War collapsed in a single day — on April 30, 1975. If you've been keeping track, the sequel returned 46 years later when America's 20-year Afghan War collapsed in a single week. And for the prequel, in 1842, British troops were forced to retreat from Kabul during the First Anglo-Afghan War. Of the 16,000 British soldiers and civilians guaranteed safe passage to their garrison in Jalalabad by Afghan tribesmen in 1842, only one European made it to safety. The rest were massacred or died of exposure.

During Vietnam's collapse, the nation's first couple, Nguyen and Madame Kỳ, were rescued by helicopter atop the U.S. embassy and fled to the United States, where they adopted their new all-American roles: running a liquor-deli convenience store a few miles from Disney-

land. That's right. After our nation shov-
eled 60,000 American lives and a trillion
current dollars to prop up a geopolitical
sinkhole, the tragic irony of the dramatic
universe showed its hand. South Vietnam's
flash-in-the-pan leader, a playboy partial
to purple scarves, upscale nightclubs, and
beautiful women, was now selling booze by
the pint, beef jerky, and Hustler magazines
over the counter in a derelict neighborhood
in Garden Grove, CA. This scene became
indelibly etched in my consciousness. Toto
had pulled back the curtain to reveal the
Great and Powerful Oz – a mere humbug.

Nguyen Cao Kỳ

After days of student protests, the Great and Powerful Trustees invited
William Kunstler back to campus, this time to a crowd three times larger
than the first. The dramatic arc of apparent chaos etched into my being. I
saw how the present moment stretches, and how the inherent irony – the
truth of the story – is revealed. Whether that truth is greed, hypocrisy,
meanness, or weirdness, irony shows its hand through opposites.

Consider the 43rd President: After sending thousands of troops to
death and disfigurement for an immoral war, George W. Bush chose
a compulsive new hobby for his golden years – painting portraits of
dogs and cats, still-lifes, landscapes, two self-portraits *en toilette*, and a
collection of portraits of veterans. I don't want to psychoanalyze, but his
integration journey would have been better-served painting portraits of
the 151,000 Iraqi civilians who died from the war or those captured and
tortured at the hands of the CIA.[4]

Nguyen Cao Kỳ shape-shifted to reveal his own ironic truth. After his
liquor store failed, he tried the seafood business. This also went bankrupt.
To cap the couple's legacy, his wife attempted suicide at the luxurious
Manila Hotel. I don't feel sorry for grifters. You have two choices in life
– ride the pendulum or get hit by it. You can't outwit it.

Like Kỳ, the Woodstock promoters learned how sudden reversals of fortune signal plot points in the dramatic universe. When the pendulum swung — collapsing their Woodstock business dream — they didn't panic or try to protect their losses. Instead, they let Reality play out in real time: they opened the gates to the hippie hordes. The promoter, Michael Lang, remembered:

> "We wanted to ensure that anybody who came to our event was welcomed. Of course, in the original plan, we had gates and ticket booths… The counterculture was heading to an event run by their own. We just avoided the silly confrontations that stupid rules can create".[5]

Lang put a hippie spin on his reversal of fortune. The suddenly free festival left him and his partners with $1.3 million in debt (a $9 million loss in today's dollars), but the pendulum of risk swung again. They made it all back from album and movie ticket sales.

History textbooks don't focus on pendulum swings; they teach history as a string of discrete events because that's how books are written: one chapter after another. J.G. Bennett's four-volume magnum opus, *The Dramatic Universe,* saw all of history as a single dynamic story guided by a demiurgic intelligence. If the universe is indeed *dramatic*, some being must write, cast, and direct the play. This intelligence has traditionally been called the Demiurge — from the ancient Greek, *Dēmiourgos,* the *Craftsman.* If God is the Boss, the Demiurge is "God's fixers."

Defined as "a *being* responsible for the creation of the universe," the *Demiurge* is neither an absolute God moving the pieces nor the random-chance mechanics of subatomic particles. Bennett defined *Demiurge* as a "mode of Being associated with intelligence higher than human and with a far greater Present Moment." In this way, the Demiurge works on a bigger stage than our day-to-day lives can take in.

Bennett explained to his students, when "I use the word *Demiurge,* I mean the same as the writers of Genesis meant when they used the word Elohim."[6] In Genesis, Elohim (God) is both the *He* who created heaven and earth and the *Us* who created man in *"our"* image. In Psalm 8:5, Elohim is also translated as *angels*.

Is the Creator a *He,* an *Us,* or the *Angels?* Take your pick, but I'm sticking with the Demiurge as the *Creative Imagination* that fashions our world. In this way, the dramatic universe plays out as the higher mirror of our impulses — a conscious intelligence stumbling through a game board of chance, making it up as it goes along. The emergence of life, the appearance and disappearance of species, the rise and fall of civilizations, and the redemptive arc of human history are inseparable from the demiurgic angels who help us find a parking space — or even the psychedelic spark that imagined a new species of *mouse.* Thank you, Doug Englebart.

J.G. Bennett (1897 - 1974) was a British scientist, technologist, metaphysical teacher, and author. During World War I, he was blown off his motorcycle by an exploding shell, then taken to a military hospital where he remained in a coma for six days. This precipitated an out-of-body experience that launched his lifelong inquiry into the deeper reality.

In 1923, Bennett met the Russian philosopher and mystic, G.I. Gurdjieff, who introduced him to the esoteric workings of the universe and the techniques that could transform humanity.

J.G. Bennett

Bennett melded Gurdjieff's metaphysics with the discipline of his scientific life. As a unified vision of reality, *The Dramatic Universe* challenged the reader from the first page. One commenter warned, "In reading it, you feel as though you need a Ph.D. in history, physics, philosophy, chemistry, and bi-

G.I Gurdjieff

ology. Being able to speak Latin and French would also be useful, as he'll often use those languages without translation."[7]

Anthony Blake, Bennett's editor and protege, wrote in 1976:

> The publication of The Dramatic Universe was one of the major
> intellectual events of this century and, in keeping with all major
> events, passed almost unnoticed by the world at large... Bennett
> had set himself to give a framework for understanding the whole
> of human experience.[8]

Whether it's a unified field theory or a Web conspiracy, it's human nature to seek a theory of everything — a finishing puzzle piece to explain the complexities of life. Everything can't fit into a theory, nor should it. It's a noble task, and this book follows that quixotic spirit — to find a unifed understanding of Uplift.

Unlike Bennett's masterwork, my question has been more humble and childlike. I asked it on page one: "Where is the Uplift?" If we're released into life like a glider pilot flying on a cushion of air, gravity slowly, then suddenly pulls us to our fate. How does the leader of the free world end up painting still-lifes and pets? How does the Premier of the Republic of Vietnam become a humbug selling pint liquor for his second act?

Experienced glider pilots know where to find the next Uplift — the column of rising warm air that lifts the glider to continue the journey. In this way, Uplift holds the secret to continuous renewal.

Uplift provides an anti-gravity force for continuous renewal like a hot air balloon releasing its ballast to chart new horizons. This periodic flush-cycle of mental ballast extends the range and enlarges the map. It expands *the present moment* — the place of pure action and freedom that is not constrained by the past nor crippled by anticipation of the future.

When Bennett devoted his final volume of the *Dramatic Universe* to the history of the human mind, he sought a stage large enough to cast his story. He enlisted the *present moment:*

> All experience is contained within the present moment. This is the
> only immediate and irreducible certainty. The present moment is
> not a dimensionless point but a finite region of experience that
> never changes inasmuch as it is always *present* and yet always
> changes inasmuch as it is in a state of *flux*.[9]

Bennett's present moment was not the linear sequence of Kunstler, dormitories, cops with clubs, and broken windows. Bennett defined the present as the content of human experience — the *total immediate experience.*

Think of the universe as a big TV with 8 billion streaming channels (including your own) – channels that flip from retro to romance and from hell to healing. In this larger present moment, those channels constitute one big show, a timeless redemptive drama where Indochina's corrupt colonial history juxtaposes with protests at a corn belt university. Unlike physics which measures the dimensions of space and time, Bennett's present moment is bounded by the dimensions of human experience — through autonomic, sensory, and conscious awareness.

My teacher, Bhagwan Awatramani, narrowed it further when he explained to me: "The present is not a moment." In Bhagwan's explanation, the present is not a moment; it is outside of time. When I kissed Karen in the elevator to seed the book in your hands, the creative imagination spawned it whole even though it would take over a year of hard work for *time to catch up* with that present moment.

I remember watching *This is Your Life* as a child— possibly the first "reality" TV show. The host, Ralph Edwards, surprised guests in front of a live audience by reciting the story of their lives. Long lost colleagues, friends, and family would step out from behind the curtain while Edwards narrated the guest's life story. The U.S. Army spawned the idea for the show when they asked Edwards for help rehabilitating injured soldiers. The Army felt

Ralph Edwards – This is Your Life

Ralph Edwards could help war-stressed soldiers integrate the stories of their lives. The surprised guests who burst in tears offered more than vicarious entertainment. They illustrated the "expanded present moment" and how gratitude and redemption emerge when time catches up for Ralph Edwards to declare, "This is Your Life."

Consider a very different present moment in the dramatic universe — the storming of the Capitol on January 6, 2021. The nation shuddered for six violent hours – from 2 pm when the Electoral College count was halted until 8 pm when the Senate resumed. Instead of six hours, you can enlarge that moment to the two months of attempts to illegally overturn the election — from November 3 to January 6 — or the eight months of false assertions that voting by mail constituted fraud.

Expanding the present further, the Capitol insurrection was also telegraphed four years earlier when Trump oddly inserted "American carnage" into his inaugural address (followed by Kellyanne Conway "throwing some mean punches" at the Inaugural Ball).[10]

"American carnage?" I pondered, "What the hell is he talking about?"

When Trump spoke those words at his inaugural, my present moment expanded, and not in a good way. Just two weeks earlier, Barack and Michelle Obama had joyously hosted the cast of *Hamilton* in the East Room — and now, *boom*, Trump changed the channel to *carnage*. Years before the storming of the Capitol, Trump's foreboding fetish with violence foretold what was to come with Charlottesville, Portland, Lafayette Square, and the attack on the Capitol.

The four Trump years was not the launch of a *new* era. Author Anand Giridharadas described it as a convulsive backlash against the future – a temporary recoil against the storyline of the dramatic universe:

> [The Trump era] is not the engine of history. It is the revolt against the engine of history... We are living through a revolt against the future. The future will prevail.[11]

Whether we face a future of carnage or caring, it is not out of our hands. The Greek philosopher, Heraclitus, said, "Character is destiny." In this way, the insurrection played out as the imprint of character captured in the seed impulse — Trump's obsession with *carnage*.

A seed impulse can also be called *will*. Will is not complicated, but it is also sacred. The entire Quran is said to exist in the opening *Bismillah* — that in its authorship, the sacred text manifested when the quill touched the parchment. *Be, and it is.* From the Quran:

> He is the One Who has originated the heavens and the earth, and when He wills to (originate) a thing, He only says to it: 'Be,' and it becomes. 2:117

In Arabic, the imperative verb for *Be* is *Kun*. *Kun fa-yakūnu* — Be, and it is.

> His command (of creation) is only that when He intends (to create) something, He says to it: 'Be,' so it instantly becomes. 36:82

We experience God's command, *Kun*, through the action of Will — not my will or God's will, but simple, non-complicated will. Will sees the play while moving it forward. Will is the driving force for Uplift. As the actors of our stories, we embody this Will. Whether we sit in meditation, place a quill to a parchment, or go fishing, the present moment enters the action through Will — the perfect cast (*Kun*) that lands a trout.

This is the creative imagination in action — Engelbart *envisioned* the information age, Trump *willed* a coup d'etat, and I *saw* the span of history on my violent college street. Instead of "I'm hot, and my feet hurt walking to this muddy music festival," the creative imagination senses the larger present moment, *"The times, they are a-changing."*

Will witnesses the dramatic universe in a transformative arc – the half-century that connects Edgar Hoults (d.1969), to George Floyd (d.2020). One died in obscurity, and the other convulsed the nation and the world for weeks of protest. It would take 50 years for the nation's majority to become "woke" to "Black Lives Matter." As Edgar lay in a pool of blood after working the night shift at Follett's, a sounding note was struck – a dark chord that ultimately summoned a national movement and renamed the avenue in front of the White House, "Black Lives Matter Plaza."

My present moment stretched that night in Champaign, Illinois. I didn't recognize the full irony of my school's decision to bar William Moses Kunstler, a lawyer who gave a lifetime of work to the principle of equal justice under law. Kunstler stretched the American present moment in his unpopular defense of Communist revolutionaries, the Freedom Riders, the American Indian Movement, Black Panthers, Attica Prison rioters, a string of notorious mobsters, and, at the time of his death, the Blind Sheik, Omar Abdel-Rahman, for his role in the 1993 World Trade Center bombing. He was also a special trial counsel to Martin Luther King Jr. True to form, Kunstler claimed he was headed to the airport to represent Lee Harvey Oswald on the morning Jack Ruby gunned Oswald down in Dallas.

In my hometown, Chicago, Kunstler put Allen Ginsberg on the stand to chant "Om." He also defended two cases of flag burning before the Supreme Court. Always ahead of his time, Kunstler understood the exercise of Will. He described himself as a "legal performance artist." He understood that "you always want to be in the media, no matter what gets you there."

Kunstler's final role as the nation's moral performance artist would have to wait thirty-five years after his death. The 2020 movie, *The Trial of the Chicago 7* put a mirror to the *Trumpian* moment. In 1969, the government staged a show trial to send seven random white peace activists (plus Black Panther, Bobby Seale) to prison for a decade for protesting the Vietnam War in Chicago's Grant Park. In 2020, for the crime of protesting unwarranted police killings, the federal government conscripted a faux military from various agencies to stage "show riots" in downtown Portland and Lafayette Square with the cynical intent to foment riot footage to promote the Trump campaign.

From Grant Park 1968 to Lafayette Square 2020, life unfurls in a circular motion. We experience the circular rhythms of day and night, the four seasons, and our revolution around the sun. Life also spirals — spiraling up as growth and spiraling down as decay. Political promises spiral down while pole beans planted by urban pioneers in abandoned city lots spiral up.

Time marches forward – often like a needle stuck in an LP groove. Continuous renewal coaxes Uplift from these grooves. Glider pilots catch thermals and follow the updraft in a spiral flight path. We don't have wings to catch an Uplift, but we have an active imagination that can jettison mental ballast and re-imagine our possibilities.

When I was three years old, lying in bed one night and unable to sleep, my creative imagination took a strange turn. Like an ever-rising drone shot, I saw my immediate world — people going to work, politicians on TV, and everyone worrying about money — all out of sync with our true circumstance as a floating speck in space. As the drone pulled up, I saw cities and forests, mountains and oceans. I also saw other lands with different customs and cultures. As I continued to pull up and away, I saw planet earth hanging in space. Apollo hadn't taken our selfie yet, but I imagined what it would look like. And then I got scared.

I hadn't heeded the advice of poet, Nick Flynn:

> Children under, say, ten, shouldn't know that
> the universe is ever-expanding, inexorably pushing
> into the vacuum, galaxies swallowed by galaxies,
> whole solar systems collapsing, all of it
> acted out in silence.[12]

Yep, I was under ten and wondering, "What's outside our solar system? And what's outside of that? Where exactly are we?" This vast gap between our tedious, goofball lives and the majestic reaches of space made no sense. Hitchcock should have yelled, "Cut!" and summoned the script girl to explain the continuity gap to me. Even at that young age, I sensed a dramatic story at play, that humanity performs in a "theater of the absurd" — the present moment.

Feeling freaked, I shuffled my pajama feet down the hall.

"Mommy, I can't sleep."

"That's okay," my mom reassured. "It's okay just to rest."

And that is where I am, writing this oddly non-linear chapter on my initiation into the dramatic universe on the morning of our first COVID Christmas. (I know the Capitol insurrection is 12 days away, but I bop around as I write). You probably have a vivid memory of this particular Christmas. Someone you love may have been sick or even passed away. Maybe you opened presents with your hygienic family pod around the tree. I'm preparing for an antiseptic family Zoom. Either way, the dramatic universe changed your holiday plans.

My "holiday" message is to fire up your creative imagination and stretch the present moment of all your Christmas memories until the pieces of your story fit together, your heart feels safe, and you know you're loved. Like the message a previous generation learned from Ralph Edwards: if you embrace the larger present moment, it returns the favor by remembering you in love.

As I fumble with the kettle and prepare for an empty-nester holiday, I look out our frosty cabin window and realize that Santa has delivered the rarest of gifts — a winter wonderland of white fluffy Christmas snow in the Deep South. Maybe the dramatic universe still has some Uplift up its sleeve.

Endnotes

1   J.G. Bennett, "The Image of God in Work: Talks at Sherborne House 1973-4

2   Corbin, Henry. Alone with the Alone. Translated by Ralph Manheim, Princeton University Press, 1998.

3   theguardian.com/artanddesign/2017/may/11/design-museum-california-designing-freedom-tech-design

4   World Health Organization, https://www.who.int/mediacentre/news/releases/2008/pr02/en/

5   https://www.mojo4music.com/articles/5282/inside-woodstock-with-organiser-michael-lang

6   Bennett, J.G.. The Image of God in Work: Talks at Sherborne House

7   Will Szal, Dramatic Universe review on Amazon.com

8   jgbennett.org/the-dramatic-universe-commentary-by-a-g-e-blake

9   Bennett, J. G. (1997). The Dramatic Universe, Volume 4: History (3rd edition). Bennett Books.

10   https://www.thedailybeast.com/cheats/2017/01/24/report-kellyanne-conway-punched-man-at-ball-inauguration

11   Anand Giridharadas. "We are falling on our face because we are jumping high." https://the.ink/p/hope

12   "Cartoon Physics, part 1" by Nick Flynn from Some Ether. Copyright 2000 by Nick Flynn. Reprinted by permission of Graywolf Press.

Chapter 2
KATABASIS

"It's all right if you grow your wings on the way down."
~ Robert Bly

THE POUNDING SURF SENT RAINBOWS INTO THE SKY.
Fluorescent shades of orange, purple, and pink played hide and seek while my inner Walt Whitman pranced among the colorful sea anemones. Yes, a single toke could boost my Body Electric – and to the credit of THC, it could bury my pain. Like Certs "two mints in one," smoking weed boosts and buries — a phenomenon known as "spiritual bypassing."

I inhaled the last ounce from my Illinois baggie, and with it, I let my link to my college buddies drift into smoke. I had lived a non-stop creative life at the University of Illinois — a counter-cultural circus where music, art, politics, and adventure melded to form a new Bruce identity. Sadly, my college capers were receding into the rearview mirror as I sunk into an existential funk – an altogether new experience for me. Still, you have to put 20 years of Uplift into reverse at some point.

As I walked the beach, I savored the night we piled into Scott's VW

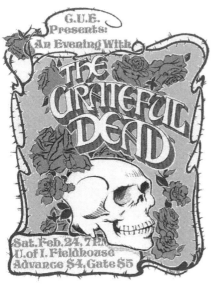

Bus (no heat or fourth gear) for the five-hour drive to see the Grateful Dead in Iowa City. The show got underway with a "hippie bucket brigade" that joyously and illicitly passed hundreds of university-mandated folding chairs into precarious piles. With the floor wide open, we danced ecstatically into the night. One Dead Head commented: "Proof that drugged-out anarchy is not chaotic!"

Another night, we drove to Chicago to see The Doors, right after Jim Morrison's famous Miami bust for indecency — yes, the one where he whipped it out (you can look it up). Morrison's dark, sullen mood was epic.

And how could I forget the wind-whistling night we drove to the Voorhies Castle — a full-moon Sendak nightmare in the middle of the Illinois prairie. In 1867, Nels Larson, a Swedish farmer, built a wooden palace in the style of his homeland while waiting for his fiance to arrive. They lived lavishly until 1914, when his wife Johanna crumpled suddenly and was found dead at the foot of the stairs. (I know a thing about crumpling wives).

Distraught, Larson abandoned the castle with its 70-foot clock tower barn that very day. Ghost lore has it that Johanna never left the house.

Being pre-Wikipedia, all we knew

was what was in front of our eyes — a creepy decrepit farm palace atop a windswept hill. With shafts of moonlight guiding our way, we crept up the stairs like the Hardy Boys on weed. My roommate, Rich, poked into a bedroom just as a cold screeching blast sent tattered curtains flying, timbers creaking, and Rich screaming like a bat from hell. Five years later, a tornado destroyed the clock tower — and presumably the ghost.

But here I was at Malibu beach, desperately trying to connect with the ghost of my previous college life. My Body Electric and my Uplift began to lose their buzz, so I retreated across the parking lot and waited to cross all six lanes of Pacific Coast Highway.

Why California? This particular story started in middle school — the day my creative imagination ignited — yes, the creative imagination that Ibn' Arabi talked about, where "theophanic visions… appear in their true reality."

While poking in a closet at the budding age of 13, I found an old 16 mm film camera — the one used by my parents to capture my babyhood. I studied the shutter, sprockets, and pull-down claw. With my new-found Excalibur in hand, the power to warp the physical universe entered my brain: shoot with the camera upside down, rewind the footage end to front and project normal life backward. No big deal in the digital world, but in the analog age, seeing Rob purge beautifully formed spaghetti onto his fork distorted space and time in a way Einstein couldn't touch.

I became a budding film wunderkind in my high-school years, showing films on the coffee house circuit and as part of our high school musicals. For *Bye Bye Birdie*, I scripted Conrad Birdie stepping out of a Boeing 707, then chased by a crowd of screaming fans out the jetway, through the concourse, down the escalator, and out the terminal. Back in that age of innocence, a high-school filmmaker could casually stroll into an empty American Airlines jet, frame the shot, and call, "Action!"

During my high school senior year, I studied experimental films at DePaul University – a course hosted by my boyhood hero, a young Roger Ebert. Roger had been hired as a freelancer to write fluff for the Chicago Sun-Times Sunday magazine until the paper's lone film critic retired. In a stroke of fortune, the 24-year-old Ebert became Chicago's full-time movie critic.

In 1969, avant garde artists pushed against cinema's edge, and here I was, a skinny high school kid, watching and listening to them — the Kuchar brothers, Robert Nelson, Bruce Conner, and Stan Brakhage. My mind blew past the boundaries of what "movies" can do or even be. Brakhage took film stock, painted it, burnt it, and even glued translucent moth wings to it. The older folks in the audience didn't know what to do with ten minutes of epileptic flicker, but I settled into a deep connection with Brakhage's vision — a meditation on the luminescence of consciousness itself. Brakhage's 1959 film, *"Window Water Baby Moving,"* photographed his wife in childbirth as an orgiastic swirl of pleasure, pain, exhaustion, and exaltation. Watch it online.

My camera captured the pent-up angst of youth in college and found ecstatic release in nature. My visionary romp, *Monsieur Gardei,* about a student fleeing the shackles of his mind, won the University Film Festival and earned my ticket to UCLA film school.

It takes forever to cross Pacific Coast Highway, so let me add more. My 16mm camera awakened a sense of purpose at a young age. Watching Tony die in Maria's arms in *West Side Story* kindled a soul desire to channel pure feeling onto the screen, and with it, pursue my lifelong inquiry into Uplift.

Everyone seeks a sword of purpose. My dad's mission emerged at the end of WWII when he peeked into GE's top-secret lab. His illicit glimpse catapulted him to become a pioneer of the high-fidelity industry.

After GE, my dad and pregnant mom moved to Chicago, where they found a one-bedroom walk-up apartment. The government had halted residential construction during the War, so with housing tight, my infant brother slept in the bathtub. Following the pent-up post-war boom, my parents sought open spaces in the suburbs where I was born. With every-one making babies, hordes of kids roamed our newly-built neighborhood in dawn-to-dusk unstructured play.

My dad's dream took him to Radio Crafts-man, a manufacturer of audio amplifiers built from heavy transformers, chrome chassis, and heat-generating vacuum tubes — a ton of wattage to power 18-inch woofers and  Electro-Voice horns that 1950s martini dads installed in their walls. Back then, the sound of needle against vinyl signaled Uplift to my LP-wired brain — a sound that accompanied adults mixing cocktails, free-wheel-ing laughter, and Sinatra's *Songs for Swingin' Lovers*.

In 1953, at age 32, my dad left Radio Craftsman to start Sherwood Electronics. The high fidelity revolution in the fifties mirrored the personal computer revolution  of the eighties. Instead of Apple, IBM, and Atari, audiophiles reveled in McIntosh, Fisher, H.H. Scott, Harman Kardon, and Sherwood.

As a kid, I grew up with sine waves and stereo effects ping-ponging  across our living room as my dad tested speakers and amps. He made two significant contribu-tions to the industry: the world's first FM stereo broadcast (using his technology on WKFM in 1961) and, in 1967, the first 100% solid-state audio receiver. Neither family

Ed Miller (L) at WKFM

nor friends understood Ed's accomplishments. That's because at dinner parties, while the guests mingled inside, my dad would be digging garden borders in the host's backyard.

I never understood how my dad's obsession for gardening fit with his brilliance as an engineer. Dirt and digital seem opposed, but maybe transistors, resistors, and capacitors mingled in my dad's mind like marigolds, magnolias, and boxwoods.

Ed Miller was deep, quiet, and self-contained — a Scorpio type — so I never grasped his inner world. Maybe he had Asperger's, but this was four decades before the diagnosis was coined. What I do know is that his trips to West Coast hi-fi shows got him hooked on the California dream.

In the sixties, the Golden State's movies, bikinis, and palm trees lured every Midwesterner like a siren song — especially Chicagoans who endured bleak winters and sooty snow from November through March. My dad spent these winter months reading entrepreneurial magazines while secretly plotting his escape to the sun. One winter, he famously used a propane torch to plant bulbs in the frozen soil. OCG (obsessive-compulsive gardening) deserves a spot in the DSM manual.

When I left for college, Ed Miller sold his share of Sherwood Electronics. Without much consultation or consideration, my dad purchased a car wash in Torrance, California — a wet and clangy mechanical underworld where fancy cars got damaged by tow chains and motorized brushes, customers complained, and guys off the street performed wipe-downs for tips. Multiply a few bucks per car, 100 cars per day, times 30 days, subtract loan payments and overhead — and that's the business.

After my freshman year, my brothers and I drove the family station wagon from Chicago across the Mojave Desert to begin our California lives. Cars were funky back then, so with the 100-degree heat, we ran the heater full blast to keep the engine from overheating. Soaked in sweat, we finally pulled off the 405 freeway and into the "family car wash" to meet our destiny. To my shock, my famous dad, with his industry accomplishments, was hunched in a dingy office sorting credit card slips. Back then, car wash owners got together weekly to trade charge card slips. If you sold Chevron gas, you swapped slips with the Shell and Mobil guys — like exchanging currency from different countries.

"Hi, dad, we made it," I announced. "Wow…this is something."

"Can you vacuum?" my dad asked.

So, we got to work.

During dinner that night at a local Denny's, I sensed something was wrong. My ashen dad stared into an unseen void. I was too frightened and ill-equipped to handle the dark side of my dad's emotional moon, so I froze, too — we all did.

My mom was still back in Chicago, packing the family home and closing her budding PR agency as one of the first women to break that ceiling. Did she know what was going on? Was she equipped to break the emergency glass?

Finally, I worked up the nerve. "Dad, what's going on?"

"I've put an offer on a house in Palos Verdes; we can see it tomorrow." Then he down-shifted: "The car wash… business has been falling off."

My dad's dad, Sydney Miller, was a gambler who launched a Kentucky distillery that failed. Sydney failed again at a parking garage. And after that, he spent his golden years studying race results while his obese Kentucky wife berated him. We ignored these family dynamics as kids, and only later did I crack the family code as an adult. Today, we talk about *intergenerational trauma*. I got my dose that night at Denny's.

In 1970, researchers had just sequenced the genetic code, but the "karmic code" — the idea that behavior has a genetic component — was novel. That explains why nobody rang the alarm when they saw my dad's big gamble. Only a gambler would leave his business and career behind, not to mention the friendships, our temple, and the home he and my mom built — all to put his winnings on a lame car wash.

My dad's "Sea Biscuit" car wash was located in the heart of the Southern California aerospace industry. It seemed like a good bet, but there was no Internet back then, so you couldn't Google "aerospace employment" and discover that it peaked at 1.4 million in 1967 and slid precipitously to 900,000 by mid-1971. Aerospace production workers, engineers, and scientists all fell by nearly 50 percent — as did car wash revenues.

In Greek mythology, the Sirens lured sailors to shipwreck on a rocky coast near the Ionian Sea. This analogy speaks to me because years later, I gambled on a sunny Ionian sailing holiday in the iffy month of October. There were no Sirens, but we were slammed by a week of Sirocco winds and hellacious storms.

The guy selling the car wash was not dressed as a Siren or even a mermaid, but with his finger on the local pulse, he knew to sell his sinking business to a Midwest rube with golden dreams. Odysseus was also a dreamer. He longed to hear the Siren's song – so much that he ordered his soldiers to tie him to the mast while they blocked their ears.

The moral of Odysseus is presumably to lash oneself to the mast of fortitude — but the real story is told by the sailors who sank to the bottom.

The Greeks have a word for this, *katabasis,* which describes the inevitable sinking in every quest. By definition, *katabasis* means *descent,* such as heading downhill, the sinking sun, a military retreat, or a trip to the underworld. We have many words in the English language for sinking, but only *katabasis* captures the fateful sinkholes that swallow a heretofore lucky life.

Suzuki Roshi, who brought Zen Buddhism to the U.S., described *katabasis* more succinctly: "Life is like stepping onto a boat which is about to sail out to sea and sink."

Robert Bly, in *Iron John,* the seminal 1990s book behind the men's movement,

described how men experience the intensity of their buried wounds through *katabasis:*

> When katabasis happens, a man no longer feels like a special
> person. He is not. One day he is in college, being fed and housed
> – often on someone else's money – protected by brick walls men
> long dead have built, and the next day, he is homeless, walking the
> streets, looking for some way to get a meal and a bed.

A switch gets flipped in *katabasis.* More than a life transition, the rug gets yanked, triggering a pivotal life change. Bly continues:

> It's as if life itself somehow 'discharges' him. There are many ways
> of being discharged: a serious accident, the loss of a job, the break-
> ing of a long-standing friendship, a divorce, a 'breakdown,' an
> illness.

> The way down seems… to require a fall from status, from a human
> being to a spider, from a middle-class person to a derelict. The
> emphasis is on the consciousness of the fall.[1]

Having waited forever for the light to change at Pacific Coast Highway, I finally crossed all six lanes to face my *katabasis.*

After the car wash debacle, my mom scuttled my dad's dream house. She insisted that they move into the Edgewater Beach Towers apartments near Santa Monica — where Sunset Boulevard meets the sea. The funk factor was high with its creaky elevator and desolate corridors, but my mom needed the ocean to regulate her frayed nervous system.

My mom and dad were both forced to get jobs. Nann Miller leveraged her *katabasis* to reinvent herself as a spokesperson for the LA fashion industry and ultimately build one of the first women-owned PR agencies.

My dad never rebuilt his career. He got a job as an engineer, then later started *Great American Sound* to manufacture high-end audiophile components. My parents purchased a beautiful home in Malibu with sweeping views of the mountains and coast by this time. Without telling anyone, my dad used the home as collateral for an SBA loan. When *Great American Sound* failed, the house went too. They sold it to Simon Le Bon of Duran Duran, who sold it to Roy Orbison's widow, who enjoyed it until a massive wildfire swallowed it to ashes — yes, *katabasis*.

My parents paid off the loan and bought another house, further out in Malibu, but with more land for gardening. Was this a failure or a success? You tell me.

I crossed the highway, headed up the apartment elevator, down the corridor, and stopped. I shook off my Walt Whitman buzz and entered the door. My mom was watching *60 Minutes* while my dad read the paper. My brain circled in wonder: "Who are these people claiming to be my parents?" (Word of warning: Don't hang with your parents while stoned.)

As a rule, college students should spend as little time as possible with their parents. Transferring schools shouldn't have been a big deal, but after a 20-year golden childhood, this was my first experience of descent – yes, a first time for everything. I didn't know about *katabasis* or that the Greeks figured it out 2500 years earlier. What I did know was that my emotional power grid had shut down.

A word about shutdown: According to the *polyvagal* theory, the vagus nerve *wanders* through the body to form two circuits that regulate our emotional regulation system — one social and one restorative. In the same way that thermoregulation keeps our temperature at 98 degrees, our autonomic nervous system keeps our emotions on an even keel.

When our comfort zone is upset, the depressive state kicks in as an adaptive response to adversity — and not a disorder. Okay, it's a theory.

With polyvagal theory, when we feel threatened, we try to reestablish our sense of connection and safety through the *ventral* vagal circuit — the social Uplift circuit situated around the lungs, heart, and facial muscles. If that doesn't work, we progressively resort to evolutionarily older defense strategies. First, we will draw upon the *sympathetic* nervous system to activate self-protection. Here, we might feel shaky, anxious, or panicky — traditionally called "flight or fight."

If this sympathetic response doesn't reestablish a feeling of safety, we default to an even older part of the vagus nerve, the restorative *dorsal vagal complex* centered in the gut. The *dorsal vagal* functions in this primitive way – like a train engineer who pulls the emergency brake. The dorsal circuits engage shutdown strategies where you feel collapsed, depressed, or numb. A mouse playing dead in a cat's mouth is a dorsal survival strategy.

At the Edgewater Beach Towers, I shared an apartment bedroom with my little brother. Feeling hopeless and collapsed, I hung onto a slim thread of my Body Electric. I slipped on my Koss headphones, randomly tuned into underground rock KLOS-FM, and prepared to self-isolate. I sunk into my state like a frozen mouse, centered into *dorsal,* and let *katabasis* envelop my depressed cocoon. An unexpected voice suddenly awakened the center of my lizard brain:

> "Let me introduce myself. My name is Ram Dass. *Dass* means servant, and *Ram* is one of the names of God — that which is nameless. Prior to being Ram Dass, I was Richard Alpert, Ph.D. in psychology. I taught at Stanford, Cal, and for five years, I was an assistant professor at Harvard University. My research took me into consciousness-altering and mind-expanding chemicals in 1961 with Tim Leary, and we did quite a bit of work together. That work led to my dismissal from Harvard because that was such controversial research."

My vagal nerves tingled from the sound of this Ram Dass guy's voice. He continued:

> "In 1967, I went to India, mainly because every map that was written about what we were experimenting with came out of the Indus Valley in the Himalayas. So, I went with a friend in a Land Rover looking for Whirling Dervishes, Indian mystics, and we ended up in Nepal. I met a young American who knew a lot more about what I was looking for, and I stayed with him for several months. He ultimately brought me to a man up in the Himalayas who, within a few minutes, showed me that he knew everything that I thought and everything that I was in my past. In addition, as I got

to know him, he represented everything I was trying to achieve with psychedelics. He was that statement all the time."[2]

I wasn't interested in gurus at this point, but the interviewer, Elliott Mintz, suddenly asked a question that went straight to my funk.

> **Mintz:** For those who are listening right now, and are so desperately seeking a way out — or a way in — what do you have to do?

> **Ram Dass:** The first thing you do is dig the humor of your own predicament of being on a desperate search.

You kidding me? *Dig the humor* of my predicament?

> "It's just another set of thought-forms," Ram Dass continued. "Everybody that's on a journey, the first thing to realize is that you are already here. When you get to the end of the journey, you realize that you were here all along. It's not really much use to know you're already here when you don't know you're already here."

I confess. I wanted *not to be here* in my predicament. But the following words triggered a spiritual crisis:

> "This is a trip you take right here, right now. There's nowhere to go, nothing to do. It's about learning to watch your drama unfold. It is important to expect nothing, to take every experience, including the negative ones, as mere steps on the path, and to proceed."

Even the negative ones?

> "So the game is to get rid of all the thought-forms that keep you from being here. They are only thought-forms in your head and they're usually connected to past or future. Because all of your thoughts are in time, and those are what keep you bound in a certain stuck place where you're searching or suffering or it's not enough."

Well shit. I didn't realize it at the time, but Ram Dass had planted a seed — a small particle of self-awareness deep in my subconscious.

I didn't understand co-regulation at the time, but according to the polyvagal theory, we seek help (from a friend, lover, or a pet) to reset our nervous system. Ram Dass had that effect — up-regulating me from *dorsal* to *vagal* — deep inside my Koss headphones.

A few months later, I invited my Illinois buddies to visit for a spring break romp through Big Sur and San Francisco — a whole week of co-regulation and renewed buoyancy. When they arrived, I tried to ignore the karmic split our journeys had taken, so I invited everyone to the beach to smoke some weed. I didn't realize it, but I was already on the Ram Dass path, learning to embrace every experience, *even the negative ones* — so I declined a toke.

To be honest, I couldn't wait for my friends to leave. I wanted to dig into a strangely printed book of Ram Dass discourses I found in Berkeley — *Be Here Now* — a publishing experiment created by young seekers at the Lama Foundation, a spiritual commune in New Mexico.

Ram Dass described the publishing process:

> "They start with these four-foot pieces of cardboard, and this book is 108 pages and each day they meditate from five to eight in the morning – there's a group of five of them – and then all in silence… they hand rubber-stamp each page, all the letters of the page, and then the artists do all the sketching around the thing. Then the whole thing is photo-reduced and shipped to Japan where it's printed on rice paper, and hand-stitched because it's an experiential-type document."

What was I to make of this odd square book printed with different inks, different papers, and meandering text? Was it a talisman, scripture, or a hologram? Whatever it was, it was sucking me into an unknown dimension. I let the words penetrate:

"BEAUTY = TRUTH = PURITY. It's all the SAME TRIP, It's all the SAME. Any trip you want to take leads to the SAME PLACE."

Well damn. There's nowhere to go, nothing to do. With that, Ram

Ram Dass

Dass became my spiritual tour guide.

A few weeks later, Ram Dass came to UCLA. I had never seen a gossamer audience float into Royce Hall before, but they did. In 1967, everyone wore tie-dye. In 1969 it was army surplus. And now, in 1972, we were Mexican peasants. Disco fashion would come two years later. I surveyed the dreamy-eyed crowd and felt at home. These were my people.

Ram Dass became our New Age Johnny Carson. He cajoled us with spiritual one-liners and mystical wit — all tailored around the "inside joke" — that living on the material plane was a big trap for those not in the *know*, not in the *now*.

Treat everyone you meet like God in drag.

~ Ram Dass

Whether by oversight or design, I overlooked Richard Alpert's most important teaching — the one alter ego Ram Dass rarely talked about: His spiritual awakening resulted from a massive dose — not of psilocybin — but *katabasis*.

Sara Davidson, in a 1972 interview for Ramparts Magazine, captured the shadow side of Ram Dass' transformation from Harvard to the Himalayas:

> At Harvard, Alpert taught psychology and practiced psychotherapy. He flew his own plane, collected antiques, cars, a sailboat, and scuba-diving equipment. Although he had spent five years in psychoanalysis, he says, he was tense and suffered diarrhea every time he lectured. He drank heavily and was a closet homosexual, "living with a man and a woman at the same time in two different parts of the city – a nightmare of hypocrisy." He looked at his

colleagues on the A team at Harvard and saw that none seemed fulfilled or content. He feared he himself would wake up 40 years later no less neurotic or more wise, and he panicked. "I thought the best thing I can do is go back into psychoanalysis. But then I started to have doubts about the analyst. Is his life enough? Whose life is? Who's saying, right, it's enough?"[3]

In 1961, as part of his Harvard research, Ram Dass took the infamous tab of psilocybin. By 1963, he was fired. Davidson continued:

> By 1967 Alpert was in a state of despair, the dimensions of which must have been truly hideous. He had cut all his lifelines and was adrift in the midst of nowhere. He could not go back to the straight world, and after hundreds of acid visions, neither he nor anyone knew how to make constructive use of the experience.

> His mother died early in the year, and when a friend invited him to travel across India, he accepted not in hope of learning any-thing, but because, oh well, what else? He watched the countryside go by, and his depression never lifted.

Before psychedelics, Ram Dass had been an atheist, but even then, a spiritual sinkhole was opening beneath his feet. The formative work of his destiny was well underway.

Long before my bouts with *katabasis*, I had been fascinated by sink-holes. How is it that these geologic "*kata-basins*" suddenly emerge from the earth? One moment, kids are riding bikes in the cul de sac, and the next, an angry chasm swallows the neighborhood.

Take this metaphor on any level you wish: The ground beneath our feet is not as solid as we think. Solid ground is made from dirt, rocks, and minerals. Our "solid selves" are woven similarly from thoughts, patterns, and memories. Water, like spirit, seeps into the under-ground structure to erode the limestone and sediment. Similarly, spirit dissolves our hopes, needs, and expectations. When the flow of water reaches a tipping point, the subterranean structure collapses into a void. *Katabasis!*

The power of *katabasis* is not in the descent (the rollercoaster ride) but in *facing* the bottom. It comes from realizing the *nothingness* at the heart of every charade. Robert Bly called this realization *ashes*. Ashes play a significant role in every culture. On Ash Wednesday, the ashen spot symbolizes death and repentance. Human remains become ashes. And after a raging forest fire, heartbroken home dwellers sift through the ashes of their lives. In alchemy, *nigredo*, or blackness, describes the stage of putrefaction or decomposition that forms the philosopher's stone — another term for building an immortal soul.

> Ready must thou be to burn thyself in thine own flame; how couldst thou become new if thou have not first become ashes!
> ~ Friedrich Nietzsche, *Thus Spoke Zarathustra*

As my new life descended toward *katabasis*, I redirected my journey to the path every golden child takes — to avoid *ashes* at any cost. I had no idea Richard Alpert faced the black hole of *katabasis* to become Ram Dass. Like so many New Agers, I was drawn to the off-ramp — the spiritual bypass that keeps *katabasis* at bay. Kirtans, yoga, vegetarian food, peasant blouses, and feel-good gatherings created a counter-culture – a sunny premature retirement in our twenties.

I also had no insight into *katabasis* because Robert Bly's book would not be published for another two decades — when I was age 42 — the official year to have a midlife crisis. If you're wondering why this book on Uplift insists on dragging you through *katabasis*, a little reminder: stairwells, escalators, and elevators go both directions. *Going down?*

Robert Bly ends *Iron John* with a curious list of eight men who faced *katabasis* – men "who are open to ashes." A little research shows that they all faced loss, grief, or disgrace in some manner. What's not clear is whether Bly is lauding or lamenting their stories (with my notes in italics):

1. **Richard Pryor**, comedian
   Spent five months in jail for drunk driving and subsequently lit himself on fire with 151-proof rum while freebasing cocaine. He was treated for burns covering more than half of his body.

2. **James Baldwin**, author
   Baldwin left his cruel and judgmental Pentecostal stepfather to become the first civil rights activist to come out as gay when "closeting" was the norm. He self-exiled to France.

3. **John Cassavetes**, film director
   A long-term alcoholic, Cassavetes died from liver cirrhosis at age 59. At the time of death, he had amassed a creative stockpile of forty unproduced screenplays, three unproduced plays, and one unpublished novel.

4. **C. Everett Koop**, 13th Surgeon General
   Koop was recognized for his landmark work on cigarette use, AIDS, and children with disabilities. As a young man, Koop spent a year in the hospital after a brain hemorrhage from a childhood skiing accident. His son died in a climbing accident while at Dartmouth.

5. **Woody Allen**, Director, writer, comedian
   Allen was described by Roger Ebert as a "treasure of the cinema" for his prolific body of work, including the eerily prescient "Crimes and Misdemeanors" about a man who arranges a hit on his wife and gets away with the crime. Woody Allen's public life spiraled into disgrace when he married his stepdaughter — 35 years younger. Around the same time, Allen was accused by his adoptive daughter, Dylan, of sexual abuse. After a high-priced legal fight, the Connecticut state attorney dropped the case because young Dylan was too "fragile," and (life imitating art) Allen was never charged with the crime.

6. **Cesar Chavez**, Farm labor activist
   After founding the United Farm Workers, Chavez became a hero of the left for his work on behalf of migrant workers. Later in life, as a political figure, his authoritarian leadership, need for the spotlight, and association with a cult-like organization, Synanon, generated controversy and strife within his organization.

7. **Jimmy Carter**, Former President
   After being elected to restore ethics and morality after Nixon,

Carter had the bad luck to oversee the Iranian hostage crisis and command a disastrous rescue mission in the desert. Carter's warmth and authenticity were painted as weakness by the Republican right-wing. This, plus a possible plot by Reagan to delay the hostages' release, caused him to lose reelection in a humiliating landslide.

8. **Reshad Feild**, Author, spiritual teacher

Raised in the British aristocracy, Reshad (Timothy) Feild performed with Dusty Springfield before his inner yearnings took him on a spiritual journey to Turkey to meet the Whirling Dervishes. Feild's new age classic, The Last Barrier, drew countless seekers to the spiritual path and brought the mystical poet Rumi into public awareness. From an ashes point of view, Reshad suffered a long dependency on alcohol, went through four marriages, faced financial and medical difficulties, and couldn't form enduring relationships with teachers and mentors. Reshad jokingly called himself "Father Figure Anonymous," which explains how he became my teacher for nearly three decades. Always an enigma, Reshad rarely acknowledged his ashes, but he never hid them either.

Endnotes

1   Bly, Robert. Iron John: A Book About Men. Da Capo Press, 2004

2   Reprinted with permission from ElliottMintz.com

3   Sara Davidson, "The Metamorphic Journey of Richard Alpert," Ramparts Magazine, February 1973. www.saradavidson.com

Chapter Three
THE ENERGY MUST
GO THROUGH

"You write your own book as you go along.
But you can't really make it up as you go along
unless you know you're loved."
~ Reshad Feild

"CAN YOU COME DOWNTOWN AND SHOOT A PHOTO?"

"Okay, okay, Mom, sure. What, when?"

"Five o'clock. NBC's Tom Brokaw is coming to the Hyatt."

My mom's celebrity wall of photos needed one more trophy, so I obliged. What I didn't expect was that this gig would change my life.

I was living in my parents' house in Malibu a year after college – the Duran Duran/Roy Orbison house that later succumbed to wildfires. After the car wash debacle, my mom's career blossomed to become the PR Director for the Hyatt Regency Los Angeles. As a spiritual by-passer, a big career was not on my list, so I moved into my parents' garage, rent-free, where I built a film/photo studio. I also constructed a tiny loft — my pooja pad for reading *Be Here Now.* I preferred the ocean views and mountain scents to the hellish drive downtown — but when my mom rang, duty called.

Katabasis rebooted my life to become a spiritual seeker. Life's compass ultimately points in one of two directions: living outward or turning inward – one, a path of ambition, and the other, self-inquiry and reflection. The inward path is supposed to wait until after career and family — but like many in my generation, I reversed the order. In addition to inward and outward, a third direction is possible, "turning inside out." I'll get to that in the Epilogue.

First, the backstory: A year before Tom Brokaw, I was reading *Be Here Now* when Ryan, the sixteen-year-old sadhu of Malibu Beach, strolled unannounced into my puja pad.

"Hey, man," Ryan asked devilishly, "Have you experienced the states Ram Dass talks about?"

I should complete the picture. Ryan carried an ever-present plastic bag of rotting fruit in one hand, Vivkekanda's *Yoga Sutras* in the other, and didn't seem to bathe.

"States? Not directly," I answered, keeping my cool. "But, I intuit the truth of what Ram Dass is saying."

"You need to try some organic mescaline," Ryan suggested bluntly.

Until then, I wouldn't have taken that bait, but my desire to get it over with — like a first try at sex — led me to take Ryan up on the offer. Together, we took off in my VW bus to Reyes Peak, where we camped, fasted, and ingested the drug.

Your results may vary, but at elevation 7,000 feet, I lost my spiritual virginity. More so, I dissolved into cosmic consciousness (that's what I called it at the time). While under the influence, I entered eternity, which was terrifying because eternity is a very, very, very long time.

After this stunt, I made two resolutions — 1) to dedicate my life to awakening because I experienced the truth behind the curtain, and 2) don't try it again.

About a week later, while walking up Janss Steps at UCLA, I spotted a hand-scrawled sign that read: "FESTIVAL OF LIGHT."

Changing course, I followed the sign toward a young flutist who was ignored by the passing students. Sam, the flutist, must have spotted me because he put his flute down and announced: "Mr. Mory Berman is here today. If you are interested in cosmic consciousness, he would be happy to meet with you."

I sputtered in my tracks, "*Cosmic consciousness?*"

Without introduction, Mory, an elderly Jew from the Old Country, approached with fire in his eyes. I turned as Sam approached from the

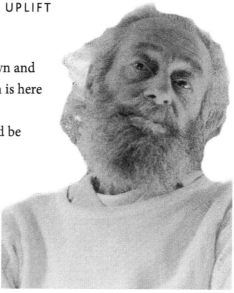

Mory Berman

right, "Can you do Thursday at four?" Sam asked.

"What is this about?" I probed, feeling bewildered.

"This is very important," Mory explained. "You are the racehorse, a thoroughbred. That's who I am looking for."

Thursday at four arrived, and the Thursday after that. I spent a year with Mory, driving him to the bank, drugstore, and the wholesale fruit market (he was a fruitarian) — all while learning the path of service. Mory never shared the purpose of our relationship or what was supposed to happen, but a mysterious something was transmitted.

"I talked to you in your dreams last night," Mory announced one Thursday. He dropped little nuggets that seemed benign but jolted my guardrails. For example, the time I played him a Ram Dass recording:

"That's me! That's me talking!" Mory exclaimed as if obvious.

When I told him I wanted to become a film artist, he reacted in horror: "*Ar-teest?* Did you say, *arteest?* You just end up in the cuckoo house!!!"

On the Thursday afternoon that became "Mory Graduation Day," no one answered when I knocked at his door. After convincing the Armenian landlady to let me in, I found Mory in *savasana,* the yoga corpse pose — and very much a corpse. I imagined he followed the yoga cue, *let go,* to its full expression. Mory once told me he was a "stepping stone" on my path, so I sat quietly and meditated. None of the yoga books laid out the protocol for a dead teacher, so I eventually called the police and his family. My meditation came to an unsettling close when the forensic squad arrived, taking flash photos. When they left, I "borrowed" Mory's complete set of Khalil Gibran books and drove away feeling that my spiritual life had launched.

Mory's *"ar-teest"* comment hit deep. I sold all my film gear because Mory was right — without real knowledge, I would end up documenting my neuroses and projecting them on the screen.

Without much direction, I bopped around spiritual events. I even got "shakti-bopped" by Swami Muktananda's famous peacock feather — but without any effect. On the way out, I grabbed a flyer: " *Reshad Feild — The Reappearance of the Christ, Ambassador Hotel, December 19, 1974."*

I crammed the flyer into my pocket, thinking, "Unlikely... but, if I happen to be in downtown Los Angeles Thursday night...."

Yes, the Tom Brokaw night.

Back then, people didn't use Jung's word "synchronicity," but new age seekers were convinced of their specialness when the stars aligned. Call it spiritual narcissism, but the new age was actually *new*.

The author, James Joyce, was a big believer in synchronicity, but without the narcissism. He viewed fortuitousness through the meat-and-potato lens of coincidence. He reportedly told a Swiss friend, "Chance furnishes me with what I need. I am like a man who stumbles along; my foot strikes something, I bend over, and it is exactly what I need."

Joyce would have set my spiritual narcissism straight — but I didn't read the classics. Many years later, while I was trying to unravel the conundrum of Fortune, I asked my meditation teacher, Dr. Bhagwan Awatramani about synchronicity. His eyes rolled, dumbfounded by my question.

"Synchronicity?" Bhagwan replied in a fuddle. "What do you mean, synchronicity? The whole universe is synchronous."

One way or another, the synchronous universe timed my photo gig so I could dart from the Hyatt to the Ambassador Hotel – the storied setting where the Rat Pack performed, Judy Garland staged her comeback, seven U.S. presidents stayed, and where Sirhan Sirhan assassinated Bobby Kennedy. In 1974, the once-glamorous hotel was inching toward demolition, but the magic was still there.

I looked around. "Who are these people?" Unlike the spiritual hippies of the Ram Dass scene, the Reshad Feild folks were more serious. Reshad's call for epochal change and planetary consciousness was heady stuff, but I wanted Reality without a side of sentimentality, so I fit right in.

"We are preparing the groundwork for the Second Cycle of Mankind," Reshad heralded. "This change can come about through the transformation of consciousness that is needed at this time. We are starting this school for the shortest possible time — forty days. Our goal is to work together, then go back into the world, fulfilling our obligation in being born man and woman. And this means to come to know who and what you are. Only then can you be of real service to the reciprocal maintenance of the planet."

Reshad wound up his pitch as electric guitars rocked Kyrie Eleison and lifted us to our feet. The arched ballroom took on a UFO glow as the Uplift swooshed away every drop of *katabasis*. Don't get cynical. This was the dawn of the New Age, and I was hooked.

"I can come back to Los Angeles and start a school," Reshad offered, "but you have to do all the work."

I liked the hit-and-run nature of the school — just forty days. I signed my name to the list, moved out of Malibu, and offered my unfired soul to the Kiln. We rented a vacant mansion in the Wilshire District and launched the Institute for Conscious Life.

The Institute for Conscious Life

Thirty-five aspiring students moved into a house built for eight. No one had money, so we lived on rice and pinto beans — hardly today's yogini scene of Maui, Costa Rica, Bali, and Tulum. The spiritual cauldron included a concert cellist, Jewish stripper, Afghani dervish, drywall installer, biker girl, Berkeley Communist, and a B-movie comic actor. Rumi famously described the cooking pot:

> "Why are you doing this to me?" the chickpea complained. The Cook knocked him down with the ladle: "Don't you try to jump out," the Cook scolded. "You think I'm torturing you. I'm giving you flavor, so you can mix with spices and rice and be the lovely vitality of a human being."

Spiritual schools famously gathered an odd mix of spices to stoke the heat needed to dissolve mental gristle. The Institute for Conscious Life was no different. Reshad cranked the temperature through the pressure of time. We woke at 5 am, prayed at 6 am, then cooking, cleaning, classes, study, more cooking, cleaning, exercises, more cooking, cleaning, evening class, how about some more cleaning, and bed at midnight. People also kept vigil through the wee hours, transcribing talks. On top of this, we staged weekly public performances.

I had no idea what I signed up for; no one did. We gathered for "zikr" on day one, linking arms and chanting "Allah-Allah-Allah." A stray

thought occurred, "What's a good Jewish boy doing in a place like this?"

I decided not to identify with the Allah business. I was here for Uplift — but that required living in compressed time. A stove-top pressure cooker boils two-hour beans in 30 minutes. A spiritual pressure cooker is no different — the minute-by-minute intensity forced us to live in the present moment.

We think of time as a measurement — a constant ticking of the clock on the wall. But time is also a mental energy that vibrates through us — at a languid pace while sipping a pina colada or with electric intensity when the pressure cranks up. Compare the pace of a 30-second commercial from the 1960s to a TV spot today. Somewhere along the way, humanity's capacity to absorb accelerated time received an upgrade.

So what was I doing in a place like this? I'm not particularly religious nor interested in belief systems. As an aspiring filmmaker, I wanted to learn the mechanics of creative living — how to flush old patterns and renew the creative spirit. On Reyes Peak, I encountered the deep programming that drove the story of my life. At 7,000 feet, I faced the existential predicament of "Bruce" and asked the obvious question:

"Who am I?"

It's not a question that can be answered scientifically, intellectually, emotionally, or even religiously. Reshad offered an answer that was as good as any:

"According to Mr. Gurdjieff, what you are is a cosmic apparatus for the transformation of energies. There is nothing romantic about it. You are basically a tube through which subtle energies are transformed."

Okay, a tube.

This goes to the heart of the matter, so let's pause. All tubes function the same way. Something goes in; something comes out. Food in, shit out. Oxygen in, carbon dioxide out. That's easy. What about ideas, impressions, and experiences? What comes out? How are subtle energies transformed?

Unlike food and respiration, you can't measure subtle energies. But they can be felt. In the Reshad school, we became adept at allowing the energy to "go through." I apologize to the skeptics — there's no way to identify what energy we're talking about or where it's going. But you can't *sense* the moon pulling the tides either. Try kayaking against the tidal current. Yes, it's a thing.

It's humbling to the intellect, but the *Roto-Rooter* plumber has a better grasp of what's "going through" than a cognitive scientist. Good plumbing makes for a happy home. And letting the energy go through is the key to health, wealth, creativity, relationships, endurance, and maintaining an erection. This question, "Did the energy go through?" carried mystical significance at the Institute. We were practicing to become tubes.

At the end of every workshop, someone asked the ardent question: "Did it go through?" *It* being a mysterious energy seeking to manifest in this world — or so we were told.

The movement of energy became our singular concern. Reshad taught us to feel energy blocked by asphalt and from violence to the land. We learned earth acupuncture and how to drive iron rods wrapped in copper to guide the earth's energy into areas of depletion or violence. We also learned how a Whirling Dervish channels energy like a DNA helix in motion.

We sensed two simultaneous vortexes during meditation — one clockwise and the other counterclockwise. Through visualization, we learned how to anchor this mysterious energy into the world. Reshad warned, "This is highly esoteric and potentially dangerous; don't share this practice with anyone." I came to understand why. When Reshad

NBC News visits the Institute

described "the walking wounded of the spiritual path," I realized how the spiritual path invites occupational hazards. Too much of a good thing (without sufficient grounding) is too much.

Our energy sensitivity got crazy — sounding the *Hu* while kneading bread, washing the walls with rosewater, burning Epsom salts and alcohol to clear thought-forms from a room, and visualizing the beginning, middle, and end before every undertaking.

When Bhante Dharmawara, a Buddhist monk who lived to be 110, visited the Institute, per his instructions, we covered the walls in green fabric to channel the healing powers of the color green — something Bhante discovered in the jungles of Cambodia. Bhante bounded into the room at the sprightly age of 86 and instantly ignited my curiosity. If anyone exemplified continuous renewal, Bhante was the fountain.

Bhante prayed with us:

> *O Green Rays of Balancing Cosmic Force,*
> *Thou art the Source of Strength, Energy, and **Youthfulness**,*
> *Flow on me thy Eternal Rays of Wisdom's **Source**,*
> *Make my Mind and Life Evergreen and Fresh,*
> *O Emerald Rays of Great Harmonizing Light*
> *Make me thy Instrument, fit to serve*
> *Mankind.*

I prepared for Bhante's famous green meditation by hanging stage lights with green gels in our meditation space. I hadn't

Bhante Dharmawara

anticipated that the heat would soar to 100 degrees, but there we were, sitting with Bhante in the sweltering *green heat* of our "Cambodian jungle." I soaked to the skin, but his prayer sunk deeper. Life is "evergreen," ever-reaching toward self-renewal. Bhante bestowed a gift — that the knots of self can untie. No effort is required — only trust.

Reshad closed the evening singing the Roberta Flack hit, *The First Time Ever I Saw Your Face* — a song penned by Reshad's singing mentor, Ewan MacColl. Everyone ooh'd and ahh'd with sentiment, but I became fascinated by the energy and how it would shift from uptight skepticism into tears of release – the Uplift. Unlike the tearful folks, I watched closely for the "sleight of mind." I was the cynic scrutinizing Siegfried & Roy materialize a white tiger. Okay, Reshad, show me the Uplift trick!

The guy's a performer, I reasoned. He sang with Dusty Springfield, but something else was happening — all these hearts opening in unison. What sort of plumbing materializes tears?

The answer came when J.G. Bennett's students arrived from England to lead a workshop on the Octave — knowledge that came to the West via Gurdjieff and was chronicled in *In Search of the Miraculous*, by P. D. Ouspensky.

Bennett met Gurdjieff in 1919 in Istanbul, visited him again at his Institute near Paris in 1922 and again at the end of Gurdjieff's life in 1948. Despite their short time together, Bennett became a leading exponent of Gurdjieff's work. When Bennett passed away in December 1974 (almost to the day Reshad spoke at the Ambassador Hotel), I saw how one door closed while another opened. And now, we were together — Bennett's students and our motley crew — at the Institute for Conscious Life in Los Angeles.

"Two fundamental laws govern the universe," Doug, a mathematician from the Bennett group, explained during the workshop.

"Two laws?" I wondered. I was hoping for one, but okay, but I could go with two.

"Two laws, the Law of Three and the Law of Seven," Doug continued. "The Law of Three speaks to *relations*, and the Law of Seven, also called the Octave, speaks to *transformation*."

My brain tick-tocked as Doug spoke: Okay, a *relation* is like having a girlfriend. *Transformation* is how dating morphs into marriage. Having a teacher is a *relation*. Being in a school is a *transformation*. The Law of Seven is the process of getting cooked.

Doug continued, "Gurdjieff referred to the Law of Seven – the Octave – as *Heptaparaparshinokh* and the Law of Three, as *Triamazikamno*."

Now I was lost, but I sensed that the Octave was a big deal — the Big Tube Reshad had mentioned.

"Every phenomenon in the universe is the manifestation of three forces," Doug explained. "And every process follows the seven steps of the musical scale — Do, Re, Mi, Fa, Sol, La, Si, and Do. When you sing these notes, they sound whole and complete, but the way they move up from note to note doesn't proceed uniformly. Look at a piano. A black note sits between every key — except between Mi and Fa and between Si and Do, where the black key is missing.

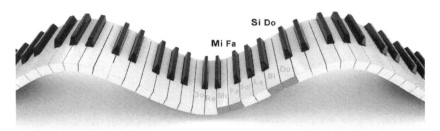

"We use the musical scale to talk about the Octave, but this is not about music. We are exploring the transformation of energy – how our efforts get stuck, why communications break down, and why it's so difficult to change our ways.

"Like playing notes on a piano, the Octave of transformation moves effortlessly up and down the scale, except at two junctures – the Mi-Fa and Si-Do. At these intervals, the movement is checked, and new energy must be summoned for the Octave to proceed along the original path."

Okay, slow down, Doug. I don't remember my fingers getting "checked" playing *Heart and Soul*, so this business with the intervals was confusing.

Instead of a piano, I mused on the steps of a staircase, uniform steps. When a carpenter builds a staircase, the steps proceed uniformly. The rise of each step is seven inches. If the steps aren't uniform, they don't pass inspection. Why? Because they present a *hazard*. Doug must have picked up on my muse.

"J.G. Bennett observed Hazard as the creative force in the universe," Doug explained. "Hazard explains how chance enters into a process as an outside force. There is an element of risk in every matter of significance.

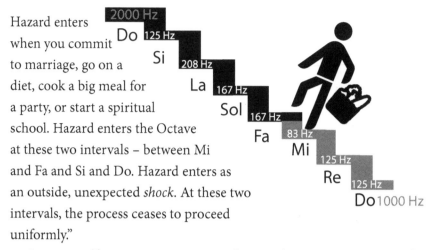

Hazard enters when you commit to marriage, go on a diet, cook a big meal for a party, or start a spiritual school. Hazard enters the Octave at these two intervals – between Mi and Fa and Si and Do. Hazard enters as an outside, unexpected *shock*. At these two intervals, the process ceases to proceed uniformly."

I saw myself carrying groceries up the initial stairs, Do-Re-Mi, with the proper rise. In my dream, I was excited to cook fettuccine *aglio e olio* for my girlfriend, Penny. I must have been thinking of sex when I hit the shorter step — the Mi-Fa step that didn't pass inspection. With this unexpected shock, a carton of eggs flew out, and after a few expletives, I opened the carton, saw that most were cracked, and (change of plans), I decided to make a soufflé.

"Bruce, I love soufflés. They're sooo fluffy," Penny cooed. Fluffy being the code word for let's have sex… Snap out of it, Bruce.

Doug began to explain the math. "Don't get hung up on music theory, but Pythagoras discovered the notes of the major scale by plucking various lengths on a string. Plucking the string at half the length sounded the same note, but an octave higher — from Do to a higher Do. Pythagoras

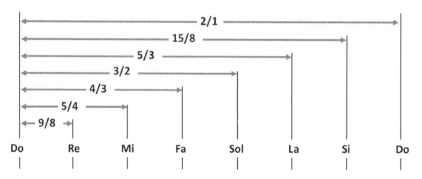

found the other notes by plucking different interval ratios: 3:2 (perfect fifth or C to G), 4:3 (perfect fourth), 5:4 (major third). If a note has a frequency of 1000 Hz, one octave up is 2000 Hz — designated as 2:1. Whole number ratios explain why the notes sound pleasing to the ear."

Doug had us sing the scale. The sense of completion at the top felt obvious — and glorious.

My thoughts went back to the stair-steps. On the piano keyboard, the rise between notes is not uniform. Most notes have a black key in between, but between Mi and Fa, there's no black key. Going from C to D is a full step (major 2nd), but going from E to F (through the Mi-Fa) is a half step — a minor 2nd that feels foreboding.

In the stairway chart (left), if Do is 1000 Hz, the rise between steps starts evenly (like good carpenter steps) — 125 Hz, then 125 Hz — then slows to 83 Hz (you'll trip on this one), then rises evenly, but faster — 167 Hz, followed by 167 Hz — then speeds up 208 Hz and then slows back down to 125 Hz until we hit the top at 2000 Hz. The uneven steps illustrate why there are no straight lines in nature. Energy zigs and zags.

Doug read from *In Search of the Miraculous* to explain the uneven rise:

> "The principle of the discontinuity of vibration: all vibrations in nature, (whether ascending or descending), do not develop uniformly but instead with periodical accelerations and retardations. At a certain moment, a kind of change takes place in the impulse, and the vibrations cease to obey it, and for a short time, they slow down and may even change their nature or direction."

Got it. I'm climbing the stairs — clomp, clomp, clomp — mindlessly following the measured clomp in my step. I know how to climb stairs. I sense the first rise when I lift my foot, which sets the pace. Even if grocery bags obscure my feet, I sense where to place my foot. But with uneven stairs, the periodic retardations throw you off — "a kind of change takes place," according to Gurdjieff. When I stumbled with the groceries, my body "ceased to obey" my impulse (my will) to get to the top and a "change of direction" ensued. Instead of fettucine, it was now souffle, and with a stroke of luck — even sex.

The energy wasn't going through at this point, maybe because I was daydreaming. Unlike Reshad, Doug wasn't skilled at "changing gears." If you've sat through a boring lecture, you know the feeling when people start nodding off. Sensing this sluggishness as the Octave bogs down is the key to allowing the "energy to go through." Reshad sensed this shift and barged in.

"Don't get into the mind," Reshad exhorted. "This is about love, making love possible on earth. Do not take any of this for granted. One day, you will have the responsibility for holding a thousand people."

Without explaining "holding a thousand people," Reshad quickly changed gears, "You know how two porcupines make love?"

I wanted to blurt out, "SOUFFLES!"

"VERY, VERY CAREFULLY," Reshad guffawed.

Reshad laughed at his joke, and everyone followed suit.

With the energy shifted, Doug continued, ascribing qualities to each note of the Octave.

"Take these as a guide," Doug explained. "They are not absolutes because we are talking about qualities that describe an energetic journey."

Doug assigned qualities to each note of the Octave (the parenthetical descriptions are mine).

Do — *Intention*

(The first note in the Octave activates a process or launches a journey to fulfill a decision. So often, we stumble into things without a sense of initiation or beginning. Writing a paper begins with a blank page. The husband carries his bride over the threshold, and a job candidate has a day one. Four percussive notes launch Beethoven's Fifth and set the mood for the symphony as a whole.)

Re — *Rhythm*

(The second step establishes the beat. With Re, the process moves forward with momentum and a sense of doing. Like a wind-up toy releasing its spring, the propulsion from Do can only carry us so far. The mechanical momentum from Re puts points on the scoreboard that we can draw from when the going gets tough.)

Mi — *Identification*

(Mi rhymes with "me." In any process, the energy of self-absorption turns in on itself. This is where we begin to think about ourselves — "I'm tired, I'm distracted, what's in this for me?" *Do-Re-Mi, Do-Re-Mi* loops like a rotating machine — so much so that Mi can short-circuit our efforts to go further. Modern pop and hip hop songs use sampled loops and mechanical beats. They can also fail to evolve, as do our routines of work-eat-sleep-work-eat-sleep.)

Mi-Fa — "Chaotification" — *Barzakh*

(Doug referred to the Mi-Fa interval as "chaotification," but I think of it as *barzakh* — Arabic for the intermediate realm. It's the veil or a barrier between two states, also described by the mystic sage, Ibn' Arabi (1165 - 1240), as the *isthmus*. This "no man's land" between Mi and Fa creates a feeling of instability when the rate of climb suddenly slows (the funky step). Imagine a manual gearbox when the clutch briefly disengages between third and fourth gear. In the Mi-Fa, with gears spinning, nothing pulls you forward. In this lull, you could just as easily downshift into second as up-shift into fourth. Remembering one's intention while spinning out of gear is the key to moving through the Mi-Fa. Importantly, an outside shock enters this intermediate realm to move a process forward. If you were a fruit tree, bees serve as the outside shock. They form an essential part of the pollination process for the formation of fruit.

Fa — *Expansion of the Heart*

(The *I Ching* refers to "Crossing the Great Waters." Leaving behind that which no longer serves you lets you arrive at the uncharted terrain of the heart. Imagine climbing a hill and reaching the top of a rise — from Mi into Fa. You expect to see the verdant valley of Fa, but it's shrouded in fog. You can't know Fa until you step beyond the mist of the mind and into the energetic heart of love. Indiana Jones took this step crossing the bridge of faith in *The Last Crusade*. Fa is synonymous with Uplift.)

Sol — *The Thing Itself*

(Sol rhymes with Soul. It captures the whole journey — the love, pain, sacrifice, and realization. It follows Fa like a second act. The "mid-point crisis" functions like Sol in a story structure. In *Raiders of the Lost Ark*, Indiana Jones finds the Ark to fulfill his quest but is left to die in the crypt.)

La — *Negation*

(In Islam, *"La ilaha illallah"* means "there's no God but God." La means "no." We must sever the past and shed beliefs that no longer serve us to move forward. In a story, Act Three starts with the final clash between the protagonist and the antagonist, but in this case, it's with the self — the delusions that hold us back.)

Si — *Surrender*

(In the Octave of transformation, we are changed. Who you are in the beginning is not who you discover yourself to be at the end. This self-image is surrendered into the cauldron of actuality — like the alchemical process of transforming a base metal into gold.)

Si-Do — *Gratitude*

(During childbirth, the mother, exhausted from labor, experiences a surge of gratitude as the baby's head emerges. The Si-Do is the "crowning" of the Octave. This interval heralds new life coming into this world. Relaxation and gratefulness, and not effort, move us through the Si-Do because the future is coming *into the present* from the world of possibility.)

Do — *Completion*

(A feeling of realization provides the capstone of every effort. In the Octave, this note signals a harmonic sense of glory and fulfillment. The new Do mirrors the sounding note, but at a higher vibration to describe the spiral nature of life.)

"Perfect timing," Reshad announced. "Now, it's time for lunch. Thank you, everyone. We set the lunch hour to coincide with the note Fa — the expansion of the heart. Can you feel it?"

Reshad was right. Suddenly, I felt lighter and more expansive — as if a weight had lifted. With this buoyant feeling of release, chatter erupted like mice escaping from a cage.

"S T O P !!!" Reshad bellowed to freeze the scene. After a long pregnant pause, he spoke softly, "Please respect the energy that is being born. We are making love possible in this moment and not some other moment. We are here, now, for the future of mankind. Now, please, gently, continue."

I ate my pita sandwich with fitful chews — not wanting to upset the future of humankind or yank the energy into an unexpected direction.

After lunch, I closed my eyes and settled into the stillness. According to the program, we were in the note Sol — *the thing itself* — the entirety in a single note. In Sol, we face ourselves, not in a confrontational way, but in the mirror of self-reflection.

Donna Bell

"I am going to invite Donna to take us on a journey with her cello," Reshad instructed. "Don't listen to this as a piece of music, but allow the energy to move inside you. Leave behind the baggage that no longer serves you — the hurts, and expectations, and the shocks. Let these crystallized patterns of the past be healed in this moment if you allow."

Donna centered herself, lifted her bow, and began to play. I felt the energy begin to move. Was Donna doing this? Was Reshad playing through her? Did we invite this energy?

Years later, while meditating with Bhagwan over Skype, I marveled that the energy moved through me the same way as decades earlier with Donna on the cello. Bhagwan described the phenomenon:

> "What is this energy that we are discovering? It is something that can't be seen, that we can't think about or imagine. So, how do you know it exists?
>
> "You know it through its effect on you — how it affects you intimately. Does it become a part of you? Is it what gives you life? Does it give you an awareness? This energy affects you intimately to bring about the awareness that this Being is yourself. Ordinarily, there is no awareness of Being. This mysterious energy infiltrates your body and becomes your Being.

"There are many forms but only one Being. This mysterious energy is your Being. It is beyond the universe. So are you beyond the universe? You can't answer that; you can't think about it. But this is the truth — the truth of yourself, the truth of your Being."

Donna finished the meditation with a slow draw of her bow culminating at the final Do. Tears flowed into the pin-drop silence.

That night, the tears in the house became sobs and bawling and even wailing into wee hours. I laid still in my Army surplus metal spring bunk, mindful not to add squeaks to the release of emotion upstairs.

"Just let it go," I could hear Reshad coax. "It's okay, dear. Just let go of the pain, the hurt, the violation of your being."

"No, no, no... I can't!!!" the sobbing continued.

My god, what's a good Jewish boy doing in a place like this? Indeed.

My Octave initiation did not come in the middle of the night or with tears. It came through an act of abandon on a hot July night. Reshad's son, Oran, had been born in the house earlier that day. Right after dinner, Tom Springfield walked in. I didn't know the guy, but he was Dusty Springfield's brother, an Oscar nominee for *Georgy Girl,* and Reshad's former bandmate. Let the alcohol begin.

After Tom and Tim (aka Reshad) downed a few gin and tonics and swapped stories from their chart-topping days, out came the guitars, drums, and tambourines. Feeling bold, I grabbed a conga drum. Tom launched into *La Bamba,* which his sister Dusty (aka Mary) recorded a few years earlier. You may know the Richie Valens hit, but you don't know the Institute for Conscious Life version. Imagine Tom and Tim leading a forty-person conga line through the house, all bellowing the *Bamba* refrain — louder and looser with each verse.

Here comes my initiation: I was insanely shy as a 24-year old, barely able to utter a word in public. But with sufficient focus, I could keep a good beat. Suddenly, the conga line steered Reshad into my orbit. "Oh, boy," I thought, "Here we go."

Reshad positioned himself face-to-face, eye-to-eye, and countered my beat on the drum. Reshad drummed faster, challenging me, *mano a mano*, to a conga duel. Faster and faster. To keep up, I would have to *let go*. And I did.

With the conga line snaking, dancers erupting, *Bamba Bamba... Bamba Bamba,* the Octave energy grew wild.

Without thinking, I looked into Reshad's eyes — drunk smiling eyes, yet he was present, free in himself, channeling creative energy from some distant star.

Para bailar la bamba se necesita una poca de gracia!!!

Like a Latin jet engine thrusting mysterious energy, the roof started to lift, releasing that same Uplift I tasted at the Ambassador Hotel, but now chaotic and more dangerous. I felt the same foreboding that signals the crash of a tray of drinks, but instead:

"STOP!!!!!!!!!!"

At the top of the stairs, a Sikh doula, shrouded in white, crowned in a turban, and armed with her ceremonial sword yelled STOP, bringing the chaos to a crashing halt.

"Denise is resting with the baby and has asked for the celebration to end," she announced as if a military communique.

Amid the sheepish shock and sudden self-restraint, I remembered the mantra: *The energy must go through.*

Kazoom, it went through, all right — through the neighborhood, the city, and probably the universe.

Oran: I hope you're reading this. I think it went through you.

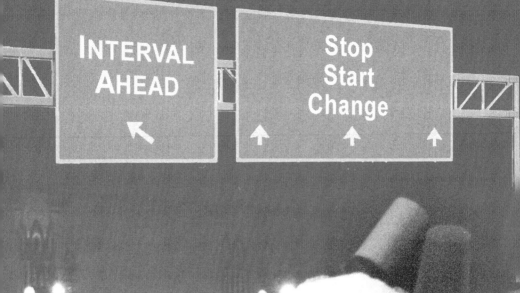

Chapter 4
I AM THE OCTAVE

"Nobody can stop time; we must accept that.
The universe turns, and the days fall, one after the other."
~ Suleyman Dede

IF THE OCTAVE APPEARED AS A HIGHWAY SIGN, it would read:

INTERVAL AHEAD
STOP-START-CHANGE

A few days after Oran's La Bamba celebration, we received the STOP in the form of a stern letter from the city: *This cease and desist order is to inform you that you are operating a school in a residential zoning.*

There it was – the outside shock.

I reflected on how our forty-day intention became eighty and how the pressure inside the chickpea pot pushed the Octave past its due date and finally burst. I remembered the night we dragged Reshad's mattress down the stairs so he could stay up all night until we "learned to love each other." And, the 6:00 am chanting in the basement vault, the vipassana meditations at noon and the Arica exercises at 4:00 pm,. Then there was the parade of guests including NBC News, Governor Jerry Brown, Linda Ron-

The Silverlake duplex

stadt, Ellen Burstyn, Pir Vilayat Inayat Khan, Yogi Bhajan, and the supernaturally young Bhante.

Like chickpeas on the run, we dispersed in four directions to *Start* over. Reshad and family found a garage apartment near the Whisky-a-Go-Go, and I moved back to Malibu.

The Berkeley contingent wanted distance from Reshad, so they moved into half of a duplex in the Silverlake area. That strategy succeeded for a few months until the second half became vacant, and bingo – Reshad and family moved in next door.

We followed suit and moved into the Silverlake neighborhood. I took up residence in the garage. With the team back in the boiling pot, we crowded into Reshad's side of the duplex one afternoon while he read from his new book. Reshad paused, put the manuscript down, and announced, "I have been communicating with Suleyman Dede, the sheikh of the Whirling Dervishes in Konya, Turkey. He's never been to the States, but if you raise the money, we can invite him to Los Angeles."

It seemed like a benign request. I had a vague sense of Suleyman Dede from Reshad's book, *The Last Barrier*. In the story, Reshad's teacher, Bulent Rauf, asked Reshad to pray at Rumi's Konya tomb, knowing it was verboten. When furious security guards arrived barking orders in Turkish, Suleyman Dede suddenly appeared and rescued Reshad from his breach of decorum.

To understand why praying at the tomb was verboten, you must go back to 1926 when Turkey's first president, Kemal Atatürk, shut down the dervish lodges and tombs and forced the dervishes to conceal their Sufi ways from the authorities. Even using the word "dervish" invited imprisonment. Suleyman Dede was just 21 years old when he started his dervish training until – *stop-start-change* – Atatürk dissolved the Sufi orders, banned the use of mystical names, titles, and costumes, impounded assets, and prohibited their meetings. He ordered the Mevlevi lodge and Rumi's tomb to cease its religious function and become a museum. Dede spent the next several decades cooking for the poor (an approved function) while practicing the dervish rituals secretly – and illegally.

Suleyman Hayati Loras Dede

Flash forward fifty years. The now elder Dede, age seventy-four, landed in Los Angeles with a mission. "I come to plant Mevlana's message of universal love in this soil," Dede announced. "The way of Mevlana, of Rumi, will grow in the West in its own way."

1976 was ripe for a Rumi resurgence. Nixon was behind us, the New Age had arrived, and more importantly, Rumi (1207-1273) had reached his seventh centennial – a significant number if you are counting octaves.

Our Silverlake duplex filled quickly with guests, talks, initiations, and whirling. And here's the CHANGE part of *stop-start-change*. Overnight, the Institute for Conscious Life morphed into the Mevlana Foundation. Dede gave us new marching orders – to bring the mystical poet Rumi to America.

Stop-start-change enters a process as an outside shock – a sudden snap-out-of-it that upends one story and advances another, often fulfilling a historical imperative. The dramatic universe always performs its magic this way – through the Octave in action. Bennett explained:

> "It is through the unforeseen openings of Hazard that something
> new can come in from the Future... those cracks that let the light in.[1]

In the dramatic universe, the same blocked energy that stifles a business meeting operates on a cosmic scale. If you ever sat around a conference table, you know the Octave. You've seen how everyone fights sleep or fiddles with their phones while the boss drones on, reading a

Powerpoint. Suddenly, and mercifully, the crack opens, someone blurts out the real issue, and the meeting jolts back into motion with a creative urgency.

In a meeting, checking off boxes on the agenda gives the appearance of change – *click-click-click* through the presentation. But if the unfettered exchange of ideas and voices is absent, there's no opening for the outside shock. What looks like forward motion is actually a downward spiral of energy. The drooping energy goes unnoticed – unless the vector of change – the blurt – upsets the status quo and moves the mission forward.

Two weeks after Dede arrived to plant the seed of Rumi in America, a continent away in Maine, the poet Robert Bly handed a stack of Rumi poems to a young poet from Georgia, Coleman Barks. Bly famously requested: "Release these poems from their cages." Coleman Barks, originally from Chattanooga and now an English professor at the University of Georgia, had never heard of Rumi. But, he dutifully worked and reworked the translations every afternoon in a coffee shop for seven years before even thinking of publishing.

Atatürk was prescient when he reportedly stated after shutting down the Mevlevi lodges:

> "You, [the followers of Rumi] have made a great difference in combating ignorance and fundamentalism for centuries, as well as making contributions to science and the arts... Nonetheless, the ideas and teaching of Rumi will not only exist forever, but they will emerge even more powerfully in the future."[2]

Mustafa Kemal Atatürk (middle) and the Mevlevi Order, 1923

Atatürk couldn't foresee that an unassuming cook from Konya and an English professor from Chattanooga would jump-start Rumi's reemergence, but that's how Rumi went from total unknown to the most-read poet in America.

Vectors of change alter the historical landscape. In 1492, Columbus "discovered" America and, with this "outside shock," brought Catholicism, conquistadors, and foreign diseases to the New World. In 1893, Swami Vivekananda, a wandering Hindu monk, followed his intuition and traveled by steamer and train to Chicago's Parliament of the World Religions. Vivekananda lacked an invitation, but he found his way to the podium through a series of flukes. He cracked open the world of organized religion when he announced:

> "Sisters and Brothers of America... I am proud to belong to a religion which has taught the world both tolerance and universal acceptance... We believe not only in universal toleration, but we accept all religions as true... all lead to Thee."[3]

The universality of God was a novel idea in 1893, but Vivekananda's speech, captured in headlines, lifted people from their seats for a three-minute standing ovation. Vedanta had come to America, ultimately influencing Joseph Campbell, George Lucas, and even Star Wars.

An "outside shock" also changed the course of Tibetan Buddhism when, in 1950, the People's Republic of China forcibly annexed Tibet. The tension between Tibet and its overseers built until 1959, when the Tibetans revolted, and the Dalai Lama fled to Dharamshala, India. With tragic irony, China's suppression of Tibet catapulted the hermetic religion into a worldwide phenomenon.

Even benign vectors force dramatic change: When your partner announces, "We need to talk," life takes off in a new direction. I would add biopsy

Swami Vivekananda

results, letters from the IRS, layoff announcements, and even parking tickets to the list of outside shocks. They all force open cracks to the light. Unexpected shocks shift the mechanical trajectory of Do-Re-Mi into a place of Hazard – into the Mi-Fa interval. Shocks reflect God's attribute, *Al-Fattah*: *He Who Opens All Things.*

Using Malcolm Gladwell's tipping point metaphor, an outside impulse appears as a tipping point at a moment of critical mass – a game-changing shift that you don't see coming. Today, we see tipping points across the planet: hundred-year floods, record storms, a semi-permanent El Niño, and the collapse of the Antarctic ice shelf.[4]

Tipping points also explain why venture firms initially give their product away for free. They want to achieve scale and jolt the status quo through rapid adoption. The tipping point also explains why Amazon. com was willing to lose money for 17 straight quarters – to change the face of retail forever.

Tipping points explain why, in his first year, President Biden wanted to pump trillions of dollars into the poor and middle class. He sought to change forty years of politics skewed to the wealthy. Well, he tried.

At first, an outside shock appears insignificant. When Steve Jobs introduced the iPhone to a crowd of techies in 2007, he announced, "We're going to make some history together today." But no one imagined that a pocket device would change the course of civilization.

The product had a 3.5" screen, an 8-hour charge, and only worked on AT&T's crappy network. It should have failed as a product, but as an outside shock, Jobs surprised the world when they realized that one device in your pocket could lay 20 products to rest.

Little vectors force bigger change. The coronavirus is a case in point. In one scenario, the worldwide pandemic was triggered by a single person feasting on a bat-bitten ferret badger who got sick and visited a crowded market in Wuhan, China, in October 2019.

From CNN:

> Only bad luck and the packed conditions of the Huanan seafood market in Wuhan – the place the pandemic appears to have begun – gave the virus the edge it needed to explode around the globe, the researchers reported in the journal Science.
>
> "It was a perfect storm – we know now that [the virus] had to catch a lucky break or two to actually firmly become established," Michael Worobey, a professor of evolutionary biology at the University of Arizona who worked on the study, told CNN.
>
> "If things had been just a tiny bit different, if that first person who brought that into the Huanan market had decided to not go that day, or even was too ill to go and just stayed at home, that or other early super-spreading events might not have occurred. We may never have even known about it."[5]

Maybe it was a bat, an anteater, or maybe, the virus escaped from a Wuhan lab.[6] Regardless, the coronavirus stayed "over there" until February 2020, when two cruise ships signaled *stop-start-change*. A single sick person (a vector of change) infected hundreds of people aboard the Diamond Princess in Yokahama. One month later, its sister ship, the Grand Princess, moored for a week off the California coast until it was permitted to dock in Oakland on March 3, 2020.

"I like the numbers being where they are," Trump said in a Fox News interview. "I don't need to have the numbers double because of one ship that wasn't our fault."

Americans watched in dread as healthcare workers in

hazmat gowns wheeled sick passengers off the ship. One week later, a wave of panic rolled from coast to coast as frantic customers emptied grocery store shelves. Buzzfeed named March 11, 2020, "The day COVID swallowed everything." That was the moment the coronavirus pierced our veil of normalcy as an outside shock.

MSNBC's Chris Hayes remembered that fateful day:

> "I felt like we were all standing on a beach, and this wave, this tsunami was building on the horizon, and people couldn't see it, and you're screaming for people to get off the beach."

Astead Herndon, a national political reporter at the New York Times, remembered:

> "I'll just never forget turning my phone back on after the [Broadway] show. My first text was from my friend. It was an all-caps 'FUCK.' I remember saying aloud to her, 'Oh my god, Tom Hanks has COVID. Oh my god, the NBA shut down.' That ride back from the show was so eerie. I remember some teenager who ran into the subway, dramatically sneezed and spit and yelled, 'CORONAVIRUS!' and then ran away. It was the one day the reality was starting to set in, and it was suddenly deeply uncomfortable."[7]

The hallmark of an outside shock is a sense of "reality starting to set in." On that same night, I decided to stock up on disinfectants. I entered a Walgreens at 10 pm and eyed the ransacked shelves. "Holy shit," I thought. So, I drove across the street to what's billed as the World's Biggest Kroger. Inside, I found a scene from "War of the Worlds," the Orson Welles 1938 radio drama that sparked a national panic. The virus particles had not yet entered our atmosphere, but shoppers were heaving everything from toilet paper to Cheeto's into carts while children screamed in exhaustion.

Thus began our big national problem – an alien invasion that exceeded anything Orson Welles could have conjured.

Reshad explained, "There's no such thing as a problem, just an unattended situation." The idea of "no problems" seemed preposterous at the time because, as twenty-somethings, we had lots of problems – all stemming from unattended situations! Failing to check the engine oil, balance your bank account, pay a utility bill, remember a birthday, call your girlfriend, and on and on. For the longest time, I considered *problem versus inattention* a question of semantics.

But, three months earlier, on January 3, 2020, the Trump administration proved Reshad right. After being briefed that day on the outbreak in China, administration officials let three *unattended* months go by before enacting any mitigation efforts. Like an earthen dam inching toward collapse, the three months of inattention crept toward the inflection point of March 11. Engineers release the floodwaters through a spillway so the dam doesn't collapse. The energy is allowed to go through.

"Honey, we need to talk," signals the pressure. "Okay, what is it?" opens the spillway.

I hadn't put it together, but Reshad had given me the ingredient. *Attention* to signs, signals, and importantly, the energy is the key to moving through the Octave.

Working with Reshad, I began to focus on the question: Is the energy going through? I became sufficiently versed in feeling the energy to become Reshad's Octave Apprentice. And like the Mickey Mouse character, I put on my sorcerer's hat and started teaching the Octave. There's no degree in Octavology, but as a school for spiritual transformation, the Octave became the primary merit badge and the steam that powered our ship.

Reshad would often ask, "Where are we in the Octave?" "Mi-Fa!," we'd reply. Like atmospheric pressure before a storm, we would sense the intensification. Glassware would break in the kitchen, the sound system would fail, or the chaos of nervous banter would escalate. And when the energy went through – like the sun breaking through the clouds after a storm – hearts would open into Fa, into the Uplift.

As the Octavologist, I gave classes, explaining to new people how the Law of Three produced the steam for our school for transformation, and how the Law of Seven piloted us through the breaking waves.

I began each Octave class presenting evidence for the Laws of Three and Seven. My flip chart listed the following:

Expressions of the Law of Three
(Third force in italics)

- Gurdjieff
  Affirming, Denying, and *Reconciling*
- Electricity
  Positive, Negative, and *Ground.*
- Atomic Structure
  Protons, Electrons, and *Neutrons*
- Weather
  High pressure, Low pressure, and *Precipitation*
- Mediation
  Affirming, Denying, and *Mediator*
- Law
  Plaintiff, Defendant, and *Jury*
- Marriage
  Husband, Wife, and *Child*
- Christianity
  Father, Son, and *Holy Spirit*
- Taoism
  Yin, Yang, and *the Tao*
- Physics
  Space, Time, and the *Continuum*
- Sitcom
  Set-up, Complications, and the *Resolution*

Every relationship (two forces) invokes a third force that reconciles the two opposing forces and allows the energy to go through. For example, the judge instructs the *jury* to remain impartial to reconcile the conflicting claims between the plaintiff and the defense. With the weather, temperature variations create high and low-pressure areas that reconcile as rain. On a sunny day, the pressure is high. When low pressure moves in, high and low collide. The air is free to rise into the atmosphere, where it cools, condenses and returns to earth as rain.

In spiritual transformation, the desire for freedom (active) encounters fear and resistance (passive and denying). The Third Force (a mysterious energy) releases our stubbornness (mental identification) through *grace and humility* – fancy words for letting the energy go through.

Bhagwan's "mysterious energy" also described the Third Force:

> "What is this energy that we are discovering? It is something that can't be seen, that we can't think about or imagine. So, how do you know about it?

> "You know it through its effects on you – how it affects you intimately. Does it become a part of you? Does it give you an awareness? This mysterious energy is conscious. It is life energy – the energy that keeps you alive. It affects you intimately to bring the awareness that this Being is yourself."

To demonstrate the Third Force, I asked people to perform a simple yoga stretch and sense the three forces:

"Okay, everyone, stand up and get ready to stretch. Reach toward your toes (active), and feel your tight hamstrings resist the effort (passive). Now breathe (third force) into the tightness and feel your muscles release. Feel how it affects you intimately."

Flipping the chart, I moved to the Law of Seven (also called the Octave), which describes how events unfold to create our world:

The Law of Seven in our World

- Bible
  Six days of creation and the seventh day of rest
  Seven years of famine and seven of plenty
  Seven deadly sins
- Periodic Table of Elements
  Seven periods – each with the same number of atomic orbitals
- The Natural World
  Seven seas
  Seven continents
  Seven ancient wonders of the world
- Esoteric Body
  Seven chakras
- Solar System
  Seven observable celestial bodies: Sun, Moon, Venus, Jupiter, Mars, Mercury, and Saturn
- Light
  Light refracts into seven colors
- Surfing
  In surfer lore, a "set" is a series of ocean waves that travel in groups of seven, with the seventh wave being the biggest and most powerful.
- Cognitive Psychology
  In 1956, George A. Miller of Harvard argued that the average number of objects a human can hold in short-term memory is seven. This is the don't go shopping without a list theorem.
- Greek Mythology
  The Seven Sisters, or the Pleiades, were the daughters of Atlas's marriage, who held up the sky.

- Disney
    Snow White and the Seven Dwarfs – each a unique archetype
- Marriage
    Marilyn Monroe as the marital disrupter in The Seven Year Itch (See my "Seven Stages of Marriage" in Chapter Six)
- Musical Octave
    In Western music, seven ear-pleasing tones generate from the ratio: 3:2 and culminate in double the original frequency.

As I write, a noisy tufted titmouse has been attacking his reflection in my kitchen window, twelve hours a day, for two weeks now. According to the bird book, the titmouse is trying to establish dominance, but more interestingly, the titmouse sings with perfect pitch.

Some birds sing melodies, like the mourning dove who serenades Bb-E-B every morning. Bird songs reveal how the natural world is wired harmonically. The Octave is not new-age woo-woo or music theory. but evidence of the universe's design.

When I gave my talks, I saw the Octave as a formula – notes on a piano, but I came to realize that focusing on the sequence of notes obscured the Octave as the animating force – the pianist playing the notes. The Octave-as-formula distracts from sensing the life force in the mourning dove's song. Or my decision to jump into the unknown and write this book. More than a measure of topography, the Octave lives in the hiker's **stamina, pushing her limits toward** the top of the hill.

My screenwriting studies helped **and** hurt in this regard. When I studied with the guru of story structure, Robert McKee, he broke a story into formulaic parts to which I applied the Octave:

- **Do-Re** – As a film begins, we are introduced to the world of the protagonist. In *When Harry Met Sally*, Meg Ryan pulls up on campus to pick up her ride, Billy Crystal. She lays out the journey: "I have this figured out," she explains. "It's an 18-hour trip which breaks down to six shifts of three hours each."
- **Mi** – As we see more of Harry and Sally's world, we discover what makes them tick. Harry and Sally argue about whether men and women can ever be platonic. "What I'm saying," Harry announces after an awkward silence, "and this is not a come-on in any way, shape, or form – is that men and women can't be friends. The sex part gets in the way."
- **Mi-Fa** – The central plot point, or inciting incident, radically upsets the balance in the protagonist's life. This event is often benign. It can occur early or later in the story, but always in the first third. Sally's faked orgasm after ordering lunch derails Harry's know-it-all theory of women and sex and pulls him into his saga with Sally. In one of the most famous comedic scenes in film history, Sally climaxes, yelling, "Yes! Yes! Yes!" Sally caps it with a slap on the table, a triumphant bite of coleslaw, and a smile. For the kicker, Estelle Reiner (the director's mom) deadpans from another table, "I'll have what she's having."

Here are other Mi-Fa moments that pushed the protagonist into a new direction:

- In *Sleepless in Seattle*, Tom Hanks calls into a radio show to talk about how much he misses his deceased wife.
- In Hitchcock's *Rear Window*, JB hears a woman scream, "Don't!" and the sound of breaking glass.
- Army intelligence sends Indiana Jones to beat the Nazis in retrieving the Ark of the Covenant.
- The attempted theft of a Gran Torino launches an unlikely friendship with Clint Eastwood's racist character.
- And in *Die Hard*, Bruce Willis realizes that he is the only one who can save the hostages from the ruthless killers.

- **Fa** – Having passed through the Mi-Fa point of no return, the protagonist begins their hero's quest. Progressive complications ensue.
  - Ten years later, Harry and Sally meet again at a bookstore, and in the company of their respective best friends, attempt to just stay friends without sex becoming an issue between them.
  - Indian Jones meets Marion (Karen Allen) in a bar in Nepal, where she drinks him under the table. After a fiery scuffle with the Gestapo, Indiana teams up with his old flame on a journey to find the Ark.
- **Sol** – A mid-point loss forces the protagonist to face a dark night of the soul:
  - At a New Year's Eve party, Harry and Sally confront the complex tangle of emotions they feel for each other.
  - In *Raiders of the Lost Ark*, Marion is seemingly killed in Cairo, leaving Indiana Jones despondent.
- **La** – A confrontation with the antagonist or self builds to a dramatic climax.
  - Harry and Sally fight at their friend's wedding and stubbornly refuse to accept that they are a perfect match.
  - Indiana Jones recovers the Ark from the snake-infested Well of Souls, but German forces surround the entrance.
- **Si** – The final resolution reconciles the crisis and delivers a new understanding.
  - Harry tells Sally that he

loves her at a New Year's Eve party. They kiss and later get married.

- The Germans open the Ark to discover it contains nothing but sand as malevolent spirits explode the Germans' skulls.

- **Do** – With the epilogue, the character arrives in a new place where the strands of the story are pulled together and the credits roll.

  - Several old married couples tell the camera how they met. The last interview features Harry and Sally recounting their zig-zag relationship and how they got married.
  - The Ark of the Covenant is stored in a government warehouse back in DC. The camera pulls back to reveal row upon row of similar crates.

As McKee lectured from his giant notebook – I became confused whether screenwriters write from formula or inspiration. Like a food scientist analyzing a chicken nugget, McKee reverse-engineered every film from *Citizen Kane* to *Chinatown*. He flipped through his big book while we scribbled notes – *exposition, deus ex machina, beat, sequence, arch plot, mini-plot, internal versus external conflict*, etc.

The film industry people in the room went on to make big bucks writing formulaic sequels, sitcoms, and series. I also followed McKee's formula, but my scripts failed. I couldn't crack the soul of my characters to capture their driving forces. If the Octave is like a wild stallion, I was afraid to push my characters to the limit and hang on for the ride.

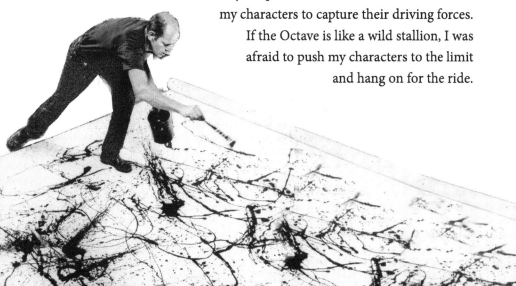

My Octave classes reminded me of the McKee playbook. I was the food scientist, or better, the museum curator discussing Jackson Pollock's painting technique while missing the central fact that Pollock lost both parents, was expelled from schools, drank heavily, cheated on wives, flipped his Olds convertible while drunk, and killed 25-year-old Edith Metzger, the friend of his mistress who sat in the passenger seat.

During the last three years of Pollock's life, the artist struggled with periods of prolonged inactivity, deep mental anguish, and a paralyzing spiritual crisis. If we follow Pollock's Octave, all of his efforts at redirection had failed. If a potter fails to kick the wheel, the whole enterprise collapses into mud.

Each person's Octave is unique. Bob Ross, the frizzy-haired guy on the PBS "Joy of Painting," gained acclaim for his happy trees and cheerful skies. Compare Ross' sunny scenics to Pollock's angry globs. Pollock sought to capture the life force of nature itself.

"The painting has a life of its own, and I let it come through," Pollock declared.

Reshad, like Pollock, dipped liberally into the forces of life. If the Octave got stuck, he might pour a bowl of soup over his head, or threaten to climb out a second-story window, offer spontaneous healing, sing a sentimental ballad, tell a naughty joke, or bend spoons in a fancy restaurant to our horror – always with impeccable timing.

One of his students explained, "He did not teach by words at all, but rather by sound and pattern. It was his voice, his look, his heart, and his very being which exercised impact and fostered understanding."

One night, after a lecture in New Mexico, I probed, "Reshad, if I understand this right, the Octave rises from our intention, and God responds in kind. This seems to be a call and response."

Reshad kept putting on his hat and coat. He was tired, but I persisted.

"So, if we call God's response the *Octave coming in*, here's my question: Does God's Octave coming in face the same hurdles that we encounter?"

Reshad stopped. I suddenly felt small. He looked me in the eye and announced after an uncomfortable pause:

"I am the Octave."

I'm not sure if Reshad was pulling aristocratic rank, sabotaging my train of thought, or simply drunk. Reshad had the rare gift of uplifting a roomful of hearts – so maybe he was the Octave. Like Judy Garland segueing from "Swanee" to a tear-jerking "Over the Rainbow," I found Reshad's magic compelling. If the Octave is a doubling of frequency, Reshad's presence raised the game. Our spit and polish of cooking, cleaning, timing, and attention quickly elevated when he entered a room. More than military duty, the heightened attention raised our vibrational state. The room sang with love.

And like Judy Garland, Reshad used his broken vessel to channel a soaring spirit. What did he even mean, "I am the Octave?" What mattered was that my question was barking up the wrong tree. "I am the Octave" became my riddle, my koan, and a mystery to be solved.

Following my new path, I decided that the Octave technicians had it wrong. The Octave is not a pattern, a scale, a map, or a formula. *You are the Octave.* The Octave launches through intent and proceeds through the heart of the beholder. The Octave is a mysterious energy, channeled through the being of the pianist – and not the piano or the score.

I began to see the Octave as a whitewater ride through the rapids. Even if you've guided a raft down the river a hundred times, Hazard looms at every surge. Today, the flow might be different, or the paddlers may space out when you command:

"Give me two hard strokes on the right!"

A few years back, we were rafting the Olympics section

of Tennessee's Ocoee River. The river meanders through several stretches of whitewater and then heads down the renowned 1996 whitewater slalom course where – one after another – it surges through a sequence of turbulent crescendos. "Humongous," a Class 4 rapid, provides the finale.

The excitement arrives when the river pours into the Humongous Hole and then shoots back as a powerful opposing wave. Ahead of us, a group of rafters headed into this hydraulic volcano under the command of their guide. If you approach Humongous at the wrong angle, you will flip. If you hit it with insufficient speed, the raft will stall, slide backward, then spin slowly until the raft flings everyone into the drink. Imagine a mechanical bull tossing a group of riders. I mentally steeled myself as I watched Humongous swallow the raft ahead and jettison the paddlers into the raging river. After rescuers pulled out the traumatized paddlers, it was our turn. *Gulp.*

"Stroke hard," Tully, our guide, commanded. Not wanting to repeat a humongous mistake, all five of us pulled like banshees, ramming our raft through the raging water. Kawomp! We over-shot the pool below and slammed our raft into a group of innocents chilling at the river's edge.

"Excuse us," I said, feeling sheepish as we extricated our raft from the tangle of paddles and people.

I have retired from rafting, but I hold my whitewater memories as an Octave analogy. From the Olympics course description:

> The course consists of Best Ledge, Smiley's, where a midstream boulder splits the stream, Slam Dunk, the Conveyor Belt wave train, Callahan Ledge, and Humongous. Humongous is the steepest and most constricted rapid, with a wave train on the left and two big drops on the right – Godzilla and Humongous Hole. To avoid getting stuck in the Humongous Hole and missing the rest of the gates, slalom racers needed to catch the Godzilla wave to stop their downstream momentum when entering the eddy and catch it again to surf across the current toward the upstream gate.[8]

That's a lot of river talk. Stated more simply, the river's twists and turns make life interesting – and hazardous. But you chose to raft the river.

If you're inattentive, you will capsize, get pulled under, maybe wedge against a rock and die. If you stay engaged, the river will guide you to a gentle pool and offer the sense of satisfaction that you have conquered the elements.

The missing black notes on the piano had been my catechism, my profession of faith in the Octave. But there are no piano keys on a river. "I am the Octave" forced me to abandon the keyboard, the funky stair steps, and the theory.

In YouTube videos of Humongous, some paddlers emerge triumphantly, and others not. On a destined-to-capsize raft, you could always spot the paddler not paying attention, drifting along as fate approached. Sure enough, *kaboom*.[9]

The river taught me that the Octave forces a confrontation between paddler and river, decision and hazard, planning and risk, and known and unknown. The paddler must face each obstacle with a measure of active versus passive – a Law of Three jujitsu – where just the right moves invite the Third Force.

If "I am indeed the Octave," who is this "I?" Psychologists who study resilience call it the locus of control.

Locus of control is the degree to which people believe that they, as opposed to external forces (beyond their influence), control the outcome of events in their lives.[10]

This so-called locus of control can't control the universe, let alone a river. And internal versus external forces are open to debate, so let's settle on *Will* as the "I" in "I am the Octave." The capacity to steer the boat through Hazard and the unknown is a measure of Will – and Will is the product of Attention. The paddler attends to the external forces of the

Approaching Humongous on the Ocoee River

river and the internal forces of instinct, kinesthetics, and intuition.

To find the river on my piano, I graphed the rising frequencies of the Octave.

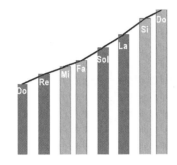

Nice, but not what we experience. So, I replaced the whole thing with a swooping squiggle. This is how we experience the Octave.

I replaced the Mi-Fa and Si-Do intervals with loop-de-loops – the raft flipping over. What had started as a fun boat trip – *stop-start-change* – suddenly became a desperate swimming exercise. The raft hit the Humongous back wave, stalled, and was pushed backward. On the piano, the generous steps of the rising scale compress at the half-steps – yes, those tight little loops. A lot is going on when hell breaks loose.

My friend, Penny, remembered rafting on the Kern River with some cock-sure male companions who failed to give the river its full respect:

"My friends weren't paying attention, and suddenly, we were thrown out of the raft," Penny recalled. "It happened so fast; I was trapped underneath amid the rushing water. An impulse came to me, 'swim away from the raft,' which I did until I resurfaced, grateful to catch a gasp of air."

The swooping squiggle is shorthand for, "Oh shit, we're in the loop." "Swim away from the raft" is the locus of control that knows when and where to swim. Life suddenly goes upside down and backward. The Mi-Fa pushes us into the new normal – capsized in Humongous.

I would end my Octave classes with a sonic experience, using two CD players to live-mix the feeling of Uplift. This was before mp3s and playlists. Fading "Bolero" into "Axis Bold as Love," and into "The Lark Ascending," my clever mix raised the energy, and the audience applauded. Reshad took the microphone and challenged us with a real Octave:

"Thank you, Bruce," Reshad announced. "We are now moving into the note Fa – the best time in a seminar to have lunch. Get in your cars and find the right spot for a picnic lunch. Plan to eat at 12:30. Good luck, and see you back at 2 pm."

These instructions seemed simple enough, but in an esoteric school, the pressure was on – the *right spot* better be perfection. We were in Lucerne, Switzerland, so I let my hosts do the driving. We drove in circles, hit dead-ends, backed up side streets, and followed spiritual instincts that delivered one dud after another. You can't force serendipity, so I expected to eat in the car. I forget who noticed it first, but an unassuming archway beckoned – a stonework at the dead end of the street with a small imposing sign warning us off: "PRIVATE."

Paying no heed, we drove through an *Outlander*-like portal to discover a bucolic pasture where farmers raked hay in a wildflower field. We parked, smiled as if we belonged, hiked across the pasture, climbed a hillock, set our blanket, and absorbed the Alpine scene. In my imagination, Ralph Vaughn Williams' *Lark Ascending* began to play – the ultimate musical expression of Uplift.

I looked at my watch. It was 12:30 pm."

Endnotes

1   Bennett, J. G., & Blake, A. G. E. (2012). Talks on Beelzebub's Tales. Bennett Books.

2   For an in-depth exploration, see my book, "Rumi Comes to America.

3   https://www.artic.edu/swami-vivekananda-and-his-1893-speech

4   Gladwell, Malcolm. The Tipping Point: How Little Things Can Make a Big Difference. Back Bay Books, 2002.

5   https://www.cnn.com/2021/03/18/health/coronavirus-bad-luck-genetic-study-scn/index.html

6   https://www.science.org/content/article/why-many-scientists-say-un-likely-sars-cov-2-originated-lab-leak

7   https://www.buzzfeednews.com/article/buzzfeednews/march-11-covid-tom-hanks-nba-who

8   https://en.wikipedia.org/wiki/Ocoee_Whitewater_Center

9   Ocoee Rafters Flip on Humongous. Jul 14, 2008. https://www.youtube.com/watch?v=FE1mQ6LLsyU

10   Wikipedia. https://en.wikipedia.org/wiki/Locus_of_control

Chapter 5
DIFFERENT WORLDS

*"It is by going down into the abyss that we recover the treasures of life.
Where you stumble, there lies your treasure."*
~ Joseph Campbell

IT WAS THE SEVENTH YEAR OF OUR MARRIAGE (Si-Do), and three years after moving from our tiny L.A. bungalow to a *Tara*-like money pit in Georgia (Mi-Fa), and exactly forty-two years into my life (mid-life crisis) when Karen motioned me to another room. An emotional low-pressure system signaled the approaching storm as I closed the door.

"I want a separation," Karen said calmly.

"You what?" I stammered.

I won't bore you with the details except that the mother of all *katabasis* delivered my ashes.

A few days later, Karen sent over a couple of goons with a truck to move furniture out of our house. ("They were not goons!" Karen objected as I read the draft to her.) At the time, I was paralyzed, watching the citadel of our marriage crumble. But, the tide of events was irreversible. My options seemed limited to just one: fully experiencing the crushing pain in my heart.

The thing about grief is that it is tangible, intense, and palpable. So, I chose to go with it.

I dragged myself to the back of the now-empty house where I had built an audio control room — part of my unsuccessful business plan. I shut the door, collapsed to the floor, and curled into a fetal position. I let the sobbing course through my body and surrendered to an emotional whirlpool that had no bottom. Yes, the Infinite runs in both directions.

Thus began a difficult three years that upended my expectation of a spiritual marriage. Like so many, our perfect union went into the marital dumpster.

Unlike most flirtations with divorce, the deep dive of our three years apart ultimately brought us together. From Robert Bly's ashes came a second son, a successful business, and, all praise to Uplift, a renewed love.

"You need to write a book about THAT!" my friend Jamie suggested. Jamie was one of the smartest, wittiest, and most talented of our friends. She also suffered a knock-out-drag-out divorce from her mendacious lawyer-husband, lost a child to a drug overdose, and broke up from a string of relationships. I understood why Jamie sought the magical ingredient for *divorce reversis*. I can even see the gauzy commercial in my marketer's eye.

> *Ask your doctor about Divorce Reversis. No karma, no dharma —*
> *just pure marital Uplift in a pill.*

There is such an ingredient. But sadly, it's *katabasis* — the willingness to compost your dreams, turn the soil of your life, and let reality bloom from the ashes.

Reversis may not exist in a pill, but in our pillow talk, Karen and I frequently talk about a mysterious ingredient we call *Bondo* — not the auto body filler — *but the capacity to form and maintain intimate relationships*. Some people seem to have ample supply, and others do not.

Karen and I must have had enough *Bondo* to save our marriage, but I'm unsure how it intervened. We study relationships in hopes of understanding the mysterious *Bondo* in action:

> **Me**: "So, you seem to have *Bondo*. How is that?
>
> **Karen**: "My mother was hardly attentive. I spent the first year of my life in the crib while she took care of my sister. And my parents fought constantly. It's a mystery."

Bondo doesn't fit into a formula. And unlike physicists trying to observe the first quark, there's not even a real word for the sub-atomic particle of intimacy.

The Yiddish word, *mensch*, describes someone who has *Bondo*, but a *mensch* is a person, not the ingredient itself. Rabbi Neil Kurshan, the author of the book *Raising Your Child to Be a Mensch*, described *mensch* as:

> Responsibility fused with compassion — the sense that one's own personal needs and desires are limited by the needs and desires of other people. A *mensch* acts with self-restraint and humility, always sensitive to the feelings and thoughts of others.[1]

The closest psychological equivalent to *Bondo* comes from "attachment theory." According to British psychologist John Bowlby (1907 - 1990), the emotional bonds infants form from an "attachment" to a *dependable and responsive* caregiver allow the child to develop relationships safely later in life.

In his final years, the late author and acclaimed neurologist Oliver Sacks warned that the *digital inattention* of modern life might be stunting the *Bondo* of our offspring. He wrote:

> I cannot get used to seeing myriads of people in the street peering into little boxes or holding them in front of their faces, walking blithely in the path of moving traffic, totally out of touch with

their surroundings. I am most alarmed by such distraction and inattention when I see young parents staring at their cell phones and ignoring their own babies as they walk or wheel them along. Such children, unable to attract their parents' attention, must feel neglected, and they will surely show the effects of this in the years to come.[2]

Ouch. If you're looking for a quark-like explanation for intimacy, maybe it's *mirror neurons* — a special class of brain cells that can "read minds." These cells fire to discern other people's intentions, their emotions, and the social meaning of behaviors.

In 2005, Dr. Marco Iacoboni of UCLA reported that mirror neurons magically allow us to discern if a person picking up a cup of tea planned to drink from the cup or clear it from the table. Dr. Christian Keysers of the Netherlands, who studies the neural basis of empathy, found that our ability to experience and share in the emotions of others is linked to the functioning of mirror neurons. Maybe this explains how our dog knows that I'm headed to the hall for his leash and not the vacuum.

Despite Karen's *inattentive* mother (attachment theory), I married someone chock full of mirror neurons (is there a gold medal for empathy?) But mirror neurons also trigger the fundamental physics question: is light a wave or a photon? Is *Bondo* a love energy or a mirror neuron?

I prefer not to reduce life's mysteries to particles. Even though Einstein

proposed that light is emitted in little chunks of energy called photons, I prefer waves because you can't body-surf a photon. Waves transport energy (and love) from one place to another. Waves also explain different energetic worlds. They don't bounce off each other but rather interfere with each other — for example, in current politics, an authoritarian wave is interfering with the democracy wave through voter suppression laws.

As a sailor and a body surfer, I marvel how energy transports through waves — and how a body of water (or a sea of consciousness) can send wave energy from one continent to another.

With *Bondo* (and this gets sexy), when the waves come together just right, and crest meets crest, you get double waves. This pairing is called "constructive interference." In Octave talk, this is the outside shock entering a process. But sometimes, the waves cancel each other out, and you get nothing at all — an interaction known as "destructive interference." For example, how many drops in marital energy (destructive interference) does it take for the "I do" at the altar to spiral into divorce?

To understand *Bondo*, you must start with the premise that people live in different worlds — literally, different energetic worlds. Like overlapping Venn diagrams, relationships start from sparks of flirtation (constructive interference). The two shared worlds (or waves) become seriously meshed — from going steady to getting married, buying a house, and having children. After our college-age son and his girlfriend

moved in together, one day, they announced they were getting a cat. Karen and I kept our mouths shut but winked, knowing, ooh-la-la, a *shared world!*

After thirty or even fifty years, in the marriage ideal, the couple's worlds fully merge and their hearts become one. That's a lot of *Bondo!*

Years ago, I experienced my first visceral sense of different worlds. One summer afternoon, Karen and I worked in the garden when a sweetly alcoholic painter walked up to our 100-year-old house. He looked at the peeling siding and announced, "I kin paint yer house."

With nothing but a Southern drawl, white coveralls, and a toothless smile for credentials, we welcomed Tommy-the-Painter into our world. Before long, Rick, Tommy's outlaw sidekick, joined the team as chief scraper along with Tommy's girlfriend, Peggy, who commented on the work from the chaise lounge. Reports began to filter back that Tommy had been seen at one bar or another the night before, drinking away his wages. I began to realize that Tommy's long midday breaks satisfied the same urge.

Tommy helped me understand the literal nature of different worlds. Picture our neighborhood with its beautifully restored Victorian homes, turn-of-the-century courthouse, and upscale eateries surrounding the town square. It's the kind of place where small children ask to pet your dog while walkers and joggers greet you with smiles.

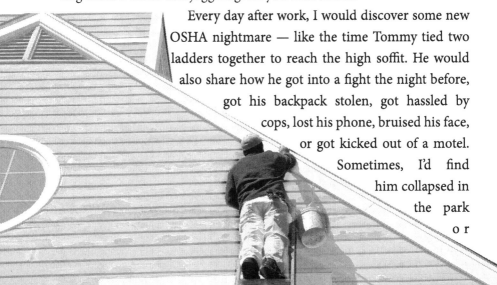

Every day after work, I would discover some new OSHA nightmare — like the time Tommy tied two ladders together to reach the high soffit. He would also share how he got into a fight the night before, got his backpack stolen, got hassled by cops, lost his phone, bruised his face, or got kicked out of a motel. Sometimes, I'd find him collapsed in the park o r sleeping on a bench. For Tommy, our *sweet streets* were *mean streets.* His stories seemed so improbable for our genteel neighborhood that it dawned on me: we lived in different worlds — not just figuratively, but literally. We lived at a different pitch, attracted different elements, and encountered a wholly different fabric on the same street. As much as I hated it, the new age meme was true — *you create your own reality.*

The Li'l Abner character, Joe Btfspik, "the world's worst jinx," personified how we live in different worlds. Joe lived under a small, dark rain cloud to transmit the luckless karma of his personal weather system.

I can't judge Joe Btfspik, or Tommy the Painter, for that matter. After Karen left me, I ate my burger alone night after night at the neighborhood bar — the same bar that became Tommy's hangout.

On many of these lonely nights, I would ask, "Why me?" The more accurate question should have been, how did I lose altitude? How did my life descend into a different world?

When the captain announces, "We have begun our descent," the sensation is palpable. The pitch of the engine shifts, flaps drop, and the airspeed slows. If you miss these cues, the flight attendant will tell you to raise your seat, close your laptop, and lift your tray table. In a relationship — or any failing endeavor — we miss the cues when our airspeed drops. The mechanical nature of daily life obscures the shifting pitch.

Gurdjieff was the first to ascribe the loss of altitude in human affairs to the Octave — the unnoticed changing of gears at the intervals. From *In Search of the Miraculous:*

> What precisely does happen at the moment of the retardation of
> vibrations? A deviation from the original direction takes place...
> After a certain period of energetic activity or strong emotion or
> a right understanding, a reaction comes. Work becomes tedious
> and tiring; moments of fatigue and indifference enter into feeling.
> Instead of right thinking, a search for compromises begins, or
> suppression, evasion of difficult problems.[3]

Using the Octave, Gurdjieff introduced a way of looking at the universe as a cosmic apparatus for transforming energies. He explained how, through self-awareness, we could participate in the creation instead of becoming enmeshed in the created.

In 1913, Gurdjieff appeared in Moscow to attract an assortment of artists, writers, academics, and musicians to his teaching. Gurdjieff was a genius at harnessing the hardships of the Bolshevik Revolution to create the conditions for inner work. He found Marxism "satanic" and fled Russia for Constantinople, then Berlin, and finally France.

Madame Jeanne de Salzmann, who later became the longtime leader of Gurdjieff's work, described her first meeting:

> "I had already been in the 'search' when I met Gurdjieff. When I saw him, and he looked at me, I knew that he was the man who could help me. He accepted me as I was – without judgment.
>
> "He was a serene, massive man who looked at one with a long, contemplative, all-knowing glance. I felt myself in a presence. He had a certain quality that one might call mythological. Later, when I came to be his student, I always felt the same way: He was a man whom you recognized but you didn't know what you were recognizing… When we were in Gurdjieff's presence, we felt his energy infused in us. He could deliver this to anyone in the room. He had something very high and not within our ordinary comprehension."[4]

A young Madame de Salzmann

Michel de Salzmann, a psychiatrist and son of Jeanne de Salzmann, also described the palpable quality of Gurdjieff's presence:

"He was always quiet, contained, regardless of the circumstances, dramatic or otherwise—and there were many such—whether he was on his way to the market or remaining with his students, presiding at his table with many guests. There was always this same kind of density of presence as if he were being seen and as if his own seeing, without judgment, was upon the world. It was contagious. When one was under the sway of this quietness, one had the feeling, all of a sudden, of seeing things from a distance, from tranquility."[5]

Religious concepts and metaphysical ideas almost always obscure the lived experience behind the teaching. Gurdjieff's teachings are no different. Today, countless Fourth Way books attempt to explain Gurdjieff's cosmology, but the challenge to move from ideas to sensations is left with the student. Gurdjieff used the language of feeling and sensation when he described the workings of the Octave:

"[At the intervals], the line continues to develop, though now not in the same direction as at the beginning. Work becomes mechanical, feeling becomes weaker and weaker, descends to the level of the common events of the day; thought becomes dogmatic, literal. Everything proceeds in this way for a certain time, then again there is reaction, again a stop, again a deviation.[6]

When I was a young filmmaker, the rhythms and patterns of life pulled at my curiosity. For this reason, Gurdjieff's teaching and the implications of the Octave hit me as a shock. Do you mean distraction, disinterest and resistance are not just human nature; they are hardwired into the structure of life?

Gurdjieff continued:

The development of the force may continue but the work which was begun with great zeal and enthusiasm has become an obligatory and useless formality... thought goes round in a circle, repeating what was known before, and the way out which had been found becomes more and more lost.

This law shows why straight lines never occur in our activities, why, having begun to do one thing, we in fact constantly do something entirely different, often the opposite of the first, although we do not notice this and continue to think that we are doing the same thing that we began to do.

My first taste of one world flipping into its opposite came in 1983. In a speech to evangelicals, Ronald Reagan referred to the Soviet Union as the "evil empire" (a line he likely stole from *Star Wars)*. Reagan doubled down and called the Soviets "the focus of evil in the modern world." I figured, if we were going to blow up the world on account of these people (who were also my ancestors), I wanted to meet them face-to-face. So I traveled to the Soviet Union.[7]

When I arrived, I expected a whip-smart superpower but was shocked to discover a hapless, backward country — a broken state with an oppressed people still stuck in the aftermath of World War II.

A year after my visit, the deviations predicted by the Octave began to sink the Soviet system like a rusting supertanker. This was a time described as *vremia zastoia*—"the era of stagnation." Two decades of leadership tried to institute reforms — Brezhnev, Andropov, Chernenko, Gorbachev, and Yeltsin — but the die was cast. Yeltsin resigned before the end of his term to install Putin to fill the leadership vacuum.

Putin's FSB (KGB) blew up some apartment buildings (blamed on Chechens) to confuse public opinion, create terror, and redirect their anger away from the corruption that had flourished under Yeltsin.

Putin seized personal power, whitewashed history, and flipped the country into a mob-oligarchy while the world barely noticed. Remarkably, many American conservatives flipped from Reagan's virulently anti-

Russia position to their pro-Russia position today. Succumbing to propaganda, they perceived Putin to be capitalistic, aligned with the Orthodox Church, and pro-family. Flip-flop-flip.[89]

Gurdjieff also watched Russia flip when the Bolsheviks launched a nearly bloodless coup. In 1917, Russia became "its own opposite" — from a monarchy to a communist dictator state.

In a staggering "flip" of values, the American Psychological Association (APA) secretly collaborated with the Bush administration to oversee its post-9-11 torture program – including waterboarding and other torture techniques.[10] Gurdjieff explained:

> All this and many other things can only
> be explained with the help of the law of octaves
> together with an understanding of the role and significance
> of 'intervals' which cause the line of the development of force
> constantly to change, to go in a broken line,
> to turn round, to become its own opposite...

Gurdjieff found a similar parallel in Christian history:

> "Think how many turns the line of
> development of forces must have taken
> to come from the Gospel preaching of love to the Inquisition."[11]

The Gospel of love morphed into the gospel of torture – from the Pope and the APA – by following the laws of nature. Disturbing my innocence, the Second law of thermodynamics and entropy describe the *natural* decline into disorder. Scientifically, "it is *impossible* for any process, no matter how idealized, to reduce the entropy of a system."[12]

Entropy raises the dystopian question, if everything is slated to fall apart, why bother with Uplift and continuous renewal? More specifically, if the downward spiral is baked into nature, "Where's the Uplift?"

I struggled for a long time to reconcile my spiritual aspirations with the futility of it all. Here's the kicker from Mr. Gurdjieff:

> In a descending octave... the greatest 'interval' occurs at the very
> beginning of the octave, immediately after the first Do...

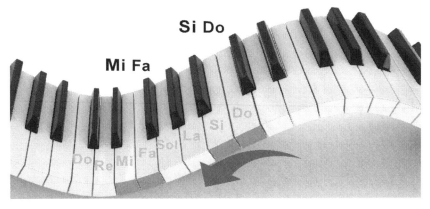

Not only is everything going to hell, but the first step will take you there. If you play a descending scale on the piano (Do, Si, La, Sol, Fa, Mi, Re, Do), the first note — the first plunk of your pinky — drops you right through the Si-Do interval. Gurdjieff explains:

> For this reason, a descending octave develops much more easily than an ascending octave, and in [descending] beyond Si it reaches Fa without hindrance.

Falling down a hill is easier than falling up. This is obvious except in human affairs. Even kids understand the descending Octave from Bugs Bunny. In *Jack-Wabbit and the Beanstalk*, Bugs warns the Giant, "Look out for that first step. It's a Lulu." Again, in *Space Jam*, Bugs tells NBA legend Michael Jordan, "Look out for that first step, Doc, it's a real Lulu." And in *Groundhog Day*, Bill Murray steps off a curb into a pothole of icy slush. A passerby mocks, "Watch out for that first step. It's a doozie!"

Doozie or Lulu, it's the same. What does matter is that nobody warns you of the second step or the third — always the first. Paraphrasing Bugs Bunny, Gurdjieff warns, "Watch out for the first step. It's a Si-Doozie!"

The first step into Lulu Land always goes unnoticed — or more accurately, descent into another world is obscured by unfulfilled desire.

Here's how I know this: To this day, my filmmaker dreams remain unfulfilled. For this reason, it should come as no surprise that the "hook" for my Lulu moment was dangled, not as a carrot, nor by Bugs Bunny, but by an Italian film producer.

The story began in 1987 when my film buddy, Nick Saxton, disappeared for a year. Nick was the kind of artistic genius who bellowed crudely at our dinner table while guzzling our expensive Scotch.

"Do you realize that I worked with Antonioni on *Blow-Up*?" Nick groused. "And George Lucas — he wanted me. Michael Jackson, 'Boogie and the Beat.' Rick James, 'Super Freak,' and 'Give it to me, Baby.' And the launch of MTV? Fucking Pat Benatar, "You Better Run." Your good friend Nicky invented the music video."

The empty bottle of Glenlivet could explain Nick's griping, but more likely it was cruel fate – Nick was now driving a cab.

Nick Saxton (I)
Director · Producer · Camera and Electrical Department

Director (9 credits)
Michael Jackson: Number Ones (Video documentary) (vide
Get Enough")
Pat Benatar: Choice Cuts · The Complete Video Collectio
Better Run", "I'm Gonna Follow You")
Michael Jackson: Video Greatest Hits - HIStory (Video) (
You Get Enough")
Pat Benatar: The Visual Music Collection (Video) (videos
Gonna Follow You")
Rick James: Super Freak (Video short)
Rick James: Give It to Me Baby (Video short)
Pat Benatar: I'm Gonna Follow You (Video short)
Pat Benatar: You Better Run (Video short)
Michael Jackson: Don't Stop 'Til You Get Enough (Video

Producer (3 credits)
Michael Jackson: Number Ones (Video documentary) (prod
Stop 'Til You Get Enough")
Michael Jackson: Video Greatest Hits - HIStory (Video) (
"Don't Stop 'Til You Get Enough")
Michael Jackson: Don't Stop 'Til You Get Enough (Video

A few days after the dinner party, Nick disappeared. No sightings or calls. Back then disappearing was a thing. No text messages, email, Facebook, credit card trails, or Find My Phone to find your friend. But we were preoccupied with our newborn and soon forgot about Nick.

Seven months later, the phone rang. It was Nick.

"Hi… can't really talk." Nick rambled into my ear without any back story. "I've been away; crazy stuff. Been to the moon and back. It will be a movie. This is very big, and I need to see you."

Nick dropped off a one-pound screenplay which I read end-to-end. The story laid out Nick's journey in excruciating detail after the legendary film producer, Giovanni Mazza, stepped into his cab.

I found Nick's redemptive story spellbinding. He had transformed from a cigarette-sex-and-drug-addicted artist to a man of purpose. Wow-wow-wow. Had Nick surrendered the mass of garbage that stood in the way of his life?

Two days later, Nick called again. He asked if I would like to meet

Giovanni. Holy shit, what was I supposed to say?

I drove to the Hollywood apartment where Nick was staying. I was startled by the new Nick — slimmer, better dressed, and more focused. Nick noticed my surprise as he stepped into my car.

"Yeah, this is my fighting weight," he laughed, patting his gut. "This is what you get after living on coffee, cigarettes, and apples for seven months — and occasionally sex."

"So tell me about this Giovanni guy," I asked, pulling into traffic. "Is he your guru or something?"

"I have no idea who he is," Nick puffed like a man of mystery, "I always wondered if a man of knowledge, a guru, a teacher, a realized being, could exist without any kind of label. A man of power but also completely hidden. Maybe, Giovanni's my answer."

"So, Giovanni is a man of knowledge?" I dug further.

"All I know is that he popped into my cab — twice — and the next thing, I'm in a kind of school without any name, without any tradition. He just pushed me to my limits."

"But he's a film producer, right?" I pressed.

"Uh-huh. Remember the campaign to save the Hollywood Sign?"

"Yeah," I said. "Late seventies. Hugh Hefner was behind it."

"Giovanni showed me this little plaque of the Hollywood Sign. He carries it everywhere."

"Like a calling card?" I asked.

"Exactly. So, I called the Hollywood Chamber. They told me that Giovanni Mazza, Italian film producer, gave $27,777 to restore the first O. Alice Cooper donated the last

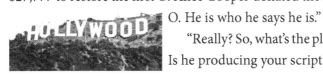

O. He is who he says he is."

"Really? So, what's the plan? Is he producing your script?"

Nick raised his eyebrows in an off-putting mystical manner. "You mind if I smoke?"

As Nick lit his second smoke, I continued driving toward Beverly Hills and fighting the surreal pull of the Rabbit Hole. Nick exhaled out the window and quipped, "If there's a plan, I will be the last to find out."

We parked on a Beverly Hills side street and Nick got out and walked toward a rooming house. I waited, unsure what to do with the portal opening under my feet.

A short time later, Nick returned with Giovanni at his side. In the script, Nick "walked like a pimp," and Giovanni "carried himself like a king." Seeing the pimp and the king together, I flashed on the great buddy films — Abbott and Costello, Joe Buck and Ratso Rizzo, Butch Cassidy and Sundance, and the Odd Couple.

"Hey, give me a cigarette, kid." Giovanni elbowed Nick playfully. "You're not holding out on me, are you?"

They both laughed. Nick pulled out a Dunhill like a gentleman.

"So, this is your good friend, Bruce?" Giovanni asked.

Giovanni was immediately disarming. Picture Danny Devito with ten times the gravitas. Or better, imagine Donald Trump the size of a cannonball, but with an Italian accent.

"I hear you want to be in the movie business," Giovanni poked like a forceful charm bomb.

"Yeah, it's true," I replied.

Giovanni's mojo quickly extinguished my skepticism. He could focus his heat-seeking charisma at anyone in sight, including a guy walking home with a pizza.

"Pizza, pizza," Giovanni called out. "Give me a piece of pizza."

The shocked passerby opened his pizza box to oblige. Sensing fortune's open door, Giovanni grabbed *two* slices.

I watched in fascination as Giovanni leaned against a parked car, folded the slices, and devoured them with pleasure. He caught my gaze.

"What? What you looking at?" Giovanni scolded. "It's no criminal to be hungry, and my good friend here is very generous. Thank you. Grazie!"

The pizza guy smiled woozily and hoofed out of the scene.

"Before we talk about movie production," Giovanni deftly interjected, "I have a little business to attend to. I need $240 to settle up where I am staying. I'm waiting on a check from Milan."

I looked to Nick. He was supposed to be my guidepost toward reality in this situation, but it was not clear whose team Nick was on.

Okay, stop the story. The astute reader probably thinks, "con man," get out of there; this is the oldest ruse since Popeye and Blimpie. But, Nick was not a con man. He was my friend, and Reshad's friend and Nick read Rumi's "Love is Reckless" at our wedding, and now had written this heavy script, and seemed transformed, and I wanted to be in the movies, and the price of admission was a hamburger today for a major motion picture on Tuesday. So, I wrote a check for $240.

As explained, the first step into a different world is the Lulu — the small check. But the next step, raising $30,000 in forty-eight hours, flowed directly from the first. The descending octave works like that, and I pushed against all my mental guardrails to avoid the rabbit hole. I have no idea if I was on the up elevator or the down. I desperately wanted to step into a different world — so that part of the initiation was a success. But, if I took the down elevator when I wanted up — it wasn't the first time. When the doors close, you take the ride you're on.

Twenty years later, I opened the New York Times to read a strangely personal op-ed. It

The New York Times

Giovanni's Gift

By Christopher Matthews
Oct. 8, 2009

f ☉ ⅴ ✉ ⌗ ⌁ ⧉

The man who called himself Giovanni Mazza had, in Conrad's phrase, an air of having been wallowing all day, fully dressed, on an unmade bed.

Bald, overweight and sweating like he had Dengue fever, he stumbled into my restaurant well before noon and, with what might have been his last breath, implored me for glass of water. He collapsed onto a banquette without waiting for a reply.

was written by Christopher Matthews, a Reuters journalist, who opened a restaurant in Rome to assuage his pain after his wife died.

The title of the New York Times piece was *Giovanni's Gift:*

> The man who called himself Giovanni Mazza had, in Conrad's phrase, an air of having been wallowing all day, fully dressed, on an unmade bed.

> Bald, overweight and sweating like he had Dengue fever, he stumbled into my restaurant well before noon and, with what might have been his last breath, implored me for glass of water. He collapsed onto a banquette without waiting for a reply.

> I brought him a bottle of green-label Nepi. It turned out that Conrad wasn't far wrong: Giovanni had slept all night, fully dressed, on a park bench.

> This was his story. While on a business trip from Los Angeles, where he produced movies, his wife's divorce lawyers had blocked his bank accounts and credit cards.

Reading the op-ed, I was mesmerized, especially when Giovanni pulled out his *wild card* — the Hollywood Sign. Matthews continued:

> Giovanni did have one claim to fame, however, and that was that he'd once paid $27,000 to rebuild the 45-foot-tall first "O" in the Hollywood sign above Los Angeles. Other sponsors included Hugh Hefner (Y), Gene Autry (L) and Alice Cooper (O).

Except for comping a few free meals, Christopher Matthews had a superpower that failed me. He could distinguish the *down* button from the *up*. He did not plunge into Lulu Land. Matthews continued:

> Fate, and his wife's lawyers, had been particularly cruel to him, Giovanni revealed forking a mouthful of Chef Angela's memorable honey-glazed coniglio.

> When the rat-trap snapped on him, he had been about to close the deal of his lifetime. He had a script any studio would do genocide for and George Clooney and Jennifer Lopez were anxious to sign

up. If only he could get back to Los Angeles.

> I naturally assumed Giovanni was a con man, and by the look of
> him, not a very successful one. So it was shocking to discover that
> the green-bound manuscript he carried under his arm was
> brilliant.[13]

Shit. Unlike Matthews, I didn't spot the con. Or, more accurately, the big con screamed like a Times Square billboard, but I suppressed it. Let me describe the moment I rebuffed my guardian angels:

I was at the bank, getting money for Giovanni when I watched him handle the cash. *A normal person doesn't handle money that way*, I thought. Something was self-pleasuring to Giovanni, even orgiastic as his fingers caressed the hundred-dollar bills. I mean, really. Who groans from greenbacks?

Yes, I spotted the con, but I had already swallowed the hook. My deep desire to break into the film business suppressed my self-awareness and sent me down the slippery slope after the manic bunny.

As with *Bondo*, the English lexicon has no word for *principal desire* — the deep need that supersedes self-protection and logic to the point where one is powerless to resist. Let's find that word:

Homeopathy talks about *miasms,* which mean *a cloud or fog in the being.* Miasms are physical and mental diseases inherited at birth that become ingrained into the fabric of our mind and body. Hahnemann, the father of homeopathy, felt that 85 percent of disease stems from a primary *miasm* called *psora,* or itch, which is derived from *tsorat* or groove. When the con man calls, do not scratch; get out of the groove.

Psychology uses *Imago Theory* to explain why we are drawn to someone who mirrors our childhood relationships. The Latin word "imago"— or "image"—refers to the "unconscious image of familiar love." If you fol-

low your *tsorat,* your *groove,* you will undoubtedly meet yourself in the mirror of life to work through unresolved mommy and daddy issues.[14]

Confirmation bias can also send us down the rabbit hole. Defined as the tendency to embrace information that supports your beliefs and rejects information that contradicts them, research shows that we feel a rush of dopamine when we process information that supports our bias. In today's politics, this is the Big Lie. In the book "Denying to the Grave: Why We Ignore the Facts That Will Save Us," the authors observe, "It feels good to stick to our guns even if we are wrong."[15]

Gurdjieff goes deeper. More than following a temporal rush, Gurdjieff explained that our *chief feature* permanently hobbles us:

> Every man has a certain feature in his character which is central. It is like an axle round which all his 'false personality' revolves... A man cannot find his own chief feature, his chief fault, by himself. This is practically a law. The teacher has to point out this feature to him and show him how to fight against it.[16]

Gurdjieff's *chief fault* suggests some kind of *original sin* — a built-in urge to do the wrong thing. I reject the "sin" word — maybe because Jews get an oil change every *Yom Kippur,* so let me offer a Lulu term of my own: *karmic imperative.*

In the bumper-sticker sense (my dogma ran over your karma) and in the Biblical sense (you reap what you sow), *karma* is a moralistic force by which every creature pays for its sins. I like the idea of *karma,* but history does not show much evidence that a moral arbiter is measuring our deeds. Despots always seem to go scot-free. Ruth Ben-Ghiat, the author of *Strongmen,* explains:

"The [personality cult] leader has to be a man of the people...They're everyman, but they're also superman. They are men above all other men. They are men who 'get away with it.' Getting away with crimes is the ESSENCE of authoritarian rule."[17]

If *karma* kept a moral ledger, George W. Bush would be performing penance for his Iraq invasion and the one million excess deaths his gambit produced. Instead, he paints portraits of dogs.[18]

Karmic imperative follows simple physics — no morality involved. In billiards, if you hit the cue ball straight on, the white ball follows through into the pocket – *plunk!*. If you add some "English" — or spin — the cue ball will squirt left or right or even hit the ball and spin back. The same holds with throwing knuckleballs, slicing a tennis serve, or spinning bowling balls to explode the pins. The ball carries the rotational *"karma"* exuded by the pitcher, server, or bowler. The spin is invisible until it collides with the world. This karmic spin applies when you kick a cat, scream at your kids, erect an ugly fence, or flip the bird on the freeway — the action carries a charge. Every *screwball* act invites a compensatory reaction when the spin of your *karma* collides with life.

With *karmic imperative,* there is no "getting away with it." Reagan suffered dementia, Saddam died in a ditch, and Berlusconi was laughed off the stage. We can't know when or if a national leader will end up selling beef jerky in a Garden Grove liquor deli. The spin on the ball takes it where it goes.

When I met Giovanni, I still carried a mighty spin from my unrequited desire to become a filmmaker. Giovanni's charisma instantly pulled me into his lusty Jabba-the-Hut world.

Michael Cohen, Trump's "fixer lawyer," also followed his *karmic imperative* — but right into prison. In his memoir, Cohen described his descent:

> "I knew what I was doing was wrong, but I couldn't stop it; I didn't
> want to stop it. I took a weird kind of pleasure in harming others

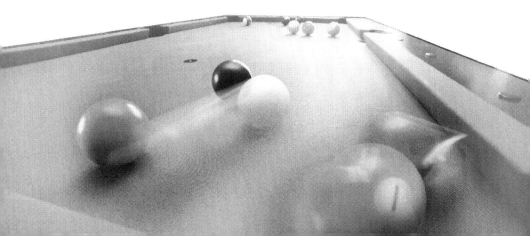

in the service of Donald Trump, to my eternal shame."[19]

Michael Cohen's *miasm* surfaced as a young lad when he worked summers for his uncle Morty at El Caribe, a lively Brooklyn social club reportedly frequented by New York mobsters. Cohen recalls watching a drunk patron skinny-dip in the crowded pool and get shot in the ass by a local hoodlum.

> "I had been an eyewitness to the whole scene. I had seen the
> shooter and could identify him, of course."

Cohen received "the glance" — a hard look from another gangster like a spiritual transmission. When the police arrived, Cohen got wise and told the police nothing. The thug slipped him $500 in an envelope. It was a formative moment. If you flashed enough cash, you could get away with anything — even shooting somebody in broad daylight on Fifth Avenue.

In 1996, Michael Cohen received a call from Donald Jr. inviting him to a meeting with his father — Cohen's Lulu moment. Thus began his intoxicating career experiencing what he described as the "pleasure of inflicting harm and exercising raw power." Despite having a disgusted wife and children who wanted him to abandon Trump, Cohen continued. Why did he stay? He explained:

> "The answer, I was coming to see, included something deeper than
> the obvious lure of money and power.... It was physical, emotion-
> al, not quite spiritual, but a deep longing that Trump filled for me.
> Around Trump, I felt excited, alive, like he possessed the urgent
> and only truth, the chance for my salvation and success in life."

Michael Cohen already owned millions in real estate and taxi franchises when he met Trump. If the pull wasn't money, it must have been his *karmic imperative* — the spin set in motion at the El Caribe.

And then there's Bill Gates. Beginning in 2011, Microsoft's chairman – notably the second richest person in the world – met with convicted sex offender and influence peddler Jeffrey Epstein on numerous occasions. According to the New York Times, Gates visited Epstein's palatial Manhattan mansion at least three times and at least once staying late into

the night. With forty rooms on seven floors, and provocative pictures covering the walls, Gates would have certainly noticed the painting of Bill Clinton in a blue dress, the life-sized female doll hanging from the chandelier, the photo-like mural of Epstein in prison, and the entrance hall decorated with eyeballs.

We're in a Different World now, Toto.[20]

But with startling understatement, Bill Gates emailed his colleagues in 2011 to describe Epstein: "His lifestyle is very different and kind of intriguing although it would not work for me."[21]

According to the Daily Beast, Melinda Gates told friends that she was uncomfortable when she met Epstein – a meeting that still "haunts" her.[22]

Stepping into a different world can be a haunting experience. Gurdjieff was possibly the first to propose the existence of different worlds. His model of the universe, the Ray of Creation, described how a descending octave of energy forms different interpenetrating worlds — from fine to coarse, from pure consciousness to physical matter, and from absolute freedom to mechanical life. In this cosmic Octave, the highest world is governed by three laws (fewer laws equals more freedom), while the lowest is governed by ninety-six laws (more laws equals mechanical existence). Gurdjieff admonished thoughtless, reactive mechanical behavior as making humanity "food for the moon."

Michael Cohen descended from fewer laws to more laws in an obvious manner. One moment he's smoking cigars with his buddies at the

Loews Regency on Park Avenue. A few days later, he was assigned to the HVAC detail at the Federal Correctional Institution in Otisville, NY — a descent from maximum freedom to maximum constraints.

I pity the indignity of Cohen's descent into the mechanical world. Cohen "hates the [prison] food," a source told Reuters. "This is a guy who ate in all the best restaurants."[23]

Cohen may be a scumbag, but he took one for Team Democracy. As the rare individual in Trump's orbit to embark on a path of redemption, Cohen's testimony before Congress alerted the Manhattan District Attorney of Trump's tax chicanery, which led to a criminal indictment of the Trump Organization. Cohen used his time in prison to reflect on his life, write a successful book, sue Trump and Bill Barr, and start a syndicated podcast titled *"Mea Culpa — Nothing but the Truth."*

I asked Karen to help me close my Giovanni chapter — hopefully forever. "Michael Cohen's wife begged him to abandon Trump," I implored. "And Melinda Gates was furious with Bill. Why didn't you stop me from venturing into the Giovanni World?"

"It happened all of a sudden," Karen recalled with zero interest in dredging the memory. "Suddenly, we were in this world. I remember reading the script and feeling heartsick. I thought this was it? This is the great script? What's worse is that Nick disappeared — not a little bit disappeared. He totally disappeared. He was not in touch with his girlfriend, who was pregnant when he left. Pretty asshole-ish."

A lower world is often served with a side of asshole-ish. My Giovanni descent set the stage for The Troubles — using the Irish term for our time of separation. Yes, it sucked, but I learned you couldn't understand the lower worlds without a visit. Joseph Campbell helped me with this:

> It is by going down into the abyss that we recover the treasures
> of life. Where you stumble, there lies your treasure. The very cave
> you are afraid to enter turns out to be the source of what you are

looking for… The purpose of the journey is compassion. When you have come past the pairs of opposites, you have reached compassion. The goal is to bring the jewel back to the world, to join the two things together.[24]

Thank you, Joseph Campbell, for extolling the merits of the cave. But allow me to *kvetch*. You didn't tell me where to find the Up button when I needed it. You didn't explain how the waves of two lovers in their separate worlds can rejoin as one.

Fortunately, I discovered that waves also take you out of the cave, and even better – the universe knows to send a train from the future to save you from yourself.

Endnotes

1   Kurshan, Neil. *Raising Your Child to Be a Mensch*. Ivy Books, 1989.

2   Sacks, Oliver. "The Machine Stops." The New Yorker, https://www.newyorker.com/magazine/2019/02/11/the-machine-stops.

3   Ouspensky, P. D. (2001). *In Search of the Miraculous* (Revised edition). Mariner Books.

4   https://www.nytimes.com/1979/07/29/archives/getting-in-touch-with-gurd-jieff.html

5   https://www.gurdjieff.org/lubtchansky2.htm

6   Ouspensky, *In Search of the Miraculous*

7   https://www.nytimes.com/1983/03/09/us/reagan-denounces-ideology-of-soviet-as-focus-of-evil.html

8   https://www.businessinsider.com/how-the-1999-russian-apartment-bombings-led-to-putins-rise-to-power-2018-3

9   https://bylinetimes.com/2021/03/02/the-network-the-american-and-russian-moralists-behind-the-january-insurrection/

10   https://www.apa.org/news/press/op-eds/bray-interrogations

11   The Inquisition was established by Pope Gregory IX c. 1232 for the suppression of heresy, often through the use of torture. Lovely.

12   Wilks, J. (1971). *The Third Law of Thermodynamics*, Chapter 6 in Thermodynamics, volume 1, Physical Chemistry. An Advanced Treatise, Academic Press

13 https://www.nytimes.com/2009/10/09/opinion/09iht-edmatthews.html

14 What is Imago Relationship Therapy?" https://harvilleandhelen.com/initiatives/what-is-imago/

15 Gorman, Sara E., and Jack M. Gorman. *Denying to the Grave: Why We Ignore the Facts That Will Save Us.* Oxford University Press, 2016.

16 Gurdjieff (as quoted by Ouspensky, *In Search of the Miraculous*, p.233

17 Ben-Ghiat, Ruth. *Strongmen: How They Rise, Why They Succeed, How They Fall.* Main edition, Profile Books, 2020.

18 .https://www.ncbi.nlm.nih.gov/pmc/articles/PMC3797136

19 Cohen, Michael. *Disloyal a Memoir.* Skyhorse, 2020.

20 https://www.thecut.com/2019/08/the-creepy-dcor-in-jeffrey-epsteins-nyc-house.html

21 https://www.nytimes.com/2019/10/12/business/jeffrey-epstein-bill-gates.html

22 https://www.thedailybeast.com/melinda-gates-warned-bill-gates-about-jeffrey-epstein

23 https://www.reuters.com/article/us-usa-trump-cohen-prison/ex-trump-lawyer-michael-cohen-loving-prison-life-hates-the-food-source-idUSKCN1T52H8

24 Campbell, Joseph. *Reflections on the Art of Living: A Joseph Campbell Companion.* Edited by Diane K. Osbon, Reprint edition, Harper Perennial, 1995.

Chapter 6
THE TWO TRAINS

"Life can only be understood backwards;
but it must be lived forwards."
~ *Soren Kierkegaard*

"BRUCE, LISTEN TO THE SOUND OF MY VOICE."

The sound of an *incoming Reshad* whistled over my foxhole like a mortar, so I braced.

"I have fixed it for you," Reshad announced.

A transatlantic phone call from Reshad always hit me like an outside shock, but this time, I mused at its oddity. *Fixed?* I was hard-wired to expect a soul-shaking when Reshad called. I had just returned from Switzerland, where I spent a week at his summer school overlooking Lake Lucerne. Something was up.

"This remarkable teacher, Dr. Bhagwan Awatramani spoke here last night," Reshad explained. "He's a meditation teacher headed to America. I told him that you are my oldest friend in the States, and by all means, he should visit you."

My immediate instinct: "Guru not wanted."

I didn't need or want a spiritual teacher to visit my bachelor life, so now

I had a problem. In our Sufi school, receiving the guest was paramount. It was called *adab,* or respectful courtesy and manners. We made a big practice of greeting guests with flowers at the airport, putting flowers in their room, and serving them a cup of tea on arrival. We also washed the walls with rosewater, prepared fancy meals — it got crazy.

"Thanks, Reshad, I… we will make arrangements to receive him. Yes, and thank you." *Click.*

I could have said no, but we were trained not to "presume" the guest. A visitor represented the Third Force, the vector of opportunity that opened your small world into a larger world — an incoming wave of constructive interference. Conversely for the guest, having left your everyday world behind, you had the opportunity to be constructively interfered — to receive new impressions and love. "To know you're loved" was the overriding theme of Reshad's school.

From my bachelor foxhole, *incoming* was more than a metaphor. For three years, I had been praying for a door to open. I was ready for a different world. I had just returned from a "magical" experience with a woman I met in Switzerland, so I wasn't looking for Reshad to fix anything. *(Note to Karen: I put snarky quotes around "magical" in case you listen to an Audible version of this book).*

Alas, *adab* is *adab.* The thought of bachelor Bruce hosting an Indian guru seemed preposterous, so I called Karen. She lived a few doors down at the time.

"Hi," Karen answered. Her tenderness caught me off-guard.

"Karen, I need your help."

"What is it?"

"Reshad is sending; get ready for this, a guru from India."

I don't know if it was adab or ulterior motives, but Karen jumped right on it.

"Okay, okay," she pounced, "Let's talk about the menu, flowers, rose-water…."

My memory of the conversation is fuzzy, so I asked Karen to fill in the details. This conversation — 20 years later takes place in bed:

"Karen, remember when I asked you to help me host Bhagwan?"

"Why are you asking me this? It's like four in the morning."

"I know. That's when I think about these things."

"Okay, but this will cost you," Karen yawned. "Yes, I remember being part of those conversations about Bhagwan coming. I think we were spending time together but living separately."

"We were co-parenting. That was all," I reminded.

"It was more than that. You asked me to come back to help you."

"Yes," I insisted, "but during Bhagwan's visit, we were still living apart."

"I had that apartment down the street," Karen reminded, "but I'm pretty sure I moved back in with you. I know I did because Bhagwan and I went to a lot of movies during his visit. Afterward, I would talk to him about our relationship. I don't think you shared what you were going through, but Bhagwan and I talked a lot."

"You talked about us?"

"Absolutely," Karen recalled. "And he would talk about the whole idea of the Lover and the Beloved and the difference between having a lover and marriage. That marriage was about having children and having a stable life. He explained that there is an ever-changing balance between Lover and Beloved.

"We saw a lot of movies," Karen continued, "including *Forrest Gump*, which was about being in the right place at the right time — just like in your book. In the movie,

Forrest fell in love with Jenny, his childhood friend. He adored Jenny, but she would never open herself to his love because Forrest was mentally challenged. Eventually, after all sorts of trials, she opened to his love. The tide turned for Jenny, but maybe too late. They got married right before she died, presumably of AIDS. But they were very, very, happy."

"Was your tide turning?" I probed.

"I think the tide was turning before Bhagwan. At the time, I wanted to reconcile and just talking to him, the tide turned, something turned."

"You felt something shift?"

"It wasn't just in me," Karen argued. "It was a door opening. It was the whole Octave thing. The door had been closing. You were pursuing this relationship in Switzerland, and I was going to do my single thing, but it seemed that there were greater forces at work. Somehow Bhagwan came at that exact time."

I avoided having my heart-to-heart with Bhagwan as long as possible until Karen gave me an intense, non-negotiable glance one afternoon.

I trudged up the stairs to an empty room where Bhagwan sat in a folding chair. Yes, the empty bedroom that had been cleaned out by Karen's mover-goons two years earlier. Bhagwan dressed like a casual tourist or a businessman in his white shorts and golf shirt — hardly a guru.

"So, tell me about this woman," Bhagwan asked.

I told Bhagwan of my "magical" time in Switzerland. I added enough synchronicity to demonstrate divine providence at work. Bhagwan wasn't impressed.

"Do you know the story of Radha and Rukmini?" Bhagwan asked.

I stared blankly.

"There were these two women in Krishna's life," Bhagwan explained. "With Radha, it was a transcendent love, *mahabhava*, the quintessence

of love. It was not a worldly love. It was beyond the
ego. Radha and Krishna are simultaneously one
and different." He continued. "Rukmini"s love is
called *kanta-bhava*, the love of wife. This love is
bounded by our duties in the world to bring
forth children and have a home. With
Radha, in your lifetime, you may never
even meet this soul. It's enough to know that
this kind of love exists. With Rukmini, this is who
you are in this world; you are bound in this love."   *Dr. Bhagwan Awatramani*

I think I heard the word "bound" and not much else. I was
still married, so I was bound. Being bound either feels good or it doesn't.
At that moment, something let go. It wasn't where I wanted to go, but I
accepted being bound.

I didn't expect it then, but a fortuitous streak began to unfold for
Karen and me. We re-fell in love and had a second child. I started a
business, solved my financial woes, and later created an alternative high
school. Together, we built a vast network of friends and bought a cabin
overlooking a mountain lake. Karen went to seminary and started a new
career as a director of pastoral education.

If this sounds like prosperity consciousness (the belief that opening your mind to opportunity ushers in wealth), it's not. It was a turning point — one that worked out fortuitously. Had we been on another
trajectory, Bhagwan could have been a charlatan who invited us into a
cult. The turning point – Reshad announcing, "I have fixed it for you," –
rang the bell that ushered the future coming in.

More importantly, we both felt the opening and said yes.

The idea that the future comes into the present seems obvious and
ridiculous. You either see yourself as the creator of your drama (now I'm
doing this; now I am doing that), or you see a divine hand shaping events
(predestination). Both views are simplistic. Neither embraces a view of a
dramatic universe where unexpected events come into your world to be
wrestled with — a world where the outcome is uncertain.

J.G. Bennett called this uncertainty Hazard. It's the same principle that governs the formation of the universe, the appearance of life on earth, natural selection, the evolution of a species, and the history of the world. Hazard is not mechanical chance or the shuffling of the deck. It is an energizing force that moves the drama forward. As a principle, Hazard is not the random chance that a tree will hit your house or that you will win the lottery. *Hazard comes into play when you invite significant risk into a situation of importance* — for example, starting a business or getting back together.

Hazard is not a blind bet or overconfidence. It's a creative force that upends the status quo. Your ability to find comfort with Hazard might draw from a dad who encouraged you to paddle through the rapids or from a mom who taught you to express your feelings. In either case, Hazard ceases to be a place of looming danger but instead, the source of creativity, dynamism, and change.

I would size up a new client in my brand strategy work by looking for cracks in their corporate culture. I would ask, how can the creative force enter this business? Is this a closed system run by an autocrat, a fearful flock of corporate sheep, or an open culture that invites many points of view? The client hired us, so I assumed they outsourced Hazard to the creative agency— but more often, corporations are tightly wired to protect against a creatively-aimed "spanner" from landing in the works.

When an Olympics skier jumps out the slalom gate, she puts years of training on the line. No matter how skilled and practiced, she pushes risk to its edge. Hazard is a co-partner in all creative work where the unknown plays a role in the outcome.

> If man sees Hazard as a misfortune rather than an opportunity, he
> will seek to close the door to freedom rather than keep it open."
> ~ J.G. Bennett[1]

"I have fixed it for you," Reshad announced.

Karen and I both said yes — but we could have said no. In that alternate universe of no, the galaxy of our second act would not have been born. But we rang the bell of yes — "gentlemen start your engines." Maybe, our marriage was scripted in the stars, but that script could not predict the yes. We had to sound that note. We had to invoke Hazard.

Reshad described two modes of time: *The Two Trains.* The incoming and outgoing trains represent the call and response of living with Hazard.

The *outgoing train* represents linear time moving forward — Chicago, Kankakee, Cincinnati, and New Orleans. Starting a business also hits outgoing mile-markers: raising capital, renting space, procuring goods, hiring help, and promotion — all moving toward your launch date.

The second train — *the incoming train* — flies headlong from the future into the present, sharing the same rail. This incoming train brings trials and pitfalls along the way — a cow on the tracks, a broken switch, or a freight train hogging the rails. In business, the city might require an unexpected $10,000 range hood for your restaurant.

The incoming train also brings lucky breaks, like getting back together after a separation. On a flight, you might sit next to a four-star chef who is looking to relocate to your town. When synchronicity strikes, you may feel that God is on your side — but it's the incoming train. Hopefully, the two trains arrive safely at the platform rather than colliding in a cornfield.

When the actress Rosie O'Donnell was starting her career, she sat down on a flight next to a bitchy woman who kept complaining to the flight attendant that she didn't get the salad she ordered. Rosie kindly offered her salad. Rosie's offer calmed the woman down, which led to small talk about Rosie's new gig on VH1. The woman shared that she was an agent from the William Morris Agency.

By complete chance, Rosie and the agent were seated together on another flight six months later.

"Well... so, what are you doing?" the agent woman asked.

"I got offered 'Win, Lose or Draw for Kids' on Disney," Rosie replied. "They're gonna pay me $50,000 a year on a five-year contract to host the show."

Her seatmate was alarmed. "No, you're not," she decreed. "I'm now your agent, and we're too close to God for me not to intervene."[2]

Rosie was lucky (twice), but this story is not about luck or that her career break was preordained. It's all about the salad. Rosie's generosity — offering her salad to console a bitchy talent agent — ignited her Hollywood career.

> All things by immortal power
> Near or far
> Hiddenly
> To each other linked are
> That thou canst not stir a flower
> Without troubling a star.
> —Francis Thompson

When I was younger, Reshad went on about this poem, stating way too often that "you cannot pick a flower without the troubling of a star." Everyone got gauzy when he read it, but I hated it. My inner Chicago cynic fumed, "Give me some evidence. Show me a troubled star!"

I'm older, maybe wiser. I now see the *flower* and *star* as expressions of harmonics. When you pluck a string — or offer your salad — higher frequencies respond. In this way, every action is part of a call and response. When you announce, "I'm starting a business," you summon the incoming train to leave its station.

By sounding the note Do, the higher frequencies respond as harmonics. Piano tuners know this. They don't just hear one note when they strike a piano key; they hear harmonic frequencies resonating above the fundamental pitch — like the harmonies sung by a choir. Harmonics exist in music, physics, acoustics, astronomy, and more.

Astronomers now know that gas in distant stars expands and contracts. This pulsating gas oscillates, producing waves similar to sound waves.

According to Tim Bedding, an astronomer at the University of Sydney, "Stars are like a musical instrument. They can play many notes simultaneously, and there are all different types of pulsations... some of these stars have nice chords."[3]

Yay, Francis Thompson!

In the world of the human heart, "harmonics" are called "angels" — not pudgy cherubs with wings, but the oscillations we feel in our heart as *conscience* and *uplift*. Just like the superpower of the piano tuner, we have the capacity to hear the call of angels. *Angel* means "messenger" from the Greek *angelos*. In the Bible, they represent God's attendants.

If you prefer Internet terminology, an *angel* is just another packet of information in the "human protocol stack" — from the crude to the sublime. When the bride walks down the aisle or your kindergartner performs on stage, you could say that the tears we feel are from angels. These harmonics of feeling are messaging a higher world of pure love.

Being a tech guy, I think of "human protocol stack" as a tech term for the Stages of Love, an idea adapted from Harville Hendrix in *Getting the Love You Want: A Guide for Couples.* Hendrix saw how relationships grow through three stages: *Romantic Love, The Power Struggle,* and *Conscious Marriage.* As adults, we strive toward the realm of pure love through relationships. Through the Two Trains, the "Love Train" enters a relationship as the future coming into the present — a train filled with angels — but these are rough-and-tumble angels inviting us on a harrowing journey. It's an Octave journey with seven distinct stages:

- **Stage I: Romantic Love — Love Under the Influence (Do)**
  When we fall in love, our brain becomes flooded with the neurochemical phenylethylamine, a compound found in chocolate that lifts our mood.

Neurochemicals like phenylethylamine increase our buoyancy, diminish pain, and cause us to feel safe. By adding sexual hormones to the mix, we become neuro-anesthetized to the degree needed to commit to a relationship. If we could see the hurdles ahead, why would anyone choose to get married?

- **Stage II: Autopilot Love — Life becomes rote *(Re)***
  Married life quickly becomes tactical. "Bring home some Pampers; let's go to Ikea; the toilet is clogged." No one is paying attention, but the tactical and practical slowly smother the magic. When we lose curiosity in the person who shares our life, the promise of love quickly flattens like soda fizz.

- **Stage III: Disillusionment — Self-Protection *(Mi)***
  Four love-killing words doom a relationship: *"Getting My Needs Met* (GMNM)." Once the phenylethylamine wears off, you face life with another human being. Think of Stage III as the masked-ball moment when the mask comes off. It's too soon to understand, but you were drawn to GMNM, not to the person. In a better system, you would choose your spouse by studying the parents, but it's too late. Your partner is facing a midlife crisis while you face your own. "Who is this person!!!???"

- **The Power Struggle --- *(Mi-Fa Interval)***
  The seeds of the Power Struggle can emerge at any time — even while planning the wedding. The feeling of disillusionment makes us dislike many of the things that attracted us to our partner in the first place. The fun-loving personality seems loud and obnoxious; the practicality and reliability suddenly become stultifying and boring. A singular issue defines your struggle: infidelity, emotional needs, financial stability, or addiction. The line in the sand becomes a wall of despair. Engaging the hidden engine of continuous renewal requires passage through this Mi-Fa interval, but what will it take? Couples therapy? Trial separation? Ayahuasca? A guru from India? A jar of Bondo™? How about good-old-fashioned grace?

- **Stage IV: Awareness — Self-reflection, Imago awareness *(Fa)***
  Marriage offers the greatest opportunity for soul growth. To
  reach Stage IV, you need to be on a soul project. This means,
  psychologically and spiritually, you subconsciously seek a
  partner who will help you become whole and complete. You
  experience how your partner pushes buttons and triggers
  wounds at this stage, but you also recognize that they are *your*
  buttons and wounds. *Imago* is Latin for "image" — the
  "unconscious image of similar love." In Imago Relationship
  Therapy, the wounding and frustrations of childhood are worked
  out in an adult relationship. Harville Hendrix discovered this
  connection soon after he signed his divorce papers.

- **Stage V: Commitment — Inner work, solidity *(Sol)***
  It's been a long journey, but the wedding vows are now realized.
  "He's not easy to live with, but I'm not going anywhere." You're a
  team — a dysfunctional one at times — but it's the team you're
  on. Your friends may wonder, "Why do you stick with him/her?"
  They can't see the deep satisfaction and synergy that comes from
  commitment. Stage V offers a shared history. You're co-starring
  in a full-length feature instead of a whimsical short. A change of
  partners can never replace the richness of your epic saga.

- **Stage VI: Constancy – A deeper connection steers the ship *(La)***
  Robert Bly described this connection as the "third body:"

  > *"A man and a woman sit near each other, and they do not long
  > at this moment to be older, or younger, or born in any other
  > nation, or any other time, or any other place. They are content
  > to be where they are, talking or not talking… They obey a third
  > body that they share in common."*[4]

What to do, what to say, and when to do it — they all emerge from a shared constancy. Even though no one is steering the ship, you follow the same guiding star. Even simple decisions, like where to go for lunch, flow from an unseen mutuality.

- **Stage VII: Conscious Love — Transpersonal, Beyond personal needs** *(Si)*

Transpersonal is beyond this world, so how can conscious love be described? Most people experience conscious love after their partner dies. When the partner's physical presence departs, the being remains. In the Netflix series, *The Kominsky Method,* after Alan Arkin loses his wife, Eileen, to cancer, Arkin continues to seek his wife's counsel as though she never left. At the funeral, he speaks to her as present company:

> *"Dear Eileen, We have been husband and wife for forty-six years. In all that time, I have never not been in love with you. I have been angry with you, confused by you, even hurt by you, but never not in love. If something good happened to me at work, it wasn't real until I shared it with you. If something bad happened, it was only tolerable because I had you to complain to. I honestly don't know how I will carry on without you, but I will because you told me to in no uncertain terms."*

A poignant beauty accompanies aging when a couple attends to each others' limitations. Because of Karen's vision disability from her brain surgery, I dutifully read every foreign film subtitle, offer my arm at street corners, and massage reflexology points in her feet. There's no scoring of points in conscious love.

Karen describes a conscious marriage, "At this point, we have money in the bank." Or better put, we found the mysterious ingredient, Bondo™.

Karen and I can only imagine that our second child was waiting in the wings when Bhagwan showed up at our door. We were summoned by the Love Train to get our asses back together. We both said yes to invite the train of the future into our lives.

Picking a flower and bestowing an airline salad demonstrate how innocuous acts change the course of history. With A-list representation, Rosie O'Donnell became a comedian, producer, actress, and author. She also hosted a daytime talk show and became an outspoken advocate for lesbian rights and gay adoption issues. All because of a salad? If a simple act can lift us into a different world, it does so by ushering the future coming in.

Jannie Jones

Consider the most far-reaching example where picking a flower awakened a star: Just like with Betsy Ross and Florence Nightingale, school children should learn the name Jannie Jones. Jannie deserves a Little Golden Book in her name because this 76-year-old African American woman may have saved American democracy and the planet itself by summoning angels with the crook of her finger. By comparison, Betsy sewed a flag.

On February 21, 2020, Jannie Jones sat quietly in a pew at St. John Baptist Church in Hopkins, South Carolina, waiting for the funeral of James White to begin. White was a local accountant who managed the books for residents for years, including for Representative James Clyburn. Jannie noticed Mr. Clyburn standing against a nearby wall. Instinctively, Jannie beckoned Mr. Clyburn toward her pew with her finger.

Clyburn shared to NPR what happened next:

> CLYBURN: "Last Friday, I went to a funeral service for my accountant, who was also a good friend. When I got to the service, I was there a bit early. I walked around the church speaking to people. A rather elderly African American woman was sitting on the front bench of the church. She called me over, just sort of beckoned me. She didn't say a word. And I went over to her, and she said to me, 'The people in this community want to hear from you. But if you don't think you want anybody to hear you, please just lean down and whisper in my ear.'"[5]

Clyburn bent down so the stranger could whisper in his ear.

141

"I need to know who you're going to vote for," Jannie asked.

And this is where the angels entered.

CLYBURN: "And when she said that to me — I don't know — it brought tears to me. I decided then and there that I would not stay silent."

Clyburn whispered his decision, "Joe Biden."

Jannie gave Clyburn a thumbs up, but she wondered if Clyburn would publicly endorse the former Vice President.

"I had no idea he was going to do it," Jones recalled in a telephone interview with The Associated Press.

Eight days later, Joe Biden joined Clyburn on stage in Columbia, SC. When Clyburn approached the microphone, he moved the inflection point:

"I know Joe. We know Joe. But most importantly, Joe knows us," Clyburn said.

"I know his heart. I know who he is. I know what he is. I know where this country is: We are at an inflection point," Clyburn said. "I am fearful for the future of this country. I'm fearful for my daughters and their future, and their children and their children's future.

"It is time for us to restore this country's dignity, this country's respect," he said.

Joe Biden with Rep. James Clyburn

"That is what is at stake this year. And I can think of no one better suited, better prepared. I can think of no one with the integrity, no one more committed to the fundamental principles to make this country what it is than my good friend, my late wife's great friend, Joe Biden."[6]

Political endorsements are not uncommon — but inflection points only come once. The week before, Biden stared into the abyss. The media watched like sharks when he abruptly left New Hampshire on the morning of its all-important primary and headed to South Carolina.

"It just felt like a dead man walking campaign for a long time," CNN contributor Van Jones said. "Obama's guy should be just sucking in money. But he's broke... He doesn't have the grassroots enthusiasm. He's not filling stadiums like Bernie Sanders."[7]

Bernie Sanders concurred: "I've got news for the Democratic establishment. They can't stop us."

Headlines at the time agreed: "Bernie Has Already Won the Democratic Primary," and from pollster Nate Silver, "Bernie Sanders Wins Nevada — Putting Him In The Driver's Seat To Win The Nomination."

The New York Times

Bernie Sanders Has Already Won the Democratic Primary

He set the tone, determined the issues and tugged the party toward him.

March 7, 2020

The Octave describes inflection points. Soon after Clyburn's endorsement, Biden won South Carolina decisively, Pete Buttigieg dropped out of the race on a Sunday night, and Klobuchar followed on Monday afternoon. Both headed straight to Dallas for a unity rally with Biden and Beto O'Rourke ahead of Super Tuesday.

Six weeks later, boom! The invincible Sanders quit the race. Octave inflection points have consequences.

I've never seen anything like it," commentator John Heilemann reported. "For Joe Biden to go from where he was, after the fourth-place finish in Iowa, fifth-place finish in New Hampshire... if you think of the way it turned around in that period from the giant victory in South Carolina and then Super Tuesday. I've never seen someone's political fortunes change from dead to nominee in the span of 72 hours."[8]

The media served up a host of postmortems explaining how the inflexibility of the Sanders campaign collided with the future coming in. According to the New York Times:

"[Bernie Sanders'] pollster, Ben Tulchin, in a meeting with campaign aides, recommended a new offensive to influence older black voters... But the suggestion met resistance. Some senior advisers argued that it wasn't worth diverting resources from Iowa and New Hampshire...

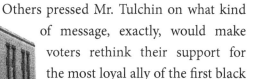

Others pressed Mr. Tulchin on what kind of message, exactly, would make voters rethink their support for the most loyal ally of the first black President. Crucially, both Mr. Sanders and his wife, Jane, consistently expressed reservations about going negative on Mr. Biden, preferring to stick with the left-wing policy message they have been pressing for 40 years."[9]

History proves that successful candidates tack to the middle. Bernie's forty-year course to the left would not get him to his destination. As a sailor, I can attest: When your sails begin to luff, you have to fall off to fill the sails or tack through the wind to stay the course.

Joe Biden's story adds the element of necessity to the workings of Hazard. Again: Hazard comes into play when you invite significant risk into a situation of importance. Necessity raises the stakes. It's the difference between *need* versus *want* in your soul project.

Necessity was on the ballot in the 2020 election. At a moment when trans-national corruption and authoritarian leadership could sink our democracy, the contest hung on a thread. As a Georgia voter, I can speak to our do-or-die effort. We scoured for every last voter to score a 12,000 vote margin. With a Luke Skywalker level of necessity, the rag-tag Democratic Party piloted its aging Starfighters into the Death Star.

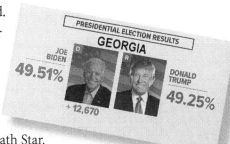

Traversing the Octave is not for the faint-hearted. Striking a mudra or chanting *Om* won't catch the wave. It requires knife-edge awareness coupled with Jedi trust that the Force is with you — even if it all goes south.

Necessity is more than paying your bill before the city shuts your water. It's finding the Uplift to move your soul project forward.

Like a Jedi knight, Joe Biden had a secret power no other candidate possessed. At age 78, having lost his beloved son, Beau, to brain cancer and his first wife, Neila, and daughter, Naomi, to a fatal car crash, Joe had nothing to lose and nothing to prove. Unlike Obama, who had to temper his words and actions as the first Black President, Joe was free to walk the knife-edge of freedom. He didn't care what people thought or said about the path he was taking:

MSNBC's Nicole Wallace saw this trait up close:

> "I think the frame on [Joe Biden] is wrong," Wallace said. "He didn't stumble into the Presidency. I think the politician who prevails is the one with the highest threshold for indignity and pain. I think he had the stomach because losing the first three or four primaries was never going to be the worst thing to happen to Joe Biden. He had so much personal tragedy — the political humiliation. Because he could endure those losses, he was able to stay in the game until he was presented with an opportunity to win.
>
> "I think that what you display when you can endure defeat and hardship and humiliation is the mettle that you need to govern."[10]

James Clyburn offered Biden the opportunity, and Joe displayed the mettle to win.

In 1987, Biden was just forty-four years old when he declared his first candidacy for President. If you remember being forty-four, running for President is an audacious act — and Biden's first campaign proved it. Hounded by multiple charges of plagiarism, inflated academic accomplishments, and a disjointed press conference to clear his name, Biden's campaign collapsed after three months.

In 2020, when Biden made his hasty exit from New Hampshire, the "Dead Man Walking" headlines must have hit hard. At age 78, death already hangs over your shoulder. Piloting an aging Starfighter into battle after losing three states likely triggered "deja vu" from his disastrous 1987 run. Biden's previous bouts of defeat, hardship, and humiliation gave him an added dose of soul necessity.

I can only imagine being Joe Biden, addressing sparse New Hampshire venues, draining cash, and having to claw his way into relevancy against a gay small-town mayor from South Bend, Indiana, who was pulling crowds. Biden could have had a nice retirement, but instead, necessity called. His fortunes began to shift when he tapped his inner fire.

One headline read: "After Iowa Stumble, Biden Goes Heart-First In Final NH Push."

> "You know, I've lost a lot in my lifetime, like many of you have," Biden told the crowd. "A car accident took away my wife and daughter. Lost my son, Beau, like many of you, have done. But I'll be damned if I'm going to stand by and lose my country, too."[11]

At the moment of death, it's said that your life passes before you. For Biden, the end of his political career was hauntingly close as the train of the future hurtled in.

We confront the Two Trains differently at each stage of life, but we first notice the incoming train at a mid-life crisis. There's no strict science here, but having observed dozens of friends go through the mid-life grinder, I always ask their age, and it's always forty-two.

Here's my back-of-the-napkin calculation of the Two Trains using the Law of Seven. Except for birth and death, your results may vary:

- **Birth**: The journey begins

- **Age 7**: Your personality is set for life.[12] According to Gurdjieff, most modern men stop growing in essence at the age of five or six as personality begins to grow instead of essence.[13]

- **Age 14**: The rites of passage. These include Catholic confirmation, Jewish bar and bat mitzvah (age 13), menstruation, and the minimum age a girl can marry in the Catholic Church(!)

- **Age 21**: Drinking age (and pre-1971 voting age). Physical growth is complete, and it's time to leave home.

- **Age 28**: The Saturn Return. When the planet Saturn travels full

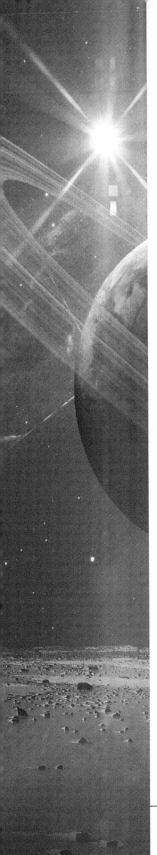

circle to its position at your birth, the planet signals a sobering wake-up call: Time to grow up! For this reason, many rock stars die before reaching 28, including Jimi Hendrix, Janis Joplin, Jim Morrison, Amy Winehouse, and Kurt Cobain. Embarking on a self-styled vision quest is not uncommon at 28. Saturn is the outer boundary of the visible solar system, and age 28 is a fixed boundary as well. Your connection to childhood completely ends when marriage, career and children loom on the horizon.

• **Age 35**: Hooray, you can be President of the United States. More likely, multiple layers of ambition and responsibility begin to pile up. At age 35, you might be comforting a crying infant late at night or struggling with pressures at work. You bought more house than you can afford and start to collect too much stuff — two cars, a jet ski, home theater, high-tech stroller, and a Peloton.

• **Age 42**: Mid-Life Crisis. At age 42, your dreams and expectations collide with reality. The person you married turns out to be a real person — one with complicated baggage and not the projection you imagined. Power struggles overshadow the love in your relationship. The stress from "having it all" affects your psyche and health. Suddenly, you inquire about therapists or get pulled into distractions like marital affairs or alcohol. What appears to be system overload is the train of the future making its first appearance — the Reality Train. Your lifetime has a fixed duration, and all limits create pressure. For example, in a TV baking competition, the ticking clock pressures cooks to panic and the cakes to collapse. If you ever raced to the airport, you understand the pressure of the future coming in. The pilot doesn't care about you or your traffic jam. The pilot had the presence of mind to leave home at 5:30 a.m. Mid-life pressures might stem from living beyond your means, being stuck in the wrong career, or living with the wrong partner. At age forty-two, the time window to remarry, change careers, or find a meaningful life is shorter than you think. You sense the pressure. The future comes in like a wave — a series of waves. You can't stop their advance, but you can capture the Uplift if you know how to surf.

- **Age 49**: Get ready for your fifties — it's your decade of empowerment in the world. Forbes Magazine selected fifty female entrepreneurs, leaders, scientists, and creators who, after the age of fifty, "are achieving their greatest accomplishments and making their biggest impact. Together, they embody a new movement of women who reject the idea that the most dynamic part of life is the first half." Consider Nancy Pelosi. She didn't run for Congress until she was forty-seven years old, and she became America's first female Speaker of the House at sixty-six.

- **Age 56**: Hooray, you are in peak power. This is the average age of an incoming CEO at a Fortune 500 firm. Even if you don't get into Forbes, having climbed the totem of career and parenting, people turn to you for advice. **Money** and relationship issues should be behind you. Using my scale of sevens (eight times seven), this is like a fresh Do. At age fifty-six, you don't feel a second Saturn Return on the horizon, but it's lurking (age 58.8). The second Return is not as obvious or difficult as Saturn's first trip around the Sun, but it brings a second wake-up call. It's a last call to complete your unfinished business. Age fifty-eight ushers deep changes that align with your soul's purpose. And if you don't realign, like my friend Nick who died at 58.8, the second Saturn boundary will call "game-over." A long list of famous people departed at their second Saturn Return,

Game over at the second Saturn Return

including George Harrison, the guru Rajneesh, Andy Warhol, James Joyce, Hugo Chavez, Chet Baker, Richard Burton, John Cassavetes, Truman Capote, and even Swami Yogananda. I'm no psychologist, but some element of rage, resentment, or despair defined their second Saturn boundary.

- **Age 63**: You sorta knew that aging would catch up, but you didn't prepare for it — because you can't. This is the Big Gear Shift from worldly ambition toward self-knowledge — and it arrives out of the blue. I was sixty-three when my business collapsed. The Social Security folks know about this age, but more than early retirement, a greater change is at work. At 63, a great realignment takes place. It's a time to pull back from business strivings to create a reflective space — a withdrawal from personality and a movement toward strengthening the soul. I was terrified at age sixty-three to discover that I had become irrelevant.

- **Age 70**: I just hit this milestone, so here's my report. The big Seven-Oh brings a subtle taste of the afterlife. You will block it from your mind, but the world and its inhabitants appear ridiculous in ways you can't pin down. Hindus call it *maya* or illusion. I had a *maya* experience at age four, and now it's back. You see all the stress and mayhem and want to nudge people awake, "Please, can you just relax?" Even if you're still super busy, there is really nothing to do, no scores to settle, or battles to win. Since the show will go on without you, why not enjoy it? My friend Chrissie discovered, "You're just no longer into material things." Hopefully, your bucket list is all checked off — and if not, you might feel some urgency or despair. You must continue to do good work at age seventy because you're still here — like me writing this book. Do I expect interviews or an author tour? Say what? This book is needlepoint for my soul.

- **Age 77**: I'm not here yet, so I asked my Canadian friend, Jane, who shared: "When I reached the end of my seventies, I was hit with disbelief that it happened so fast. You're unsure how much time you've got left — and you realize that you've taken most of it for granted. This question — am I going to be here? — forced

Jane

me to dig deep for my sense of humor. After my father had several strokes in his eighties, he had lost his memory, but he kept his sense of humor. That's what carried him through. A huge piece of aging is acceptance; you have to face it full-on," Jane continued. "I've been blessed with good health, but that's beginning to change. Inside, I feel the same age as I did in my twenties, so the only time I get shocked is when I look in the mirror. A nice side to aging is that I feel free to act on my impulses, free to have fun. Recently, my felting teacher asked me to buy some condoms to fill them with sand as pin cushion forms. I might have been shy when I was younger, but as soon as I walked in the store, I asked boldly, watching for the clerk's reaction, 'Do you mind pointing me to the condoms?' Or I might tell the person filling my car with gas, 'God, you're good-looking!' That filter is gone."

- **Age 84**: I asked my physicist friend, Joseph: "So, tell me, Joseph, what stands out at age eighty-four?"

"Being eighty-four is the third Saturn return and the 12th of the seven sequences," Joseph answered. "Living through the pandemic was a big part of my Saturn return. But just by dealing with it, I feel like a weight came off. I don't have to worry about anything anymore. If the banks fail, we'll find a way to survive. I discovered that there are good-hearted people who will help each other. This gave me a great feeling of relief. I work with the volunteer fire department, so I'm with people all the time who are there to help people. Those are the kind of people I like to be with."

Joseph

"Anything palpable to report about eighty-four?" I asked.

"Well, my mind went crazy for a while," Joseph replied. "I couldn't think clearly or remember things. Plus, I was depressed. There was no real reason for it. My energy level was low, and my thought processes became stagnant."

"Were you hitting an energetic wall?" I asked.

"I went to a neurologist, pulmonary doctor, functional doctor, and they discovered some metabolic issues. Now I have a list of supplements, testosterone injections, and a new CPAP machine, all of which changed my energy level. It's a miracle that I look this great."

"So, If the midlife crisis arrives at age forty-two," I reasoned, "then technically, eighty-four would be the end. Now that you're hitting eighty-five, do you feel like you're in a bonus round?"

"Yes, I feel that way. I've been working with consciousness all my life, and the pandemic gave me a year to become aware of consciousness without any distraction. It was wonderful. I didn't have to be anywhere, so I let go of the 'I.' It was blissful. People hang on to being the 'I' because they're afraid of what could happen if they let go — expecting the abyss. I have done that now, and it's remarkable. I understand the mystical writings because that's what they're talking about."

Okay, you're thinking, my back-of-the-napkin noodling looks like a one-way ticket to decline, so offer a reason for hope. First, Hindus celebrate *Sathabhishekam* at age 81, a ceremony to honor a couple's longevity and give them good health and strength. Having crossed 1000 full moons in their lifetime, their spirituality now grows considerably.

In life, we see flowers bloom, offer pollen to bees, proclaim their glory, and wilt and die. It's hard to see much counterforce in wilting. But this book is about continuous renewal — you are a perennial, not a wilting daisy. At the most basic level, with *Sathabhishekam*, you become wiser with age — that's a counterforce. More importantly, the higher part of your soul wants to take the reins.

David Bowie expressed it best:

> If you are pining for youth, I think it produces a stereotypical old man because you only live in memory; you live in a place that doesn't exist… I think aging is an extraordinary process whereby you become the person you always should have been.[14]

Life unfolds in the form of waves — sound waves, light waves, revolving planets, and the oscillation of stars. The Octave of your life also comes in waves — like surfing waves. Some people notice their Saturn Return, and some don't. Most everyone gets slammed by a breaking wave at their mid-life crisis. These are waves of necessity.

Farmers understand necessity. They watch the weather and wait for their pastures to dry. When the time is right, they face a tight window — often working into the night to cut and bale hay.

If you don't catch the wave, it can pull you under. As a farmer, you can lose the crop. This loss of energy is clinically described as depression — polyvagal's dorsal state. From the Mayo Clinic:

> Depression is a mental health disorder characterized by persistently depressed mood or loss of interest in activities, causing significant impairment in daily life. Possible causes include a combination of biological, psychological, and social sources of distress.

It's a Mayo-naise explanation to say depression is caused by distress. Let's go deeper:

Gurdjieff explained that we can only work with the energy we possess. In other words, you can't paddle out to meet a wave without sufficient energy. Gurdjieff's closest pupil, Madame de Salzmann, described the higher energy needed to face the wave:

> "Without the relationship with higher energy, life has no meaning. The higher energy is the permanent Self, but you have no connection with that. For that connection, a fine substance needs to be generated. Otherwise, the energy of the body is too low to make contact with the very high energy which comes from above. You must persist — stay in front of the lack. Gradually, arrange to be in conditions which help you."[15]

This higher energy with the power to persist is Will. Will is not obstinance, forcefulness, or bullheadedness. Will is like a lighthouse on a stormy shore, not buffeted by the winds of time. There is a constancy to that light. Will can play the ultimate waiting game to see decisions through — past the incoming breakers — to completion.

J.G. Bennett developed the Decision Exercise to build the higher energy of Will. In Bennett's exercise, you visualize a small task at bedtime, make a conscious decision to complete it, and fulfill the task the next morning. When I learned the exercise, it was presented as a solemn initiation because, in fact, you are building the soul's capacity.

It seems absurd that wiping the top of the fridge will set your soul free, but that's how the Will muscle is built. By carrying an intention from night until day (the outgoing train), you harness the Will needed to meet the incoming train and stay present in the discomfort to tackle big things — like your soul project. Conversely, when you fail to complete decisions, you lose energy. Even casual commitments like "let's do lunch" drain energy if you don't follow through. This is the same steadfast energy needed to get through a mid-life crisis.

The story of my yoga teacher friend, Mandy Roberts, is a case in point. When I met Mandy, she was a newly divorced single mom who had just become a yoga teacher. Through a fortunate turn of events, Mandy was invited as a newbie to teach classes at Form Yoga, a new yoga studio inside a graphic design business around the corner from my office. After a few months of teaching, Mandy's new career took a shock when Form Yoga announced that it was closing its doors.

Michele, the owner, recalled, "Our yoga business was becoming a distraction from our design business, and there weren't enough students for it to be self-sufficient."

For Mandy, the news was devastating. "I was a single mom, and I was going through a divorce," she remembered. "My child came with me to teach because I was homeschooling him at the time. I felt stuck. My head was thinking, oh great, how am I going to make this happen? What other yoga studio is going to let me drag my kid to work?"

Mandy had an idea. She offered to manage the studio and find ways to squeeze enough extra revenue to keep the doors open. Michele replied, "This sounds like a great idea. Why don't you take it and run with it."

"I started working furiously," Mandy recalled, "working the numbers, considering different scenarios, teachers, classes, and researching other studios. I had a business question as I was gearing up, so I emailed Michele. 'Hey Michele, I need to know how to handle this issue.' And she replied, 'What don't you get? It's yours. The studio is yours. I'm done.'"

I asked Michele why she gave her business to a newbie like Mandy.

"Mandy was at a time of change and evolution in her life," Michele answered, "so I wanted her to take it and run with it. She had the energy and entrepreneurial approach to do it. Unlike the other teachers, Mandy always took charge of things when she saw an opportunity — even if it scared her a bit. So, I thought, what's there to lose?"

Over the next two years, Mandy breathed new life into the business. But soon, another shock hit from the train of the future coming in: The design business lost its lease, so Mandy took a gamble and rented a commercial space of her own. As the new studio grew, Mandy found a partner to offer yoga vacations in Hawaii, Peru, Costa Rica, Mexico, and Italy.

Three years later, with her yoga community humming, Mandy took another gamble.

"I felt myself digging in too deeply with no growth and no movement," Mandy said. "I decided to move to yet another new space, three or four times bigger. This raised the financial stakes considerably. But to move forward, I needed a better location. I had to grow. Bigger classes would increase the revenue with the same effort."

Mandy saw the wave and took the plunge.

"I kept my eyes open, and I kept my heart open. I looked for opportunity and possibility, and then I would try it. If it failed, okay, let me try over here. It was an ever-evolving process of trying and failing and recalibrating." Trying and failing and recalibrating is how the engine of continuous renewal works.

I interviewed Mandy a second time for my business book *Brand Story*. By now, the once failing yoga business had blossomed into the biggest yoga studio in Atlanta. I gently prodded her, "Mandy, aren't you like 41 years old and gearing for your midlife crisis?"

"Been there, done that." Mandy scoffed, "I already had my mid-life

crisis." Mandy had a point. After growing up in a tumultuous childhood, she became pregnant at seventeen and got married with a baby at eighteen. With no financial support, Mandy and her young husband endured crisis after crisis — but Mandy was always a survivor.

On the morning of February 3, 2020, I had just posted "Happy 42nd Birthday" on Mandy's timeline when I clicked an obscure news item on USA Today:

Mandy Roberts, yoga entrepreneur,

> WASHINGTON – The Donald Trump administration declared the coronavirus outbreak to be a public health emergency in the United States on Friday… it was the first quarantine order issued by the federal government in over 50 years. …the last time a quarantine was used in the 1960s for smallpox.
>
> "The risk of infection for Americans remains low," said Alex Azar. "We are working to keep the risk low."[16]

I tried to eat my cereal, but I felt those pesky harmonics. Azar's reassurance was short-lived. One month later (March 11, 2020, "the day COVID swallowed everything"), COVID swallowed Mandy's dreams and expectations. Four months later, Mandy wrote to her students:

> At the start of the COVID pandemic, I was naive. I thought we were simply doing our part to flatten the curve by closing our doors for a couple of weeks. The idea of being closed a couple of weeks was terrifying; I had no idea if we would make it into April.
>
> As of today our doors have been closed a little over over four months… Needless to say, these sixteen weeks have been some of the most heartbreaking and challenging in my life.

Midlife crises don't mess around. Mandy continued:

"On Friday morning, June 8, my father left this world. As he left
this place, I sat on the cement, alone, in the rain on the top floor of
the hospital parking deck. I didn't want to risk exposing anyone to
COVID, so I sat under the gray clouds, praying for him to transition peacefully, without fear."

By June, yoga studios all over Atlanta were shutting down. With
nearly $10,000 per month in overhead, Mandy bravely faced the wave
head-on. She told a local newspaper:

"I was honest about my grief and the dire outlook of our beloved
studio. Our community stepped up; they generously gave back
what we have offered over the years — support. Several staff
offered to donate their pay. Someone volunteered to film classes.
Another student walked a mile for each five-dollar donation. Gift
cards were purchased, private sessions booked, cookies baked,
friendship bracelets and playlists created, home services offered,
and even an auction was suggested. It was finally safe to exhale.

"I was clear on the kind of community I wanted to create, but I had
no idea that I would need that community to survive these tough
times. I still don't know if Form Yoga will make it through the pandemic… but I vow to keep fighting and to keep breathing."[17]

After months of outdoor classes in the parking lot, installing a special
HVAC, plus masks, yoga distancing, and tons of support, Mandy kept
the business afloat by a thread. She made it through the breaking waves,
but mid-life crises are not just doom and gloom — they are about outside shocks precipitating life-altering change. A couple of weeks before
Mandy's 42nd birthday, a South African man bent on one knee atop Table
Mountain in Cape Town and asked for her hand in marriage. Mandy
shared:

"Months prior, I had all but given up on finding a serious relationship. While I had dated many fine men over the past ten years
since my divorce, and as much as I tried to make them fit, none of
them were "the one" for me. Up until I met Ruan, I usually thought

that men only wanted something from me… At that point, I believed I could not be loved and appreciated for who I was without someone trying to change me or mold me into the person they wanted me to be or break me down. And, I didn't stand in my power. I didn't speak up for what I wanted or needed; I didn't ask for my space; I didn't share all of me. I was afraid, afraid of being abandoned, ridiculed; I was afraid of not being enough.

"Ruan, you took my heart and fortified it. You made it stronger by helping me exercise my willingness to trust you with my entire being, mind, body, and soul. You treat me like a queen every fucking day, even if I don't deserve it. I don't know what I would've done without you this past year. Thank you for restoring my faith in my lovability."

Brené Brown, the champion of courage and empowerment, said it best:

Midlife is when the universe gently places her hands upon your shoulders, pulls you close, and whispers in your ear:

"I'm not screwing around."

You were born worthy of love and belonging. Courage and daring are coursing through you. You were made to live and love with your whole heart. It's time to show up and be seen.[18]

At age 42, Mandy showed up to paddle through life's three biggest waves: career, love, and death.

I've over-used the surfing analogy throughout this chapter, so on a lark, I checked to see if I'm on point. I Googled "How to Get Past Breaking Waves," and found Uplift instructions (in italics) from Kooks Only Surf.com:[19]

Watch the Waves — *Take a few moments to watch the ocean. Each spot and each day will be different. Try to gain an understanding of how long the sets take to arrive.*

Did I mention that waves come in sets of seven (anecdotally)? Watching for patterns in your world gives you the compass to navigate life.

If the biggest sets arrive five minutes apart, time your paddling out to get past the most violent section during this break. If mistimed, you may find yourself directly in the impact zone.

Timing is everything. The mastery of life is to cultivate an instinctive sense of knowing when to act.

Look for a Channel — *In some surfing locations, there is a channel where the waves are less powerful. If you spot a clearing that appears open and easy, paddle out there!*

In the Octave, channels offer Uplift and allow us to defy the forces of descent. These openings appear innocuously — an opportunity to offer your salad on a flight or beckon a Congressman at a funeral.

J.G. Bennett found similar openings in natural processes. He described how openings allow molten glass to flow. He wrote: "There are holes in the glass, and we know that these holes make it possible for one element of the material to enter into a hole and release a place for another one to enter. The melting of a piece of glass is really the same kind of process…as the game of backgammon. Someone, or something, is throwing the dice, and when the turn comes for the particular little aggregate of silicate to fall into a hole that is available, it will do so, and so the glass flows."[20]

Use the Current — *Take notes of the rip currents. If the ocean is ripping to the left, then you should walk far to the right before paddling out to let the current take you to where the best waves are breaking.*

With maturity, we discover that the Current carries us on our journey. We are taught that rip currents will kill us, but Aikido masters use this current to take down a larger opponent. Barack Obama followed his current from a community organizer working the streets of Chicago to become Keynote Speaker at the Democratic National Convention in a span of ten years.

Face the Wave Head-On — *When the white water hits you, your board should be facing straight toward the wave. Novice surfers try to punch through at a slight angle towards the wave. As soon as the white water hits the side of their board, they get pushed back or flipped off their board.*

Reshad once told me, "Until you face what you have to face, you can never be free." The willingness to face reality head-on creates an opening — the "channel" through the breaking waves.

Paddle Hard — *As you approach the white water, paddle head-on into the wave (90 degrees) to avoid flipping off. You need momentum to pass through the wave, so paddle hard.*

The conundrum between effort and effortlessness stymies all human enterprise — when to push and when to let go. Most of the time, we have it backward — except when facing a mighty breaker.

Punch Through the Wave — *As the whitewater hits, hold on tight and push your chest up to let the white water pass between your body and your surfboard. For bigger waves, duck dive under the wave, or turtle roll gripping hard, rolling your body, and traveling through the wave upside down.*

In each of these methods, you let the wave pass through you. What appears as an insurmountable wall of water is simply energy moving through your life – more like a passing weather front than an impenetrable wall.

When Karen was diagnosed with metastatic lung cancer to the brain, her diagnosis hit like a tsunami. Strangely, no one ever asked Karen how she survived a seven-month prognosis to live. Maybe, no one wanted to know. Or perhaps Karen's secret was simpler: Her soul Googled *Kooks Only Surf.com.*

After much prodding, Karen consented to an interview:

Bruce: "Karen, when I wrote 'How to Get Past Breaking Waves,' I realized, OMG, that's how you got through cancer. Can you share?"

Karen: "Okay, if you must. Why do I end up in all your books?"

Bruce: "I'm asking the questions. Let's start with the first step — *Watch the Waves.* How did watching serve your journey?

Karen: "Watching… I was always watching. After returning home from the hospital, I didn't know what steps to take, but I knew I had to keep going. I decided to watch what came my way. I practiced being open to the people I encountered and their offers to help. All sorts of suggestions came my way; I even received a colonic from a self-styled Cherokee medicine man in South Carolina. One friend suggested I call the owner of a health store. Okay. So, I picked up the phone.

Duck diving under a breaking wave

It was a Sunday, and the woman happened to be there. She prodded to see if I was open to offbeat therapies. Since I was very open, we drove out to Waltham County to see this weird guy who lived behind a big gate. We went into a small bedroom where he attached all these electrodes and hooked me to a blinking device...."

Bruce: "The Quantum Xeroid Consciousness Interface. It was developed by Bill Nelson, a genius scientist from NASA. His son had autism. It was supposed to measure the body's subtle energy systems."

Karen: "Ninety-nine percent of the diagnosis proved to be accurate. The machine even picked up the smoothie I had for breakfast."

Bruce: "I remember the machine saying there was no cancer."

Karen: "That was a surprise. Maybe on an esoteric level, I was already healed. Who knows? We didn't go back to him, but the episode gave me encouragement or permission to follow my breadcrumbs."

Bruce: "What about step two, *Face the Wave Head-on*?"

Karen: "From the beginning, I decided to face my diagnosis head-on to the best of my ability. Remember Elaine? She had me cover my feet with healing mud. She was a gifted healer, and her husband beat cancer, so I asked her point-blank if I would get through it. And she said, yes, I would definitely succeed, but there would be hurdles. I had no idea what would be required, but I knew it was possible. It was like riding a wave. I'm going to get on top and

Karen on the morning before brain surgery

162

ride it to the end. That meant reaching out, getting as much help as I could, and engaging and immersing myself in this experience."

Bruce: "Was it empowering?"

Karen: "Absolutely. When you engage something with intention, like facing the wave head-on, there's meaning in the experience. It's a chicken and egg because when you engage, the meaning develops. I don't know which comes first, but intention and meaning are connected."

Bruce: "The surfing instructions say to watch the waves for a channel to get through the breakers. Do you remember moving through openings?"

Karen: "To use your metaphor, sometimes I would paddle, and other times rest. With this kind of diagnosis, it would be too exhausting to paddle all the time. But following the channel led me to Dr. Renneker, a cancer researcher who became my patient advocate. So when Dr. Renneker suggested that we travel to Italy to meet Dr. Recchia, that was an opening — but it also took a lot of effort. You pooh-poohed the idea at first, but it felt right — that going to Italy was the next step. Whenever a door opened, I checked it out, even if I chose not to pursue it. Every person I met and worked with, however briefly, proved to be important."

Bruce: "The next instruction is to *Use the Current*. Did you find a stream of support?"

Karen: "My cancer journey took a lot of effort, but the universe also conspired to help me. The universe helps us accomplish what we long for in our hearts. I remember feeling supportive energy from everyone — even from their thoughts. It was palpable, even to the point that people volunteered to drive me to work — that was a current.

I'm not sure I understood the severity of my condition, and maybe, that was a good thing. But I stayed in touch with the journey at all times."

Bruce: "Next step is *Paddle Hard*. I remember being amazed how you started your new teaching career right after brain surgery. That took tremendous will."

Karen: "I had worked so hard to reach this stage in my professional life, and then I was hit with this traumatic event two weeks before my start date. To become a chaplain educator was my dream job; I felt called. Somehow my career opening dovetailed with my health journey, so I felt that the two callings were interrelated."

Bruce: "I remember you coming back from work exhausted, yet you chose to walk two miles each night to the post office and back — plus you swam across the lake during the summer months."

Karen: "I needed to strengthen myself. It was a way of working with the will. From the very beginning, I felt that it was more than a medical journey, particularly when they removed the brain tumor, and I felt the trauma from my childhood vanish as well."

Bruce: "Is that what you mean by not letting cancer define you?"

Karen: "Absolutely. I never talked about having cancer. I never used that language. I still don't. I say I'm on a journey — a health journey."

Bruce: "The final instruction reads: *As the whitewater hits, hold on tight and push your chest up to let the whitewater pass between your body and* *your surfboard."* What does it mean to let the whitewater of cancer pass."

Karen: "It was like going through a wall. I didn't know how to lift myself up off the board when I was going through it, but I did. The water rushes but doesn't knock you off because you're centered in yourself. It's a yin and yang of surrender and effort. I chose not to identify with the cancer because I wanted to stay connected to the journey. My experience was defined by what I had to face, what was coming next, and the strengthening of my body and emotions."

Bruce: "Was this like a wave passing through?"

Karen: "When you hold onto your intention, it's like pushing up from the board; it takes less effort than clinging with all your power. If you tighten and grimace, that wave is going to smash you. But if you lift up, you gain a different perspective of what's going on. You recognize that this "C-word" is not more powerful than you — not more powerful than the healing energies available for you. The support coming your way is greater than what's going on in your body.

Was this good enough?"

Bruce: "I love you."

After Karen finished, I remembered Bhagwan's words:

"It's all about the will to live," Bhagwan explained.

"What does that even mean?" I replied. "Nobody wants to die."

"Who we are in truth never dies," Bhagwan replied.

The will to live became my koan and an enigma. The will to live is not about desperation or willfulness. It's the task of keeping the flame lit in the lighthouse to guide the ships home.

J.G. Bennett also talked about Will. Instead of Two Trains — one coming in and one out, Bennett described three types of time. The first, clock time, allows Google Maps to calculate your arrival. Bennett called this *function time.*

The second, *being time,* is eternal. When gurus and new age people talk about living in the present or dismiss time as an illusion, they are describing *being time.* Ironically, *being time* is timeless. I often marvel at how our cute little terrier dog can hang out for hours in his dog bed, totally content, without the need for podcasts and social media. Being time is a state of fulfillment.

Years ago, when I met Bhagwan at the airport for the first time, he asked with sincere befuddlement, "What is this Octave that Reshad talks about?"

I answered with *Octave for Dummies* simplicity, "Bhagwan, the Octave is about the nature of time, how every event has a beginning, middle, and end...."

Bhagwan was drawing a blank, so I stopped. It dawned on me that Bhagwan lived in *being time.* In *being time,* we are aware of the future coming in because it's all right now. My buddy Nick's first cigarette at fourteen and his lung cancer at fifty-eight were both in one connected moment — a set of waves coming in. Expanding the present moment allows us to see these patterns of life on the back of a napkin.

Bennett's third type of time enlarges the present moment. Bennett called it *hyparxis.* He also called it *will time.* It's what carried Karen on her cancer journey. Like a breath mint and a candy mint combined, *will time* describes the Two Trains — *clock time* and *being time* — two trains at once. Clock time is mechanical; being time is eternal. With *hyparxis,* they fuse as Will — the guiding force that carries a conscious human being through the Octave.

As an experiment, hold your arms straight out for a clock-time minute — *tick-tick-tick-tick.* The strain will grow until it becomes an irritant. In a CrossFit class, your bouncy instructor will cajole you to use effort to keep them up. If you relax into stillness, they stay up without effort. The energy that keeps them aloft is will. From my years as a whirling dervish, it was a mystery how I kept my arms aloft. Bennett described how these acts of will take place outside time:

> Realization requires an act of will that is quite different from an action or an activity. The observation of our own acts of will shows that they do not happen in ordinary time. They are instantaneous, and for this reason we can never detect [the acts of will] as they occur, but only recognize them after they have occurred. Hyparxis links together time and eternity because it requires an act of will to pass intentionally from one level in eternity to another.[21]

Will carries us through the breaking waves. Amid the turbulence, a hidden channel takes us from one level to another. The impenetrable wall of water passes through us by facing the wave, paddling hard, and catching the current. You can hire surfing lessons, but for *hyparxis* lessons, you're on your own. At best, a spiritual mentor will transmit a dose of Uplift to awaken your angels.

Life presents opportunities to pass through the channels. But there's a catch. For most people, the channels go unnoticed. Life's ups and downs seem random and impenetrable. These channels open through a mysterious dance of energy called the Enneagram. Let's dance.

Endnotes

1   J.G. Bennett. Hazard: The Risk of Realization. Bennett Books.

2   https://www.wnycstudios.org/podcasts/heresthething/episodes/299360-rosie-odonnell

3   https://www.abc.net.au/news/science/2020-05-14/astronomers-detect-heartbeat-of-musical-delta-scuti-stars/12239342

4   Bly, Robert. 2000. Eating the Honey of Words: New and Selected Poems. New York: Harper Perennial.

5   https://www.npr.org/2020/02/26/809741265/rep-jim-clyburn-endorses-joe-biden-ahead-of-south-carolina-primary

6   https://www.cnn.com/2020/02/26/politics/jim-clyburn-endorses-joe-biden/index.html

7   https://www.foxnews.com/media/van-jones-biden-campaign-dead-man-walking

8   John Heilemann and Chris Mathews on "Hell & High Water," August 10, 2021

9   https://www.nytimes.com/2020/03/08/us/clyburn-biden-endorsement.html

10   Nicole Wallace on "Hell and High Water with John Heilman" - 4-6-21

11   https://www.nhpr.org/post/after-iowa-stumble-biden-goes-heart-first-final-nh-push

12   https://www.livescience.com/8432-personality-set-life-1st-grade-study-suggests.html

13   P.D. Ouspensky "In Search of the Miraculous," Chapter 8.

14   http://www.out.com/music/2016/1/11/david-bowie-obituary

15   Ravindra, Ravi. Heart Without Measure: Gurdjieff Work with Madame de Salzmann. 2004.

16   https://www.usatoday.com/story/news/politics/2020/01/31/coronavirus-donald-trump-declares-public-health-emergency/4625299002/

17   https://www.bizjournals.com/bizwomen/news/latest-news/2020/09/in-her-own-words-atlanta-s-mandy-roberts-says-yo.html

18   https://brenebrown.com/blog/2018/05/24/the-midlife-unraveling/

19   https://kooksonlysurf.com/how-to-get-past-breaking-waves/ Also: https://barefootsurftravel.com/livemore-magazine/paddle-push-waves

20   Bennett, J.G. 1991. Hazard: The Risk of Realization. Revised edition. Santa Fe, NM: Bennett Books.

21   Bennett, J. G. The Dramatic Universe: A Short Guide: FAQ

Chapter 7
THE ENGINE OF
CONTINUOUS RENEWAL

"This world is full of conflicts and full of things
that cannot be reconciled. But there are moments when
we can... reconcile and embrace the whole mess,
and that's what I mean by 'Hallelujah.'" ~ *Leonard Cohen*

BEFORE DIGITAL DEVICES, I spent hours at Atlanta's airport (the world's busiest), waiting for friends to make it through customs. Texting had not been invented, so I studied the crowd for my friend gliding up the escalator. Mother-daughter pairs piqued my curiosity, especially blossoming teenage girls alongside their burnt-out fifty-something moms. How, I wondered, does Girl (A) transform into Mom (B)?

It's a stupid question and one of mystical importance. On one level, (B)'s wrinkles, gray hair, and extra forty pounds could be explained by metabolism, collagen, and gravity. But science couldn't explain how mom's *joie de vivre* — her teenage curiosity and exuberance — sank into the tired, cynical shell of middle-age.

Watching the crowds, I imagined a sci-fi invention – an anti-gravity machine that could lift people from the steady grind of living in the adult world. In new age circles, the term "working on yourself" describes this yearning for a spiritual shot of anti-gravity. Even Dylan lamented how early career certitude robbed his primal innocence:

"But I was so much older then. I'm younger than that now." - Bob Dylan

So, when my eighty-something friends, Jane and Joseph, shared, "I feel the same age I did in my twenties," and "It's a miracle that I look this great," my mystical curiosity lit up. Can (A) slip into middle age (B) and then kick back up towards (A)? Is it possible to swim upstream in life and become younger than that now? Is there a secret to everlasting Uplift?

J.G. Bennett answered this question in his book, *Enneagram Studies:*

> "Some 4,600 years ago, there arose in Mesopotamia a brotherhood of wise men who discovered the cosmic secret of perpetual self-renewal and passed it down from generation to generation."[1]

Whoa! Did these wise men discover the anti-gravity machine — the cosmic secret for the fountain of youth? To my surprise, Bennett filled his fountain — not with a magic potion — but with the mysterious elixir we discovered in seventh-grade math class: *recurring decimals.*

Bennett wrote:

> "This knowledge was revealed to Zoroaster, Pythagoras and other great sages until the custodians of the tradition migrated northward. In the tenth century, mathematicians trained in their schools discovered the significance of the number zero and created the decimal number system which all the world now uses. It was observed at the time that a new kind of number appeared when one was divided by three or seven. This we now call a recurring decimal."

The ad infinitum generated from $1 \div 3$ revealed the messy side of math: You can't always shut the drawer on a long division problem.

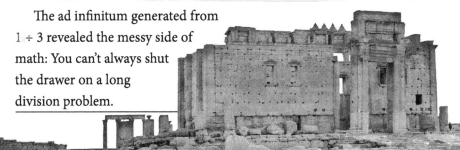

```
        .33333
3 ) 1.00000
        9
        10
         9
        10
         9
        10
         9
        10
         9
Remainder  1
```

For the early mathematicians, math was a sacred pursuit and a way to understand the hidden dimensions of life. They understood the significance of the Laws of Three and Seven. I can only imagine their wonderment performing long division with the newfound decimal thingy as it spiraled into infinity. No matter how many times they divided one by three to produce .33333̄, the remainder kept reappearing as One. With this recurring decimal, a sense of Unity lurked within the Law of Three.

If I send you to the hardware store to buy a piece of glass that's one-third of a meter square, no matter how closely you measure .3333̄, the glass will always come up a little short and leave a tiny crack against the frame. Could this be what Leonard Cohen meant:

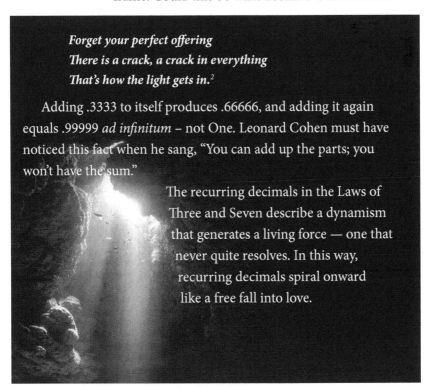

Forget your perfect offering
There is a crack, a crack in everything
That's how the light gets in.[2]

Adding .3333 to itself produces .66666, and adding it again equals .99999 *ad infinitum* – not One. Leonard Cohen must have noticed this fact when he sang, "You can add up the parts; you won't have the sum."

The recurring decimals in the Laws of Three and Seven describe a dynamism that generates a living force — one that never quite resolves. In this way, recurring decimals spiral onward like a free fall into love.

```
        .142857
  7 ) 1.000000
        7
        30
        28
        20
        14
        60
        56
        40
        35
        50
        49
        1
```

The wise men were also curious about what lay hidden in the Law of Seven. Dividing one by seven equals .142857 — also a recurring decimal with a remainder 1.

Adding the Law of Three to itself (.333+.333+.333) results in .666 and .999. Take the 3,6,9 from the Law of Three and the 1,4,2,8,5,7 from Law of Seven and suddenly all nine numbers are represented (1,2,3,4,5,6,7,8,9). In this way, the two great laws, Three and Seven, embrace all the numbers – the entire picture of life.

From this realization, the wise men overlaid the two figures (3-6-9 and 1-4-2-8-5-7) over a circle representing Unity – and voila, the Enneagram:

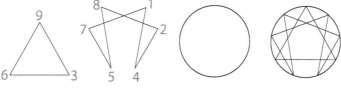

Law of Three + Law of Seven + Unity = Enneagram

Unlike other ancient symbols, the Enneagram was not found in sacred sites, temples, or ancient manuscripts. For one thing, the discovery of decimals is relatively recent. One could surmise that the Enneagram was closely held in the mystery schools until Gurdjieff introduced it to his Russian students in 1916. At that time, he announced:

> "The knowledge of the Enneagram has for a very long time been preserved in secret and if it now is, so to speak, made available to all, it is only in an incomplete and theoretical form without instruction from a man who knows"

Gurdjieff did not explain where to find such a person, but he alluded to personally meeting one:

"If two men who have been in different schools meet, they will draw the Enneagram, and with its help, they will be able at once to establish which of them knows more and which, consequently, stands upon which step, that is to say, which is the elder, which is the teacher and which the pupil."

Gurdjieff took his claim further when he declared:

"For the man who is able to make use of it, the Enneagram makes books and libraries entirely unnecessary. Everything can be included and read in the Enneagram. A man may be quite alone in the desert, and he can trace the Enneagram in the sand and in it read the eternal laws of the universe."[3]

I never met a man who knew what to do with the Enneagram, so I was on my own. In my 30 years studying with Reshad Feild, there was one word he never uttered — not even once. That word was *Enneagram*. This is remarkable because Reshad was an Octave magician — *and maybe was the Octave!* He even studied in a Gurdjieff school when he was younger. So how did he miss the Enneagram lesson?

Adding to the challenge, like a round peg in the square hole, the seven-note Octave doesn't even fit into the nine-pointed Enneagram. Sort of like shoehorning size seven into size nine shoes.

Gurdjieff admitted this "flaw" when he asked his pupils:

"Why is one of the 'intervals' which is designated by the number 3 found in its right place between the notes Mi and Fa, and the other, which is designated by the number 6, found between Sol and La, when its right place is between Si and Do."[4]

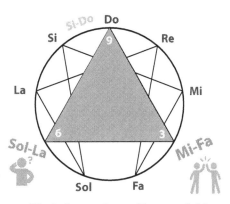

Why is there an interval between Sol-La and none between Si-Do?

Whoops.

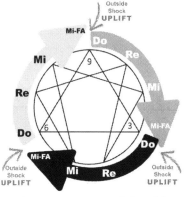

Start a new octave at 3,6, and 9.

Maybe Gurdjieff was using a Jedi mind trick, but he solved the problem by starting a new Octave at each point of the triangle 3-6-9. That's right, since the Octave doesn't line up, you can take a *mulligan* — just pick up the ball and start a new Octave at points 3-6-9. Essentially, the octave that begins at Do (9) runs out of steam at the Mi-Fa interval (3). Each opening invites a fresh impulse (outside shock) at the interval and the possibility of Uplift. It's like taking your divorce papers to the post office (Octave 1), and bumping into a long-lost friend who invites you to a dinner party (Octave 2). At the party, you meet an eligible bachelor (Octave 3). Three separate stories – the divorce, renewing an old friendship, and meeting Mr. Eligible – overlap but are distinct.

I prefer comparing the Enneagram to a potter's kick wheel. The goal in pottery is to shape clay into a beautiful pot through periodic kicks of the wheel. Similarly, a few well-placed kicks at

The Enneagram is like a kick-wheel

3-6-9 allow the Octave stories to unfold into a romance.

Another analogy for this ever-renewing circle of Octaves is the staggered start of a 400-meter race or even a baton relay. What these analogies offer — and this is the whole game — is dynamism. Gurdjieff made it very clear that the Enneagram is dynamic, in motion — like life itself:

> "In order to understand the Enneagram, it must be thought of as in motion, as moving. A motionless Enneagram is a dead symbol; the living symbol is in motion."[5]

The "original" Enneagram is not to be confused with the modern Enneagram built around nine personality types. The personality-type

Enneagram has its roots in the work of Bolivian psycho-spiritual teacher Oscar Ichazo from the 1950s and the Chilean psychiatrist Claudio Naranjo from the 1970s. Today, the word "enneagram" almost always refers to personality types (*Peacemaker, Loyalist, Achiever,* etc.). This is a different use of the symbol than what Gurdjieff introduced.

Personality Enneagram

Like a tree, the Enneagram is born from the dynamism of its source: the Laws of Three and Seven. A living tree draws nutrients from the earth, converts carbon from the sky, and circulates sustenance through its xylem and phloem. A tree produces fruit, season after season, as an act of continuous renewal. In this way, like a tree, the Enneagram functions as an engine of continuous renewal. Perhaps that's why Gurdjieff warned of the Enneagram becoming a motionless "dead symbol."

It is impossible to study the enneagram without getting tripped up by the mechanics. Since this is a book about Uplift, I prefer to focus on one's felt experience rather than theory. The *hidden engine of continuous renewal* (aka *Enneagram*) is something you feel.

People ascribe magical powers to the Enneagram, but it's just a map — a two-dimensional blueprint of the richness, hazards, and Uplift of lived experience. You can use a map of Rome to guide you to the Piazza Navona, but it doesn't show the hawkers, musicians, and gelato carts you encounter along the way. You have to live that.

Conversely, if you wander the alleyways without a map, you lose the big picture. The Enneagram helps you understand the rhythms and pitfalls of your journey to becoming a better traveler. With a map, travelers know where to expect steep hills, winding sections, and rest stops.

Similarly, the Enneagram only makes sense to *soul travelers* — people working on their "soul project." From wisdom and experience, the long uphill climbs and rest stops along the way become familiar guideposts on your soul journey.

On a soul project, we face the pressures of our growing edges – from following a guru, navigating a career, mending a relationship, clearing a trauma, mourning a loss, or following a keto diet. A zillion self-help books teach these edges. Which growing edge is best? Giovanni once explained: "It doesn't matter what you do, just as long as you do it."

Facing your growing edges

The Enneagram offers a bird's-eye perch to view life's long uphill climbs, moments of bliss, attacks of panic, and unexpected collisions. The soul's journey is inseparable from the events of life. When Bennett encountered the Enneagram as a student of Ouspensky, rather than trying to figure it out, he let it in:

> "I remember vividly when I first saw that the *Enneagram* was a picture of myself," Bennett recalled. "Mr. Ouspensky was giving a lecture on the *Enneagram* somewhere about 1924 and asked me to put the diagram on the blackboard. As I was drawing the familiar lines, I felt myself going out of myself and entering the diagram. I noticed that I was facing myself and grasped for the first time the essential difference between the two sides of our bodies. How long this lasted, I don't know, but from that evening, I was convinced that the *Enneagram* is a living diagram and that we can experience ourselves as Enneagrams."[6]

This is the starting point: Let the Enneagram in. If you take apart a watch to try to find meaning from the mainspring, escapement, wheels, and jewels — all those pieces and parts won't help you sense the moods of time. Conversely, sensing a single thread of time can open the door to the dynamism of the entire *Enneagram*. Let's give it a try:

Let's sense the Octave in a song: "Silver Springs" by Fleetwood Mac *(YouTube live performance: "Fleetwood Mac - Silver Springs - Official Music Video").* Ready? Play the song to sense the energy shifts of the Octave:

Silver Springs, live performance

Do — Intro | :00 - :14
The opening bass note for *Silver Springs* sounds a decisive *Do* — the statement of intention.

Re — Verse 1 | :14 - 1:00
Here we go. Like a train leaving the station, the song moves forward — a very slow-moving *Re.* Stevie Nicks sounds whiney but just sense the energy. It's the feeling you get waiting on hold for the DMV, watching 70 slides of Powerpoint, or sitting on the crapper waiting for movement.

Mi— Verse 2 | 1:05 - 2:17
"I'll begin not to love you." The song crawls forward but in a strange grammatic gear. *"I don't want to know"* is more whining about "me," — which is appropriate for the note *Mi.* An early song from The Beatles would be done by now, and we're still waiting for this one to take off!! You can scroll your phone while you wait. For this lesson, just feel the halting energy until…

Fa — Bridge | 2:17 - 2:42
Boom! The downbeat, key change and vocal harmonies unleash the Uplift. This is why we're here. Feel the clouds open, and your heart expand. Rewind and play the *Mi-Fa* shock lifting the song into *Fa* of the Octave. You can sense this interval in a song, but can you capture it in life? This is the thread to internalize — the moment of Uplift.

Sol — Guitar Solo | 2:43 - 3:15
The guitar Solo brings a moment of reflection. Solo equals *Sol* — how convenient. Life is ultimately a solo journey that brings us to the Self.

La — Chorus | 3:15 - 3:48
The word for "No" in Arabic is *La. No* turning back! We've said "no" to the spell of living a mechanical existence.

Si — Refrain | 3:48 - 4:24
Stevie Nicks lets loose and kicks into high gear. With her unexpected harmonics and vocal syncopations, Stevie embraces the angels. In a movie, this would be the climax. In the Octave, it's the note *Si*.

Do — Outro | 4:24 - End
Hurray! We moved through the *Si-Do* of the Octave. Even if you found Stevie's lyrics insufferable, what started as a sniveling gripe now carries depth. In this way, the Octave lifts the mundane to a new level. This is continuous renewal.

Silver Springs follows a classic song structure, but not every song moves through the Octave this way. I don't want to argue anyone's taste in music, but most contemporary pop/rap/hip-hop songs stay stuck in low gear — *Do-Re-Mi, Do-Re-Mi*. Modern songs often have no bridge, no key change, interval, middle eight, or Uplift. They stay stuck in a repetitive, mechanical structure of *verse/chorus/verse/chorus*.

To prove this point, when I give talks, I randomly visit the Billboard. com Hot 100 to see what's hot. This week, "Permission to Dance," by BTS, tops the chart. Like a car stuck between two gears, BTS hits the throttle, backs off, hits it again, back and forth until the song is over.

Our lives also get stuck — *get up, go to work, eat, watch TV, sleep* and *repeat* — *verse/chorus/verse/chorus*.

Stuck in mechanical life

The Octave breaks this cycle. It lifts life from the *mechanical,* moves the energy through the *Mi-Fa,* and engages a sense of *mission.*

Play the *Mi-Fa* section (2:15) of *Silver Springs* a few times with your eyes closed. Sense the shifting of gears at the interval. This is the feeling of Uplift. Can you remember a moment of Uplift in your life?

In *Silver Springs,* Stevie Nicks delivered a vengeful post-mortem of her acrimonious breakup from Lyndsey Buckingham in 1977. Originally a B-side throwaway for the single, *Go Your Own Way, Silver Springs* re-emerged twenty years later to receive a Grammy nomination for its 1997 live performance. In the video (3:40), Stevie turns to Lyndsey and locks eyes, *"I'll follow you down 'til the sound of my voice will haunt you."* At this point, what's happening on stage is more than a song. You feel their emotional journey. In 2005, while introducing another song, *Say Goodbye,* Lyndsey turned to Stevie and said point-blank, *"There can be little gain without some loss, and little redemption without forgiveness."*

So much for that. In 2018, (after 43 years), Stevie fired Lyndsey from the band, reportedly communicating via her manager: "Stevie never wants to be on a stage with you again." And then, in 2019, Lyndsey suffered a massive heart attack (and recovered). The Enneagram is like that.[7]

Fleetwood Mac's onstage animosity provides evidence of the Enneagram at work. When two lovers suddenly grow distant, or deaf ears ignore the demand to "clean your room," or Palestinians and Israelis dig ever deeper into their stalemate, we witness an *impasse.* An impasse starts from *identification* with your point of view (as in Do Re "Me"), followed by *distrust* of the other, and finally, the inability to *imagine* how a renewed relationship would look and feel. The polarization and distrust harden to form an impenetrable wall. My psychologist friend, Mimi, describes this wall as *sticky anger.*

Karen takes it further: "Sticky anger is when you replay a grievance over and over in your mind until it leads to an unfortunate disease."

When you hit an impasse, you're not thinking, "Oh, this must be the Mi-Fa interval." But you feel the impasse and hang tight to your position. I asked Karen to comment on how she approaches a relational impasse in order to move through the Mi-Fa interval. Like a firefighter who runs into burning buildings, Karen never seems to turn away when facing a conflict:

> **Bruce**: I've always been amazed at your fearlessness in addressing conflict. It's like a switch flips, and you go there.
>
> **Karen**: When I was a child, the prospect of conflict was threatening — life-threatening. I've learned over the years that conflict is really a normal part of life.
>
> **Bruce**: It's easy for an armchair philosopher like me to say that, but conflict is uncomfortable. No one wants to go there.
>
> **Karen**: Yes, the discomfort of conflict is palpable. And it brings up strong emotions, like anger, fear, and shame. We try to steer around conflict or put a band-aid on it. But that's not the same as addressing it. I have learned to put whatever strong opinion I have on the shelf and go towards the person, towards the conflict, and see what I can discover. It's a conscious decision.
>
> **Bruce**: You go into the burning building because there's a baby inside. But to go headfirst into conflict, do you have to see value in renewing the relationship?
>
> **Karen**: I'm driven by the possibility of transformation. That's my motivation. When there is transformation, something is liberated.
>
> **Bruce**: The Uplift. Like when a fog lifts.
>
> **Karen**: You have to let go of your position — even if for a minute. When the fog lifts, you discover something new.
>
> **Bruce**: Why is this universally so difficult? I call it *human impasse* because it's impenetrable. Is it the discomfort?

Karen: I'm on a cancer journey, so I have learned to face discomfort. The fear factor comes from embracing the unknown. When you put your hardened opinions aside, the ground you stand on becomes suddenly less secure. Few people can do this.

Bruce: It's the state of our nation.

Karen: I have two friends who would get together every morning until, one day, they had a misunderstanding. Boom! For months now, they haven't gotten back together. Letting go of a grievance risks entering uncharted territory.

Bruce: It's sad because life is too short.

Karen: Like you say, there is a failure of imagination that what lies on the other side is worth it.

The impenetrable walls – what Giovanni called the "Walls of Despair" – are the intervals. More than a wall, it's wall after wall, rolling in like waves. These walls of despair serve as the stepping stones for Uplift. The Enneagram uses these unfolding octaves as its hidden engine of renewal.

Consider the glider pilot who would steadily lose altitude if not for Uplift. Glider pilots seek lift from thermals. A plowed field, urban heat, and ridge lifts extend their range – *the hidden engine.* The pilot circles upward in a rising thermal, catches some Uplift, and reaches a new altitude. He can fly all day by spotting cumulous clouds and catching Uplifts.

The cycles of the Enneagram describe how transformative events provide the updraft, and the walls of

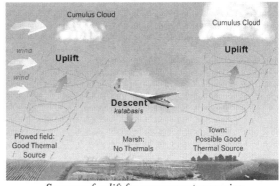

Sources of uplift for cross-country soaring

despair provide the downdrafts. Our body, mind, and emotions produce the drag.

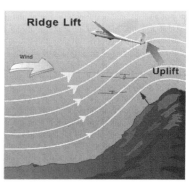

Intervals (from flatland to mountain ridge) produce uplift.

In the Enneagram, instead of downdrafts, thermals, and ridge lifts, we use the language of *shock points* or *intervals*. In the same way that thermals extend a glider flight, shock points move the story along. Each climax initiates a new starting point.

Imagine climbing a long stairwell and catching your breath at each landing. Sure, you lose momentum at each stop, but as Lyndsey said, "There can be little gain without some loss." Taking the analogy further, if you steal a kiss at each landing, the trek up the stairs transforms from tedium to playfulness. Game-changers at the intervals can also be fun.

The Enneagram keeps bringing new octaves into the story. Suppose a

distraught girl, leaving a party upstairs, comes down the stairwell while you're deep into that kiss. Suddenly, your stories intersect. In this way, the Enneagram, like a real-life movie, captures the continuous, dynamic, and multi-dimensional nature of life.

Outside shocks arrive as outside stories. In a movie, the troubled girl in the stairwell turns a quiet evening into an adventure. Imagine Meg Ryan colliding into Billy Crystal while he's stealing a kiss from Debra Winger. Film plots seem outlandish, but they mirror the rhythms of life.

If the Octave is like a piano keyboard with missing black notes at the intervals, the Enneagram follows a different paradigm. Rather than a staircase of piano keys, the Enneagram functions like a pie with three big slices — each a different flavor.

Octave: Enneagram:

Imagine a three-slice pie with butterscotch, rhubarb, and a savory slice – lamb with mango chutney – for number three. By the time you eat your way from butterscotch to rhubarb to mango lamb, you are a changed person. You're a kid who loves butterscotch, who matures into an adult enjoying rhubarb and ultimately becomes a gourmand who loves mango lamb.

Like three slices, the three-act narrative structure propels the Enneagram. In movies, the three acts are described as *Set-up*, *Confrontation*, and *Resolution*. We watch movies to vicariously experience the Enneagram in action. As spiritual couch potatoes, it's easier to watch Meryl Streep's character transform than to catch an Uplift of our own.

What kind of wings do we need to catch the Uplift? The human airfoil is our capacity to *feel* — and *act* on those feelings. You might push back, "Hey, I'm feeling all the time – and I'm feeling pretty crabby."

We experience lots of feelings. The Center for Nonviolent Communication cataloged 166 crabby feelings and 99 that describe Uplift. The crabby list paints a pretty neurotic picture. Neurotic feelings are automatic and unconscious. Can we remain conscious of our feelings?[8]

The secret behind feelings is that they are *messengers* – those angels. These are the same angels that prompted Jannie Jones to change the course of history. She spotted Jim Clyburn, had a feeling, and motioned

Feelings when my needs are fulfilled		
Physical feelings	**Satisfied**	**Thankful**
relaxed	fulfilled	grateful
comfortable	satisfied	moved
energetic	content	touched
centered		
balanced	**Cheerful**	
big	happy	**Amazed**
soft	amused	surprised
strong	joyous	flabbergasted
lively	cheerful	
in flow	delighted	

Feelings when my needs are not fulfilled		
Physical feelings	**Pain**	**Desperate**
pain	hurt	helpless
limp	lonely	hopeless
empty	wretched	powerless
small	mourning	uncertain
smothered		
short of breath	**Vulnerable**	**Skeptical**
tense	fragile	torn
wretched	uncertain	lost
sick	sensitive	bewildered
		perplexed

to him. Like with a catcher's mitt, Jannie caught the Uplift, and acted on her feeling to snag the base runner James Clyburn on second.

Let's move from Stevie Nicks to the Righteous Brothers and from the Octave in music to the Enneagram. The Righteous Brothers' classic ballad, *Unchained Melody* was originally composed for *Unchained*, a 1955 low-rent prison movie. Despite its B-film status, 670 artists recorded the song over 1500 times. The emotional power of the song's universal structure and its themes of time, longing, and freedom offer a visceral sense of the three slices of pie.

Search YouTube for *"Righteous Brothers - Unchained Melody."*

Listen to the song to sense the Uplift through all three slices of the pie:

Slice of Pie I – In a movie's first act, the *set-up* introduces the world of the story and launches the characters into the journey. In the opening verses of the song, we discover a character who hungers for love while incarcerated in prison.

The opening verse is beautiful, but life would become tedious if we

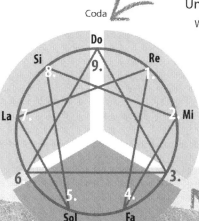

Unchained Melody

Woah, my love, my darling
I've hungered,
hungered for your touch
A long, lonely time
And time goes by so slowly
And time can do so much
Are you still mine?
I need your love
I need your love
God speed your love to me

Coda

Do

Si   Re

8.   9.   1.

La 7.   2. Mi

6.   3.

5.   4.

Sol   Fa

Mi-Fa

Woah, my love, my darling
I've hungered for your touch
A long, lonely time
And time goes by so slowly
And time can do so much
Are you still mine?
I need your love
I need your love
God speed your love to me

Lonely rivers flow; To the sea, to the sea
To the open arms of the sea, yeah
Lonely rivers sigh, "Wait for me, wait for me"
I'll be coming home, wait for me

stayed in Act I forever. Point 3 on the *Enneagram* offers an opening — the Mi-Fa interval — where something new breaks the monotony and challenges the protagonist. The key change offers a welcome shock in the song, but change is not always welcome in life. Upsetting the status quo invites Hazard and makes life unpredictable.

Slice of Pie II –In *Unchained Melody,* the second slice of pie comes at us like a completely new song, a second act, and a second octave. In a movie, this is called *the first act turn.* Suddenly, the story *turns* — thrusting the character in a new direction. In the song, instead of longing and hunger, the character steps into the river of life. In the Enneagram of life, the transformative part of the journey begins.

Slice of Pie III – The cymbal crash announces Act III, where a third octave begins. Here, at Point 6, the Enneagram raises the game from the material to the spiritual. Act III restates the opening verse of the song, but Bobby Hatfield's soaring solo lifts it to a soul level. In this way, the Enneagram functions as an engine of continuous renewal.

Imagine stepping onto the high school dance floor as *Unchained Melody* begins to play (If you're my age, this likely happened).

After some awkward swaying, the melody swoons at Point 3. The guy places his hand on the girl's back and pulls her closer. At Point 6, you lock eyes. At Point 9, you feel an urge to kiss. The Enneagram charts our capacity to *feel* — and *act* on those feelings. Even though the songwriter, Alex North, knew nothing of the Enneagram, his composition invokes the angelic world. Every classic song since Tin Pan Alley has some variation of the Enneagram in its structure — often *verse-chorus-verse-chorus-BRIDGE-chorus-outro.* You might wonder, what does song structure have to do with me? Okay, here's an example:

We just came back from a retirement party for our neighbor, Jim. We arrived late (Karen's complicated tabouli to blame), which meant the party was in full swing when we walked through the door. The decibels blasted my sensitivities, so, after grabbing a drink, I turned to the hostess: "Val, can we do a little toast or something for Jim?" Val had that deer in the headlight look: "Uh sure, but not me."

I moved to the center and bellowed, "Attention, everyone! Let's gather around!" The startled guests formed a circle. "Anyone here retired?" (A ridiculous question to ask at a retirement party). A few nodded. "Great! Since you're all experts, please give Jim a few words of encouragement."

And on it went. One person after another offered their wisdom. Jim felt shy, but he soaked up the love and fulfilled the party's purpose. Yes, Uplift.

The Enneagram is not heady stuff. It was a big moment for Jim, and I wanted him to feel the love, so I *acted* on my feelings. You can pull out your protractor and chart our entrance as the outside shock, but that's not how life unfolds. We were upbeat, buoyant, and riding a vector of love with tabouli in hand.

I study history through outside shocks, like the history-changer when fourteen-year-old Paul McCartney encountered John Lennon on the bus to school. Or, my favorite, when a young Jean Huston, the author and pioneer of the human potential movement, literally collided with Pierre Teilhard de Chardin in New York City. Jean recounted:

> When I was about fourteen, I was seized by enormous waves of grief over my parents' breakup. I had read somewhere that running would help dispel anguish, so I began to run to school every day down Park Avenue in New York City. I was a great big overgrown girl (5 feet eleven by the age of eleven), and one day, I ran into a rather frail old gentleman in his seventies and knocked the wind out of him.
>
> He laughed as I helped him to his feet, and he asked me in French-accented speech, "Are you planning to run like that for the rest of your life?"[9]

Pierre Teilhard de Chardin

A week later, Jean bumped into the 73-year old theologian a second time. This launched a magical friendship with Teilhard de Chardin that inspired Jean Houston to run towards the light for the rest of her life.

I can't compare my tabouli moment with bumping into John Lennon or Teilhard de Chardin, but the concept is the same: outside shocks shift the trajectory of a story.

If the Enneagram can enter a moment, can it shape a life?

Let's examine three brothers – the Jonas Brothers – and how their path to boy-band superstardom unfolded through the Enneagram. The Amazon documentary, *Chasing Happiness,* follows the three brothers as they rise from childhood singing in church, performing in food courts, becoming a global phenomenon, and then breaking up to marry and pursue solo careers — all predictable steps on the Enneagram.

Brothers Joe, Kevin, and Nick grew up in a conservative Pentecostal church in Wyckoff, NJ, where their dad, Kevin Jonas, Sr., was the senior pastor. It was the kind of church where children took purity oaths to protect their virginity until marriage.

The brothers' entire childhood revolved around the church. As Nick Jonas shared in the movie, "We lived two doors down from a church, and we were there pretty much every day. It was a humongous part of our lives."[10]

Music and singing filled their childhood. "It was kind of like the Von Trapp family," Kevin remembered. "Music was just always there."

What started innocently as singing around the dinner table took a serious turn at the hair salon.

"I was with my mom at a hair salon in Jersey — just hanging out," Nick remembered. "The woman next to my mom leaned over and said, 'My son is on Broadway right now doing *Les Miz.* Your son can do it.'"

Nick's mom, Denise, continued: "Nick looked at me and said, 'Mom, I'm going to be on Broadway.' Then Nick told us which shows he was going to be in. Who is this kid?"

Just like that, Nick auditioned and soon got roles on *Peter Pan, A Christmas Carol,* and *Oliver.* Joe and Kevin, feeling competitive, followed Nick's journey. "Looking up on stage and seeing Nick getting this attention, I remember saying to my parents, 'I think I want to start auditioning,'" Joe said.

"We lived 45 minutes from New York City," Nick remembered. "My mom had given birth to (fourth son) Frankie and was driving me to the city. Most days, hours, and hours were in the car, seven days a week. It was just a lot, especially with a newborn child. Sometimes my dad would do a shift on the way home. One day, he said, 'Try writing something. Start writing songs on the way home.'"

Nick and his dad sat at the piano and wrote, "Joy to the World, A Christmas Prayer." They made a scratchy recording and burned it to a CD. Maybe it was destiny, but somehow that CD landed the hands of David Massey, Executive Vice President of Sony Entertainment.

"I first met Nicholas Jonas as a 10-year-old," Massey said. "He was an amazing singer. He was really naturally charismatic, and his voice was absolutely undeniable. You could already tell at age ten that he was just that guy. I signed him then and there."

"Kevin and Joe were astounded. "I started to feel like, wow, like Nick's actually doing it," Joe said. "We started to write on our own. We were playing around and wrote a song, 'Please Be Mine.'" The song literally wrote itself in like ten minutes. That was the moment we all looked at each other and felt this could be something. Very few feelings in my life were as sure as that."

David Massey continued. "Nick wanted me to meet his brothers, and they came into the office. They told me they had written a song called 'Please Be Mine.' I'll never forget it. They stood in a semi-circle and sang

Nick. Joe, and Kevin Jonas

this great song. I was blown away by their chemistry together as brothers. I added the other two brothers to the mix, and the Jonas Brothers were born."

At the time, Kevin was 17, Joe was 15, and Nick was only 12 years old. There was one big wrinkle — the church. Kevin explained: "I was so excited, but I wasn't allowed to tell anyone that we were signed because my dad was the pastor of a church, and we weren't making a Christian album."

"You're kind of a first family in the sense of the church," Nick added. "There's a pressure to be the example. Everything should always look like this perfect family where nothing's ever wrong."

Church or not, the brothers followed their dream.

"The label had a vision that we would be a punk rock band," Nick said. "One of the fundamental issues selling the Jonas Brothers as a rock band was that we were not a rock band at all!"

The boys began their new life rehearsing at SIR Studios in New York – six days a week, twelve hours a day – to punk up their performing skills. They also began to perform – local gigs, school assemblies, and performances in New York and Boston. The growing tension between the two worlds – church and rock and roll – reached a breaking point.

"Once we started doing our own thing in music, people were starting to speak about our dad in a negative way," Kevin said.

"I think there was some judgment on us for not being a Christian band. Singing about girls started to become a bit of an issue. It freaked a lot of people out in the church," Nick added.

And then, the Pentecostal hammer came down. The church forced their dad to resign.

"It hit when we were already at a low and took us even lower," Kevin Sr. recounted.

In one swoop, the Jonas family lost their home, friends, job as senior pastor, and income. Ten years of their life was gone.

"My dad had put $90,000 of his life savings, essentially our college fund into the band, maxed out his credit cards, and had no money," Kevin remembered. "Like we were done."

On top of this, Columbia Records dropped the band. Suddenly, the boys were forced to be the primary breadwinners. They performed early morning gigs in food courts while senior citizens booed from above.

"We had to perform to survive rather than doing it as free and fun," Joe remembered. "That was a lot of pressure for somebody our age."

There was more: The Jonas family had no place to live. In an act of charity, the local police chief rented a two-bedroom house for the six-person Jonas family.

"Four boys and one bedroom... We were dealing with so much at once. It was overwhelming," Joe remembered. "And, our parents were fighting like every day."

The two outside shocks – getting booted by the church and dumped by the label – hit hard. Here's the critical question around Uplift:

How did the boys absorb these blows and bounce back better?

Instead of retreating to the basement to funk out, smoke pot, play video games, and escape the pain, the boys channeled that stress into their muse. Using the surfing metaphor: They faced the breaking wave, punched through, and rode it.

Joe recounted: "We wrote a bunch of songs in that house – out of the pain and hurt and abandonment after we got dropped by the label. We felt people didn't believe in us, so we were going to prove them wrong."

Remarkably, the boys wrote the entire Jonas Brothers debut album in the basement while their parents fought upstairs.

What explains success after misfortune? Is it 1) effort and tenacity, 2) God's destiny, or 3) just dumb luck?" With the Enneagram, all three are of one picture – the hidden engine of continuous renewal.

I think about success a lot. I have two tomato plants in my garden — one flourishing and one dead. Some mixture of sun, soil, nutrients, genetics, care, and the appetite of our nighttime rabbit made the difference. How about two boy bands? The Jonas Brothers were also blessed with a powerful nutrient — their integral sense of connection.

"The first day I met the Jonas Brothers, you just could feel that this was something unique," Phil McIntyre, their manager, remembered. "It was less about how amazing they sounded. It was more of the connection between the three of them. I just remember thinking there's something so special about this family."

Yes, the connection: *Bondo* and those angels. And then, the angels intervened.

"We got a phone call from Disney," Joe recounted. "They said, we know you need something; well, we have it. We're going to hand you a record deal. And at that time, it was a huge opportunity."

The brothers emerged from the basement, got on a plane, and flew to Los Angeles to start again. "We would write, we would play, we would sing," Kevin said. "We pumped out a song a day. Nothing was holding us back."

Fortune showed its hand again when the band released their video for "Year 3000" – a song that got squashed when Columbia dropped them.

"You're watching your TV show; here's 'Year 3000.' You watch another show, here's 'Year, 3000,'" band member Greg Garbowsky said. "It got played constantly."

"It skyrocketed," Joe added. "We were like, oh my God."

"And we got a phone call," Kevin continued, "Joe had been offered the lead in this movie called *Camp Rock* for the Disney Channel."

Their dad called the president of Disney Channel, "You can't split the brothers up! Instead of just Joe, what if it was about a band?"

The brothers flew to Canada to shoot the film in the wilderness. They were off the grid for several weeks. "What we didn't know," Kevin said, "was that in America, the band was blowing up!"

While stuck in the wilderness, the band received an invitation to perform at the Texas State Fair. They were unaware that by now, every pubescent girl in the nation had memorized "Year 3000."

"I received a phone call from the promoter," Kevin Sr. remembered. "He said there was a traffic jam to Oklahoma and 'I'm sending helicopters.' I thought the guy was crazy. And he said YOU DON'T UNDERSTAND!"

Joe and Kevin continued. "I was in the helicopter and looking down at the crowd and thinking, 'That's someone else's stage.' "There were more people than I've ever seen in my life. Thousands of people. They were singing our music back to us — 50,000 fans."

"It was so validating to all the sacrifice and to the family fighting through those tough seasons," Phil McIntyre remembered. "To be able to get to the other side and get on that stage, it was one of the most incredible moments of my career."

The Brothers quickly catapulted into the second slice of the Enneagram — the transformative journey through the unexplored wilderness of the larger world.

"We definitely hit a tipping point where we entered a new stratosphere," Phil McIntyre remembered. "It was uncharted territory for all of us."

"Two years ago, we were touring in a minivan, and now we're chartering a Boeing 757," Joe added.

From the food court to multi-platinum albums, sell-out shows, and the chaos of superstardom — the band took off like a rocket.

"The songs we wrote in that two-bedroom house in Little Falls, New Jersey, were now being sung by 80,000 people in countries where English was not their first language," Nick marveled. "I don't think I processed the magnitude of it."

More than a pop music fairy tale, this is a story about the Enneagram. It describes the path in a soul project toward individuation: The process through which a person achieves a sense of self-awareness separate from the identities of others.

Individuation is the third slice of the pie. That said, it should come as no surprise that the non-stop need to feed the beast of celebrityhood would take its toll. After a few years in the supernova, the band's fame faded, and Nick wanted out.

"A lot of people lost the appetite for what we were putting into the world," Nick told CBS Sunday Morning. "We were putting up shows that weren't selling. And we were making music that we weren't super proud of and wasn't connecting. On top of all that, at the root of these issues, our relationships were becoming strained."[11]

Nick made the call: "I want to be real with you as band members and brothers. This is where I'm at. The band is over. I want to do stuff without you guys. And I've made up my mind."

Joe concurred, "I needed to go and try to live a normal life and do my own thing. Travel, meet girls, and date. I was trying to find myself. I was really trying to prove myself — probably to my brothers, but also to show everyone out there that I can do it without Kevin and Nick."

The band canceled twenty-three tour dates in 2013. The break-up produced a lot of hurt feelings, but the third slice of the pie also created space to become adults. This new chapter brought marriages, fatherhood, creative successes and failures, and time for self-reflection.

With wave after breaking wave, the Enneagram offers a journey of continuous renewal. Each wave brings loss and opportunity. For continuous renewal, you must face the wave, experience the turbulence, and let go of the pattern of the past. Trading life as a superstar for life as a dad on a late-night run for Pampers was no small trick.

After six long years living separate lives, the Jonas Brothers began another trip around the Enneagram – but as brothers. "I feared that they would never speak to me again," Nick shared. "It took a couple of months of tricky conversations and navigating to reconnect as a family again."

The brothers let go of the hurt and found their way back together, roaring back in 2019 with a number-one hit, a multi-city tour, TV

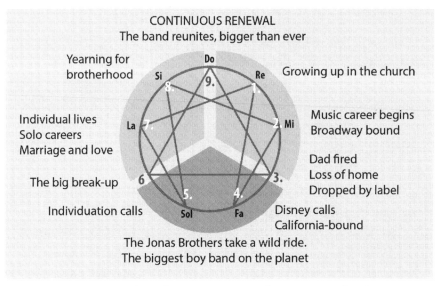

CONTINUOUS RENEWAL
The band reunites, bigger than ever

Yearning for brotherhood

Growing up in the church

Individual lives
Solo careers
Marriage and love

Music career begins
Broadway bound

Dad fired
Loss of home
Dropped by label

The big break-up

Individuation calls

Disney calls
California-bound

The Jonas Brothers take a wild ride.
The biggest boy band on the planet

performances, and a film. "We got a do-over," Kevin said. "And this time around, we're going to do it right."

The Enneagram is not about "doing it right," and it's more than three slices of pie. It teaches us how to surf breaking waves rolling in from distant weather beyond your control.

Getting kicked out of the church, signed by Disney, thrust into stardom, breaking up, and starting anew – each shock propelled a cycle of continuous renewal. If not for Hazard entering at the intervals, life would become as predictable as a slog on a treadmill. But life is more than a treadmill. In the dramatic universe, the Enneagram drives the story of our lives. The Enneagram's hidden currents guide the storyline of your life, whether you are blessed with anonymity or you live life in the public eye.

Performers like The Beatles, Fleetwood Mac, and the Jonas Brothers live in the public imagination as conduits to the angelic world. As artists, they are always reaching for that third slice where the angels live. The downside is that superstars face impossible pressures to deliver album after album from the angels without destroying hotel rooms, relationships, and careers in the process. Living life under the glare of paparazzi, adulation from fans, expectations from labels, and the weight of too many hangers-on, it's a mystery how artists make any magic at all.

For the album that became *Let it Be,* The Beatles decided to write and rehearse 14 new songs in two weeks – impossible even without the ennui, lawsuits, and drugs that colored their final year in 1969.[12]

Beatles engineer Geoff Emerick recollected, "The group was disintegrating before my eyes. It was ugly, like watching a divorce between four people... I was becoming physically sick just thinking of going to the studio each night."[13]

Peter Jackson's eight-hour film: *The Beatles: Get Back* peels back the magic and mundane of their final album. After watching *Get Back*, my friend Vic Garbarini, former editor of Musician magazine, shared how artists can tap into the angelic world even while facing the walls of despair:

> "Having interviewed all of them, including Yoko, George
> Martin, and Geoff Emerick, the period after *Sgt. Pepper*
> was pretty contentious. These amazing people had personality
> dysfunctions as well as openings to wellsprings of Creative
> Genius from higher energies.

> "Peter Jackson's film captured glimpses that correspond to what
> Sufi musicians and other master musicians I've known have said
> about The Beatles – that they were a creative matrix bringing
> higher spiritual energies into our culture.

> "Having had no inner training to handle these energies, there was
> a love that bound them – what Ringo called 'The Magic that was
> there every time we played.'"[14]

There's something in the temperament of great artists that they can channel the Magic amid the dysfunction of their personal lives. I saw this night after night as Reshad, gin and tonic in hand, peeled back the curtain on the divine mysteries.

In the Peter Jackson film, we see McCartney spin gold from straw while Lennon is stoned and Harrison wants out.

James Parker in The Atlantic described the mysterious forces that birthed iconic songs like "I've Got a Feeling" and Don't Let Me Down:"

You see them coming together, these songs, take by lumpy take, but still, you can't shake the feeling that they arrived fully formed, direct from Beatle heaven.[15]

Beatle Heaven – I prefer "creative imagination." In the film, the Fab Four slide in and out of the Magic. At one point, the Ringo's eyes start to droop, and Lennon seems asleep.

McCartney: "Wake up, Lennon."

Lennon: "Wake up, Lennon. It's about time."

McCartney: "We just sit here and allow ourselves to be embarrassed. We can't carry on like this indefinitely."

Ringo (rousing himself): "We seem to be."

Within a year, The Beatles divorced forever – but never from the Magic.

We all seek that Magic, and like The Beatles, we may have insufficient training to handle the big waves that threaten to pull us under. Bands like The Beatles, Fleetwood Mac, and the Jonas Brothers gave us master classes in how (or not) to face these breakers. You may not live in the public eye, but if you wish to open to the Magic as a budding Octave sorcerer, you need to harness the engine of continuous renewal.

Fortunately, the angels are here to help.

Endnotes:

1   Enneagram Studies by John Godolphin Bennett

2   "Anthem," Leonard Cohen © Sony/ATV Music Publishing LLC

3   Ouspensky, P. D. In Search of the Miraculous.

4   ibid

5   ibid

6   Bennett, J. G. Enneagram Studies, Weiser, 1983.

7   https://www.rollingstone.com/music/music-features/lindsey-buck-ingham-fleetwood-mac-firing-733460

8   (c) 2005 by Center for Nonviolent Communication www.cnvc.org | cnvc@cnvc.org |+1.505.244.4041

9   Houston, J. (1992). Godseed: The Journey of Christ.

10   Dialog from Chasing Happiness, Amazon Studios, Directed by John Taylor. With Nick Jonas, Joe Jonas, Kevin Jonas, Sophie Turner. 2019

11   CBS Sunday Morning interview, 6-2-2019.

12   https://www.beatlesbible.com/1969/01/02/get-back-let-it-be-sessions-day-one/

13   https://www.musicradar.com/news/beatles-geoff-emerick-abbey-road-interview

14   Copyright, 2021 Vic Garbarini

15   https://www.theatlantic.com/culture/archive/2021/12/review-the-beatles-get-back-by-peter-jackson/620872/

Chapter 8
HOW TO ASSEMBLE
YOUR OCTAVE

"The world is too much for us.
Rationality as we have come to know it works by
ignoring most of experience." ~ *Tom Cheetham*

GETTING INVITED BY A YOUNG WOMAN to her apartment for dinner was new, so I was nervous about the protocol. I met Naomi at the Institute for Conscious Life while filming her older Jewish actor boyfriend read a Rumi poem. After serving dinner and clearing the plates, instead of offering dessert, Naomi began to unbutton her blouse. As a young twenty-something in Los Angeles, I was fascinated and dumbfounded by what was supposed to happen next.

Well, next came her bra. Naomi was in control. "Do you like?" she seemed to ask with her glance.

I gathered that Naomi had presented her ampleness as an aperitif before. Still, I was unsure how to handle the dessert portion of the evening — especially with *double crème de la Naomi* served to my eyes.

Suddenly, I felt myself pull back from the timescape as if attached to a zoom lens. From my new vantage point, I could see the two of us tumble in bed awkwardly; I could see hurt feelings emerge a day or two later; and, I could see Naomi's boyfriend — with his soulful actor's gravitas — suddenly feel the hurt of a garden-variety schmuck.

"I think I'm going to head home," I announced sheepishly. "I have a big day tomorrow."

Today, scientists use quantum computers to simulate the reversal of time, but as Naomi's bra strap and blouse re-fastened themselves, I sensed the arrow of time undo what had been done — no quantum involved.

I climbed into my VW bus and paused before turning the key. The phantom images of hurt and schmuck still lingered in my sensed future. I knew nothing of the Enneagram, but I had stumbled upon one of its hidden aspects — the expanded present moment – how I describe the 1-4-2-8-5-7 inner lines.

I'm operating on intuition and personal experience when it comes to the Enneagram's inner lines, so, like writing a school paper, I turned to Wikipedia to get the official word:

> The Enneagram shows the Law of Seven and the Law of Three in a single symbol with the three forces joined in a triangle at the 3,6 and 9 points.

Sounds good. What else does Wiki have to say?

> In addition, six inner lines follow the 1,4,2,8,5,7,1, sequence. The meaning of these six inner lines is not, by Ouspensky's account, made clear by Gurdjieff.[1]

Mr. Gurdjieff, are you shittin' me? After revealing the Purpose of Life on Earth, you're going to hold back on the inner lines?

Actually, I'm grateful Mr. Gurdjieff didn't spell it out. I imagine he discovered the Enneagram on his mysterious travels, shared the basics, and then got frustrated by his overly-intellectual students or maybe distracted by the Bolshevik revolution raging in the streets. After his time teaching in Russia, Gurdjieff seems to have stopped lecturing on the Enneagram.

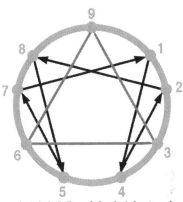

1-4-2-8-5-7 and the 3-6-9 triangle

Ben Bennett shared to our Facebook group:[2]

> The Enneagram is a mystery since almost certainly, nobody alive knows anything about where it came from, who first formulated it, or why... Any interpretation of it is neither more nor less valid than any other. To say it is designed to assist in personal transformation presupposes that you know a) who designed it and b) what their intention was.

Given this opening, I felt empowered to draw my own conclusion. I began to think of the inner lines as "angel messengers" who form our "expanded present moment." What we call *now* comes in various sizes (expanded and narrow) through a call-and-response with the higher worlds. This call-and-response is captured in the Hindu proverb:

"Take one step toward God, and he takes seven steps toward us."

Joseph Campbell replaced the appropriate seven steps with ten:

> I have found that you have only to take that one step toward the gods, and they will then take ten steps toward you. That step, the heroic first step of the journey, is out of, or over the edge of your boundaries, and it often must be taken before you know that you will.[3]

How do the gods take these steps? What pathways do they follow in call and response?

Consider the life of a toddler, running from sandbox to swing and from mom to a Popsicle. Or as a teen – leaving school, driving to McDonald's, heading to the mall, and hanging with friends. Or, as a twenty-something – one moment you're having dinner, the next moment the bra comes off and boom, you're in bed. This stream of events (around the Enneagram) filled our youth like voracious puppies consuming endless, unfolding time.

At age seventeen, the absolute freedom to bop from one thing to the next screeched to a halt: Suddenly, we were expected to think about college, SAT scores, and our plans as grown-ups. For the first time, we were asked to leave the immediacy of the present and face the train of the future coming in.

That train doesn't pull into the station on a single track. The inner lines of the Enneagram describe lots of trains pulling into the present moment. *"Now arriving on Tracks 1,4,2,8,5, and 7, Future Coming In. Head to Platform 7 for college, career, and points in-between."*

It's a lot to ask of a seventeen-year-old, but awakening to these incoming influences – "our angel messengers" – is a sign of growing maturity. As young 'uns, we live on the circumference, but with maturity, the inner lines emerge. We can sense the entire catastrophe from the snap of a bra.

As an example, in high school, my son, Jacob, was introduced to Mark, a senior industrial designer at Georgia Tech. Mark casually mentioned an internship to Jacob (unusual for a high school student), but Jacob latched on to the idea and pushed to make it happen. The two of them connected like Tom Sawyer and Huck Finn on the Mighty River of industrial design. Together, they launched Kickstarter projects, created 3D-printed camera gimbals, and toppled old barns to build a shop. Something in Jacob's soul ignited. This experience led to acceptance to a leading design school.

What was that "something" in Jacob's soul that ignited? When he met Mark, he had never even heard of industrial design. Whether you call it the "future coming in," an awakened "inner line," the "formation of *will*," or even a "messenger angel," the Enneagram of Jacob's life story opened in a moment of time.

J.G. Bennett uses the analogy of a chef in the kitchen to explain how influences from the future come into the present through the inner lines. A simple way to see these influences is to see the Enneagram as a play in three acts with the chef as the director:

In Act I, the kitchen is prepped, menu set, recipes announced, provisions delivered, lettuce washed, and vegetables chopped. The kitchen staff follows the chef's direction: "Peel two sacks of potatoes, wash a crate of lettuce, and bring up a case of wine." Chop-chop-chop. It seems pretty basic. One thing follows another.

While the kitchen staff focuses on tasks, the chef orchestrates the event. She senses the purpose of the event, the sequence of cooking, dietary needs of the guests, table settings, timing of the courses, and attention to the guest of honor. Bennett explains:

> The whole event is the manifestation of the will of the cook... This six-pointed figure in the middle, 1-4-2-8-5-7, represents what goes on in the mental vision of the cook... The deep significance of the enneagram consists in the distinction it makes between the functional cycle, which is the one going round 1-2-3-4-5-6-7-8-9, and the will cycle, which goes 1-4-2-8-5-7.[4]

While the staff is prepping the meal (1-2-3-4-5-6 etc.), the influences from the guests soon to arrive shape the kitchen activities (1-4-2-8-5-7): "We will need one serving of sauce without gluten, one without dairy," the chef commands. "Start the lamb at 5:30 pm, and fish at 6:15 pm."

While the staff chops and scrubs, the chef stays in touch with the future. The Enneagram forms a complete picture of the banquet from

creating the menu to the final toasts — the expanded present moment. The inner lines represent the influences from the future shaping the present. They allow the chef to adjust the kitchen processes to keep the event on track.

Suppose the lamb comes out dry:

"Course correction," the chef announces. "Give me a marinara sauce. We're now serving lamb ragu!" With disaster averted, the engine of self-renewal chugs on. When everything is prepped, the cooking begins.

In Act II, fire transforms the raw ingredients into cuisine. According to Michael Pollan in *Cooked: A Natural History of Transformation,* cooking with fire advanced the cause of civilization. Cooked food, being more energy-dense and easier-to-digest, allowed our brains to grow bigger. Cooking also brought us together for eye contact over shared meals.[5]

Act II of the Enneagram provides the transformation. We are "cooked" when we are thrust into life-changing soul projects and transformative events. After the Jonas Brothers left New Jersey, their seven-year streak of red-hot success cooked them to the point of splitting up.

Act III focuses on the higher energies – the guests, setting the table, announcing the menu, serving the plates, and pouring flutes of champagne. Compared to the frenzy in the kitchen, the ballroom represents the subtle world with its linens, crystal, and string quartet. From raw to cooked to heartfelt toasts and tears of recognition, the engine of renewal keeps raising the energy.

Suppose a young kitchen staffer wants to become a chef. She progresses, not by her ability to make a Béarnaise, but by her ability to take command. Her ability to stay grounded in the heat of the kitchen reflects culinary expertise, time and project management skills, business acumen, and people prowess. More than kitchen knowledge, the chef must attune to the angel messengers that orchestrate a triumphant banquet. She steps

into the kitchen and senses the entire symphony from beginning to end.

Like the chef, executives and leaders must also move from a *tactical* to a *strategic* approach. They must move beyond the Béarnaise to anticipate the future and act on it.

When Karen's non-profit hosted a symposium a couple of years ago on prison transition, several ex-convicts described the barriers they faced moving from prison to community. The audience was moved to tears and wanted to help. As I sat there, I could see the future coming in — a mission shift for her organization and an opportunity to take a leadership role on prison transition issues in Atlanta. Always watching the Enneagram, I sensed a "touched by an angel" moment for the organization – an opening to Hazard and creative opportunity.

Karen remembers, "This was the crowning moment for our organization," but the executive director couldn't see the stars align; she was tactical by nature.

As a brand strategist, my job is to see these trends and help chief executives align their organizations to the needs of their customers. By guiding them to become thought leaders, I help them shift from tactical to strategic thinking.

When I was younger, I received my first taste of becoming a "chef." Just 29 years old at my Saturn Return, an outside shock kicked off my baptism – a letter from Reshad. I had just left our Rumi school in Boulder and moved back to Los Angeles to start my life as a media creator.

I wasn't eager to open the envelope posted from Canada, but I did:

> Dear Bruce,
> Well, Paddington Bear has done it again. We have rented the
> Queen Elizabeth Playhouse here in Vancouver to present a
> performance of the Whirling Dervishes. As you can imagine, we
> are entirely out of our depth and need your help. I envision a short
> talk, some readings, a demonstration of the Turn, maybe one of
> your films, and then a performance of the full Sema.
> Please write back post-haste. HELP.
> - Reshad

Reshad missed an important point: We were both out of our depths. I was still mostly a kid, and staging professional theater was not on my resume. I drove to Hollywood, bought a book on technical theater, did my best to create a lighting plot, scripted the event, and faked the rest.

When I arrived in Vancouver with my technical plot in hand, I discovered that the group had scraped just enough money to rent the theater and pay for four hours of set-up, rehearsal, and technicians. Lovely.

Standing in the pit of the Queen's namesake playhouse, I faced a bare stage to my left, 700 empty seats to my right, and a motley group of anxious dervishes in front of me — all wondering how I was going to pull this off. Behind me, three Canadian union workers leaned against a railing, arms crossed, to see how the California kid gave direction.

I might have handled the pressure better if not for one other element — Reshad. In any room, Reshad was the sun around which all planets turned. At this moment, the sun was wobbling.

It's typical to spend weeks in production – not four hours – so you can imagine the pressure. Aiming and assigning every light, setting the projector, screen, color gels, sound levels, cues, walk-ons, and off — it all took longer than I imagined. Adding to the tension, Mr. Octave (Reshad) sensed things going awry. I didn't need an English mystic to sound the alarm; the growing horde of ticket holders outside was enough. I looked at my watch. "Holy shit, four hours of prep now down to one!"

And then, a force came over me. I became possessed — not in the *Carrie* manner of Stephen King where Sissy Spacek absorbed the abuse of her religious family to exercise newly discovered telekinetic powers — but close. The kinks in my emotional plumbing suddenly broke free — a whoosh of directorial telekinesis lifted me from scullery to chef.

"Scene 23. Dim the front lekos at a six-second rate," I commanded rapid fire. "Cue 24, bring up the red fresnels as the dervishes enter — give me 8 seconds. They will kneel, bow, then roll audio selection 4."

The hubbub in the lobby reached a pitch. "Everyone take your places," I commanded. "The show begins when Reshad takes the stage. I will give the cue."

My nerves were frayed, the dervishes whirled, and the audience moved to tears. I wondered, "Where did that come from?" My *Carrie* moment taught me about *necessity* and how the universe knows when and how to intervene. Yes, how my beloved Jannie Jones, age 76, crooked her finger to save the galaxy.

I didn't save the galaxy, but I received my first taste of the growing inner triangle – my *soul project*. The inner triangle commands the Enneagram, yet stands apart from life around the circumference, only connected at the three intervals of change – 3-6-9. The triangle integrates left and right – the *active* mode of taking charge and the *receptive* mode of letting life unfold. With each trip around the circle, your soul project grows in substance. You might even become the chef.

There are countless interpretations of the inner triangle. I see it as the great mediator of material and spiritual, effort and effortlessness, and body and soul. Whether you call it a *soul project, individuation, psychological integration, realized being,* or *will formation,* the triangle represents the conscious substance built over a lifetime. The Enneagram triangle forms the core of human experience. It is the "I."

From Plavan Go, the Japanese translator of *Beelzebub's Tales:*

> A man's real I, his individuality, can grow only from his essence. It happens fairly often that essence dies in a man while his personality and his body are still alive. A considerable percentage of the people we meet in the streets of a great town are people who are empty inside, that is, they are actually already dead.[6]

Bennett summarizes the same idea more simply:

> *The meal that is cooked in our lives is the soul.*

Gurdjieff challenged us to make use of the Octave/Enneagram, but warned it's a fruitless task "without instruction from a man who knows." Bennett challenged that the meal we're cooking is the soul. I propose an Octave Cookbook with everything included. Just add angels.

Let's give it a try:

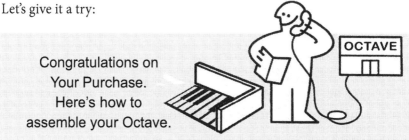

Congratulations on
Your Purchase.
Here's how to
assemble your Octave.

If you're ready to pursue your soul project — or any project for that matter — here's how to begin:

My advice is to start each day by attending to Hazard. Acknowledge the wave of the Unknown propelling your journey. Notice any sweet acts of synchronicity that may have graced your life. Maybe you bumped into an old friend who offered help, or perhaps your schedule re-arranged itself, or a cancellation opened a much-needed appointment. With Hazard, you are paddling in the unpredictable current of grace. Attention steers you around the rocks.

Hazard and the Three Balls — When you shake hands, sign the agreement, clink glasses, snip the ribbon, pull out a blank sheet of paper, decide to lose weight, repair a relationship, or decide to get right with God, your Octave clock has started. You plucked the harp string to awaken your angels – the people, providers, healers, and strategies that align like musical harmonics to launch your mission. With the decision to commence, "I'm starting a business" or "I'm going to start dating," you activate a timeline with a life of its own — so be patient. More so, stay vigilant.

Where are you now? – To keep on track, you must sense the quality of the present moment. Imagine juggling three balls representing the beginning, middle, and completion. The same principles apply, whether it's a business project or your soul project.

Present
Moment

Intention   Future
Goal

- **Ball Number One** represents the moment you set your *intention* — full of promise and purpose, but nothing to show yet. Can you remember when you decided, *I'm starting a business*, or *I need a new career*, or *I'm tired of living alone*, or *I'm going to heal my rotator cuff*. This moment might have occurred two months ago, or in a dream as a child, or maybe, you're making that decision now.

- **Ball Number Two** reflects the *present moment* – where you're at right now. Is this a happy moment watching merchandise get delivered, sending off an MBA application, choosing a restaurant for a date, or healing your shoulder? Or are you stuck in a delay, a motivational issue, a scheduling conflict, or emotional processing? Are you feeling frustrated or patient? Pissed-off or filled with promise? Think of Karen and how she faced the wave of her illness head-on. Acknowledge: THIS IS HAPPENING NOW.

- **Ball Number Three** lives in the future. It's the day you open your business or can swing a golf club again, have a six-figure career, can share your life with a newfound love, or feel buoyant and filled with Uplift. Ball Number Three is neither a vague fantasy nor grounded in reality. Strangely, the unborn future steers the whole enterprise. It's the future coming in.

- **With Ball Two hijacking your feelings**, there are always problems to fix, fires to put out, doubts to allay, and emotional flat tires to inflate. What we're describing is an attention issue. If you don't attend to Balls One and Three, the train will fall off the tracks. As an Octave sorcerer, you must maintain the presence of mind to juggle all three balls. In juggling, you don't juggle one ball at a time — all three are in motion. This is the expanded present moment. If you were reading a tense scene in a novel, you might put the book down and breathe. Mindfulness expands your time window to sense beginning to end. You invite gratitude by sensing where you started, where you are, and where you're headed. Gratitude is another word for Uplift. Let's do it:

Sense the distance. Remember the day you started with a blank page of promise. That was Ball One. Now, acknowledge the distance you have traveled (woohoo!). Even if the project stalled and complications have mounted, or you have become frustrated, you are further along than you think. Keep your momentum alive by acknowledging your progress.

Sense the present moment. What's happening right now? Don't ascribe good or bad, stuck or flowing. Just sense the quality of Ball Two – the present moment. It's just one scene in the novel and one that likely needs your attention.

Sense your destination. Reshad used to say to us, "Put time into it." Sensing Ball Three invokes the pressure of time. Setting deadlines is how things get done. Keeping your destination in focus will guide your course corrections, even in the heat of the battle.

Flush the lines. Pressures build when you drop a ball. Mistakes, setbacks, fears, and perseverating leave an emotional hangover that cripples the mission. Making things worse, they arrive as wave after wave.

With trust, learn to face each challenge fresh and let go of the outcome. Welcoming the unknown keeps your creative space open and avoids the need to judge your "failures" or prejudge the future.

Remember the mantra, "Did the energy go through?" Grieving is a natural process for letting the energy go through. Flushing the past and embracing the new is what powers the engine of continuous renewal. This isn't easy (duh). If it was, we'd all be living creative, fulfilled lives.

Don't be afraid to adjust the course. The quality of the present moment – Ball Two – is your compass. If your progress leaps forward, then stalls, this is normal. Gurdjieff warned: there are no straight lines in nature. Straight *up-up-up* is abnormal. But, if Ball Two heads *down-*

down-down, correct your course before entropy dashes your dreams.

Consider *Mic.com*. This high-hopes news site for millennials was started in 2010 by two 23-year-olds – high-school friends, Chris Altchek and Jake Horowitz. They had little work experience or journalism know-how, but they displayed remarkable comfort with Hazard.

Rolling the dice with $60 million in venture funding, 160 staffers, offices on the 82nd floor of One World Trade Center, and a $500,000 domain name, *Mic's* venture overlooked one critical fact: they never developed a sustainable business model or brand position.[7]

When you accept other people's money, it's

How to Flush the Lines – Reshad Feild taught the Clearing Exercise to flush the lines. Each night, before falling asleep, lay on your back, and settle into a deep place. Place your attention at your feet and slowly sweep your awareness from your toes to the top of your head. Do this three times. Allow any scenes or memories from the day to pop into view.

Maybe you yelled at your child, arrived late to a meeting, or received a disconnect notice in the mail. Happy images may bubble up as well – laughing with a friend, going out to lunch, or receiving praise. Don't think, consider, or analyze these images, just let them appear and disappear. Your job is to flush the lines with compassion.

easy to chuck it down a hole. In startup jargon, it's called the "burn rate." Shielded by big money and hubris, you can ignore the problem signs and signals from the subtle world for a while. Compare a flush venture to a shoestring startup where you stay closer to the ground. Sensing Hazard's pulse keeps you frugal and honest. Evidence of what's working (or not) appears quite quickly.

Your soul project is no different. A course correction might entail pulling the plug on dating sites, tossing your *Weight Watchers* meals, finding a new topic for your term paper, or leaving your guru behind. With OPM (other people's money), pouring money down the Hazard hole postpones this day of reckoning.

"We didn't really know what we were doing," one of *Mic's* founders said in 2014. "So we took a startup, entrepreneurial approach, which was to try a bunch of different things and see what worked and what resonated."[8]

Whatever you think of their spaghetti-on-the-wall approach to brand positioning, it took seven years for Mic to burn through all that pasta. If *Mic.com* had a viable brand position, they would not have competed against *Vice* and *Huff Post*. By waiting too long to rethink their strategy, the *Mic.com* guys were forced to liquidate their dream.

When the wind shifts, don't be afraid to adjust your course. Course corrections define what it means to be on an Octave journey.

As I wrote this book, this chapter was originally included in the previous chapter on the Enneagram. Suddenly, I sensed *Ball Two* losing altitude. "Man, this chapter is dragging." So, I cut the whole thing and pasted it into a new chapter, *How to Assemble Your Octave*. Snip-snip-done.

Whatever your soul project, you will be cutting and pasting as you go. Whether you call this listening to your angels — or more likely, wrestling with them — the inner lines guide your navigation in real-time.

> *The Enneagram is not something to be taken passively. It is there to be wrestled with much as Jacob wrestled with his angel.*[9]
> ~ Anthony Blake

Angel wrestling is a full-contact sport. When Naomi removed her

blouse, I wrestled with my angels. Your TV remote won't help you tune into the angelic realm because your angels have to hack through the underbrush of the human mind.

Author Tom Cheetham describes the challenge:

> The catastrophe of the West [results from] loss of contact with the worlds of the Angels... All knowledge comes from above by means of a vision of or union with the archetypes...
>
> Knowledge, whether granted freely via Revelation or gained with the cooperation of human intellect, is a result of illumination from above, not the culmination of a process of abstraction, deduction, or induction from the "data" of sense perception... The light of this knowledge "brings man to a glow." It raises us up from the world of darkness into which we have fallen.[10]

Cheetham challenges us to live beyond the world of sensory data and form a partnership with the angelic realm. I marvel at the delicious irony that Douglas Engelbart, the **Stanford Re**search Institute guy, took LSD to de**liver the** *data age* by tapping into the angelic **realm.**

Uplift is the work of angels. They **may** guide your through your conscience **or** a quiet inner feeling. If you're con**fused** by this, watch the original *Wings of Desire* by Wim Wenders.[11] Wim got **it** right. The angels hover over our **lives,** keeping the inner lines open so that we can live creative lives.

Endnotes

1   Wikipedia, Fourth Way enneagram https://en.wikipedia.org/wiki/Fourth_Way_enneagram.

2   Ben Bennett, maintains the publishing operations of the J.G. Bennett Foundation. He is the son of J.G. Bennett.

3   Campbell, Joseph. *Reflections on the Art of Living: A Joseph Campbell Companion.* Edited by Diane K. Osbon.

4   Bennett, John Godolphin. *Enneagram Studies.* Bennett Books

5   Pollan, Michael. *Cooked: A Natural History of Transformation.* Penguin Books, 2014.

6   Go, Plavan N. *The Enneagram: Living and Dead: Insights into the Gurdjieff's Vision of Harmonious Development and the Mechanism of Personality Type Formation.*

7   Inc.com, *5 Wildly Successful Entrepreneurs Reveal How Risk Taking Propelled their Careers.*

8   "Hope, Change and Venture Capital," Observer, 9-11-2014.

9   Blake, Anthony. *The Intelligent Enneagram,* Shambhala; 1st edition (October 22, 1996)

10   Cheetham, Tom. *Imaginal Love: The Meanings of Imagination in Henry Corbin and James Hillman.* Spring Publications, 2020.

11   *Wings of Desire,* Wim Wenders, Germany, 1987, Criterion Collection, Prime Video

Chapter 9
SWIMMING WITH ANGELS

"No, I never saw an angel, but it is irrelevant whether I saw one or not. I feel their presence around me." ~ *Paulo Coelho*

AT THE RIPE AGE OF TWENTY-TWO, I graduated from UCLA with nothing to do. To fill the summer, I convinced my parents to buy a fixer-upper in Ojai, California – a town down the road from my plunge into cosmic consciousness months earlier atop Reyes Peak.

If you believe the New Age folks, Ojai is centered around a massive spiritual vortex – actually, seven vortexes that tap into the Earth's electromagnetic field. This vortex reportedly saved Ojai Valley in 2018 when the area was surrounded by the devastating Thomas fire. The 300,000-acre inferno incinerated everything in its path from the mountains to the sea. According to local lore, all the important vortexes on the spiritual bucket list are connected — Stonehenge, the Great Pyramid of Giza, Easter Island, Machu Picchu, and not surprisingly, Ojai.

I was just a kid out of school, so I knew nothing about ley lines, the Earth's spiritual grid, Ojai's feng shui "dragon," or the Chumash burial grounds.

Krishnamurti under the oaks

I had a vague sense of Ojai's spiritual pedigree. Krishnamurti gave his famous talks under the oaks in Ojai, and Theosophist, Annie Besant, author, Aldous Huxley, the *avatar* Meher Baba, and numerous artists, writers, and spiritual teachers all had Ojai connections,.

As my parents and I drove past the For Sale sign and up the long dusty drive, the valley's sweeping panorama suddenly bloomed into view. At the top, a small ranch house called out, "Buy me!" I told my folks to do it, and they did.

I spent my days painting, repairing, and reading *Be Here Now* while the Earth's spiritual grid buzzed in the background. Every night, the mountains took on a rosy hue as the sun set toward the sea. I had never spent time much time apart from other humans, but suddenly found myself without TV, phone, friends, or neighbors. Days on end, I hung with the cicadas and the 24/7 streaming channel called *Bruce's Brain*.

One night, as I picked at my brown rice and peanut butter with chopsticks, an unsettling feeling came over me. I noticed that I had split into two. That's right. Two channels now occupied my bandwidth — *Bruce's*

Brain and *Bruce's Being.* To be specific, this new entity, *Bruce's Being,* had the unexpected ability to observe the non-stop chatter of the other *Bruce.* This is no big deal for people who know about meditation, but I had no one to tell me what was going on, nor could I Google it.

According to Random House:

> *freak-out* [slang] is to *enter into a period of emotional instability, as under the influence of a drug.*

Having come close to freaking out after ingesting cacti atop Reyes Peak, I tried to make this new experience go away, but it wouldn't.

The next day, I drove into town to attend a talk given by Benito and Dominga Reyes, an elderly couple who, following a vision, came all the from the Philippines to establish the world's first new-age university. Maybe, they could help me understand what was going on. When I arrived, instead of a big audience of seekers, it was pretty much me.

Benito and Dominga were no ordinary pensioners. Benito had been born in Manila into abject poverty from a mother who transitioned the dying through death. Reportedly, Benito could commune with saints in the spiritual realms. What's more, as a teenager, he had been recruited by the Theosophical Society to become a spiritual world leader in the same manner as Krishnamurti.

After the talk, I introduced myself. Dominga studied me (or, more accurately, studied *Bruce's Being*) and remarked, "I see that you have a tremendous spiritual capacity in the shape of your face and your forehead."

I assumed they were shilling for converts, so I smiled and made a hasty exit. However, they were successful in establishing The World

University of Ojai, which lasted until they died.

I returned to L.A. to become a photographer. This kept *Bruce's Brain* occupied until I got that phone call from my mom: "Bruce, I need you to shoot a photo." I hadn't put it together, but my *future was coming in.* Maybe, Reshad's "Second Cycle of Mankind" was barreling down my track.

The famed spiritual prankster and author of *The American Book of the Dead,* E.J. Gold, offered to help Reshad set up the Institute for Conscious Life. Taking him up on the offer, I walked to E.J.'s front door on Alexandria Street in Hollywood, looked up at the sign, "First Sufi Church of Christ," and *gulp,* realized I was not in Kansas (or even reality) anymore. E.J. let me in, invited me for lunch, and sensed that I was a vegetarian.

I asked E.J about promoting the school, but he changed the topic.

"Have you ever had lamb's balls?" E.J. grinned as we sat around his kitchen table. E.J. was a master at blowing the protective circuits of unsuspecting seekers.

"Uh, no."

"You can fry them, saute with garlic, any which way you like." E.J. turned to someone in the kitchen. "Richard, ever fry gonads?" If there was a shortcut to altered states, E.J. knew where to flip the switch.

Later that night — whoosh — my circuits flipped into some strong woo-woo. I assumed E.J. was responsible, so I picked up the phone.

"First Sufi Church. Can I help you?"

"Yes, can I speak to E.J.? I'm having an experience, and I'm not sure what to do."

To my surprise, E.J. came to the phone. He was quite attentive when I described my sensations, like a neurologist charting my symptoms.

"Not to worry," E.J. reassured. "I can't tell you how many times I have seen this happen, especially when people first enter the Work."

I felt relieved immediately.

"Here's my advice," E.J. offered as I strained at every word. "Either it will get better, or it will get worse."

Reshad and E.J. Gold, 1975

Fortunately, for the next 20 years, the woo-woo ceased to be an issue. That is, until one afternoon around the time of my midlife crisis, and after reuniting with Karen, getting a new baby, new job, new guru, making good money, and now working in a corporate cubicle. An unexpected dose of woo-woo-deja-vu hit while writing financial technology copy for the CheckFree Corporation.

Having forgotten the drill, I freaked out and went to the ER — a big mistake. The Kafkaesque clinicians quickly triaged me onto a gurney in the hallway. Once I realized the ridiculousness of my situation, I blurted that I was dehydrated. That worked, but not before they mainlined a bag of saline into my veins.

Five years later, Bhagwan came into my life. One day, while driving to pick him up at the airport, another spell of woo-woo forced me to pull over and stop the car. When I finally arrived at the baggage claim, I pleaded my case to Bhagwan.

"Bhagwan, something is going on with me."

Bhagwan didn't seem concerned as he collected his bag.

"I think you're fine," he announced to my relief and dismay. As a medical doctor, I had hoped that he would analyze my symptoms, but as a realized being, he saw all sensations and perceptions to be "in the mind."

Flash forward a couple more decades. I was now sixty-three — the back-of-the-napkin age when you're supposed to get your spiritual house in order. Karen had gone through chemo, radiation, and brain surgery while I was desperately trying to recover from my business crash. One afternoon, while swimming across the lake, I started feeling spacey. What the fuck? Is this a panic attack? A medical event? Something esoteric? Whatever it was, we were exactly in the middle of the lake.

"Karen, I'm feeling funny," I puffed. It was an inopportune time to create alarm, but the bottom of my being was falling out. "Karen, swim back and get the kayak," I shouted. "I'll continue across!"

Feeling agitated, I reached the dock and plopped down like a spent whale. Heart racing, I took stock of my woo-woo situation. Was this garden-variety *fana* (the Sufi term for the dissolving of the ego) or something more serious?

Karen returned with the kayak and, fearing the worst, paddled me back. My intuitive healer friend, Zora, arrived at our cabin to perform her healing magic.

"I think you're shedding some sort of spiritual skin," Zora reassured.

Karen was thinking, "terrible, horrible medical event." Whatever it was, it wasn't going away.

Not knowing where to turn, I called Bhagwan in Switzerland.

"Hi, Bhagwan. Do you have a moment to talk?"

"Well, normally, you must make an appointment," he replied, "but we can talk."

"Bhagwan, I'm concerned," I explained. "I was swimming, felt spacey, panicky, but also weirdly disconnected from my body and mind. How do you know if an unexplained experience is spiritual or medical?"

"Was it pleasurable?" Bhagwan asked.

"Uh, no, hardly."

"Hmm," he pondered. "I don't think there is any medical issue."

"Okay, that's good. But I'm feeling unsteady. My subconscious is dissolving, and I feel like a polar bear clinging to an ice floe."

Bhagwan and I breathed together over the transatlantic call for the next twenty minutes.

"It's okay to let go," he reassured.

"Really. Just let go?"

"Yes. Let go of the struggle and just be yourself."

"What does that mean, be myself?"

"To be yourself is a state of effortlessness and flow. To be the idea of yourself is a state of struggle and anguish."

"Everyone has an idea of themselves. You can't just wish it away," I rebutted.

"Stay in your center," Bhagwan instructed. "The feeling of disorientation is in the mind."

I took a centering breath and began to feel composed. We were quiet together for some time. I was startled that I could feel Bhagwan's closeness despite the phone and the distance. This was the moment Bhagwan helped me understand the mystery of synchronicity.

"Bhagwan, can I ask a question?"

"Yes."

"It's a little off-topic."

"That's okay."

"It's been bedeviling me since you were with us, and now I'm writing a book."

"Go ahead," Bhagwan replied.

"When we talked about synchronicity, you said that the entire universe is synchronous."

"Yes, every moment."

"So, what about when we're reacting, doing stupid stuff, making a mess in the world, or having weird sensations — is that included in everything is synchronous? Or just when we're harmonious?"

"Yes, that is also included," Bhagwan replied. "Something happens, then there's a reaction, then it gets worse, then there's a correction, then there's a war, then peace, then prosperity, civilizations rise, then collapse. Everything is synchronous."

"Hmm. Thanks."

I did another back-of-the-napkin calculation and noticed that my woo-woo events arrived at epochal changes of my life — the Ojai vortex, meeting Reshad, my midlife crisis, and now my age sixty-three collapse. Suddenly, I saw my mind as the Antarctic ice shelf with melting ice water seeping into cracks until a big chunk split into the ocean. *Bruce's Being* seemed to be thawing *Bruce's Brain*. Every time a "mental berg" collapsed into the sea of consciousness, it registered as a *woo-woo event*.

Here's where it got tricky. According to climate scientist Ella Gilbert:

> "Ice shelves are important buffers preventing glaciers on land from flowing freely into the ocean and contributing to sea-level rise. When they collapse, it's like a giant cork being removed from a bottle, allowing unimaginable amounts of water from glaciers to pour into the sea."[1]

My buffers were melting, and no, it was not pleasurable. But now I had a question: I understood the giant wooden hammer, but what about the giant bottle cork?

Two words: ego death.

When we returned home from the lake, I panicked, stomped my feet, and fought with the Almighty. "I don't want this! Please stop," I screamed. "All my adult life, I've been working my physical, mental, and spiritual edges — practices, studies, breath, yoga, meditation, whirling — but hear me out God, this spiritual thing, I WAS JUST KIDDING!"

My psychotherapist friend, Mimi, arrived. She and Karen wanted me to seek medical attention, but it was too late for a brain transplant, and saline solution wouldn't cut it. Kübler-Ross would have identified this stage as *bargaining*.

The cork started to ease out. Instead of every twenty years, seven years, or five years, my woo-woos were hitting every ten days. I would be incredibly sleepy for a few hours while I suffered spontaneous *kriyas* — lying in bed while my body shuddered — *zing-zang-zung*. Like an abandoned old house where one sealed-off space after another was discovered — crawl space, attic, closets — I was cracking open to let the light in. Was it pleasurable? Hell no.

It wasn't until recently, during a Skype meditation, that Bhagwan casually delivered the missing piece:

"The ability to observe your thoughts is a kind of mutation," Bhagwan explained fifty years too late. "Do not take this for granted. It is actually quite rare and should be cherished."

Oh, a mutation. I'm some kind of mutant.

Today, my back-of-the-napkin journey has taken me to the ripe young age of seventy, and with it has come a freedom of spontaneity, unfettered love, gobs of energy, and a synchronous ease of living – like injecting helium into my bloodstream for Uplift.

The cork finally fell out after my bout with COVID (caught at a outdoor, windswept wedding in remote New Mexico!). In one swoop, the top of my head filled with a swoosh of white noise and all physical resistance dropped like rusty armor falling to the ground. But was it *pleasurable?* Herman Hesse asked the same question:

> "I have no right to call myself one who knows. I was one who seeks, and I still am, but I no longer seek in the stars or in books; I'm beginning to hear the teachings of my blood pulsing within me. My story isn't pleasant; it's not sweet and harmonious like the invented stories; it tastes of folly and bewilderment, of madness and dream, like the life of all people who no longer want to lie to themselves." ~ Hermann Hesse, Demian[2]

If this book was a tragedy in nine parts, I have reached the final scene — the pivotal moment when the Greek Chorus comments with its moral authority on the dramatic action like a chorus of angels cajoling us forward.

Angels have been used, abused, and caricatured since medieval times. When I use this word, please don't picture pudgy cherubs with feathery wings, but instead, feel the archetypal realm of Uplift — the boundary between this world and the next, obscured by the mind like clouds blocking the sun.

> Angels facilitate the circulation of energy throughout the non-physical universe. Invisible, intangible, and yet within us and all around us, angels serve as the infrastructure of the spiritual world. Some have existed forever… other angels are created through our actions — good or bad. Each action creates an angel that must transmit the meaning and impact of that action to the rest of the world and in our own lives. By changing our actions, we are able to harness the power of angels, transform ourselves, and find greater fulfillment. ~ Yehuda Berg, *Angel Intelligence*[3]

The "infrastructure of the spiritual world" takes many forms — sometimes sublime, other times ruthless. Yehuda Berg became a famous Kabbalah teacher to a growing list of celebrities. Madonna, Lindsay Lohan, Paris Hilton, Demi Moore, and Britney Spears studied at the Kabbalah Centre started by Berg's father, Rabbi Philip Berg, a former insurance salesman. The elder Berg taught out of his insurance office until his celebrity cachet skyrocketed the Centre into a coast-to-coast phenomenon that brought millions of dollars into its coffers. Eventually, the Centre came under investigation by the IRS for tax fraud. Family members faced allegations of using the foundation for personal enrichment. Yehuda Berg even paid damages for allegedly sexually assaulting a student. Yes, there are bad-actor angels, too.

Lest we forget, swimming with angels is a full-contact sport. Maybe, Yehuda got in over his head, but I like his idea of angels forming a "spiritual infrastructure" – like downloading a file of angelic data from the cloud.

What I call "Uplift" and "continuous renewal" might also be called angel intelligence. This intelligence is innate. It penetrates our world in the same way the scent of a rose penetrates a room. How many olfactory molecules does it take to become aware of a rose? Reshad once explained:

> "The split second between the bud and the rose is only known to those who have become roses."

In that split second (through outside shocks and intervals), we leave the world of the bud behind and become the rose. In this way, I kicked and screamed against the woo-woo until I could finally embrace the angels guiding the show.

"It's okay to let go," Bhagwan reassured.

"Really. Just let go?"

"Yes. Let go of the **struggle** and just be yourself."

Let's recap the chapters:

- **Introduction: "The Giant Wooden Hammer"** — Your life deals Wild Cards™ from the Deck at precise yet unexpected intervals..

- **"The Dramatic Universe"** — All the world's a stage. The arc of our character swings from hubris to humility to advance the story. Paradoxically, even though the script is already written, we get to make it up as we go along.

- **"Katabasis"** — Whether you call it the *dorsal* state, *katabasis*, or garden variety depression, we grow our wings on the way down.

- **"The Energy Must Go Through"** — You are basically a tube through which subtle energies are transformed according to harmonic proportions. Life is "evergreen," ever-reaching toward self-renewal.

- **"I am the Octave"** — Your desire for freedom bumps into fear and refusal – the *denying force*. A mysterious third force dissolves this resistance when you rise above the stalemate. The Octave is not a set of notes on a piano or a musical score. It describes the inner force of the pianist who makes the score come alive.

- **"Different Worlds"** — It's easier to go down than up, so watch that first step – it's a *Lulu*. A single step can take you into a lower world, but you can't know that world without stepping into it.

- **"The Two Trains"** — Unexpected (but inevitable) events come into our life story to be wrestled with. The outcome is uncertain. This is Hazard. Each chapter of our lives unfolds from the future with the promise of transformation.

- **"The Engine of Continuous Renewal"** — While it appears as a random stream of thrills and spills, the human lifetime functions as an enormous transformation engine – also called the Enneagram. Like the glider pilot who seeks out thermals, we can use our lives for transformation and Uplift.

- **"The Inner Lines"** — Like the chef who envisions an entire banquet to the final toast, we don't have to be trapped in linear time. The inner lines expand our present moment to let angels enter our awareness. They travel on avenues *One, Four, Two, Eight, Five,* and *Seven.* We see this entire road map with their help.

- **"Swimming with Angels"** — Angels form the infrastructure of the spiritual world. Swimming with angels is more than wishful thinking. It's a full-contact sport where angels place their bets on risk, action, and follow-through.

Susan Jeffers

Famed psychologist and self-help author Susan Jeffers discovered how angels place their bets on doers — people who stick their necks out. Her celebrated book, *Feel the Fear and Do It Anyway®,* gave full expression to facing the wave head-on. A few quotes:

- "If we wait to stop feeling scared before trying to do what frightens us, we could wait forever; pressing ahead is the only way to erase fear."
- "There's no such thing as a bad decision. Each path is strewn with opportunities, despite the outcome."
- "Every time you encounter something that forces you to 'handle it,' your self-esteem is raised considerably. You learn to trust that you will survive, no matter what happens."
- "When we finally are able to let go of the need for control, for the first time, we are truly in control."[4]

Susan Jeffers learned to swim with angels the hard way. She faced a teen pregnancy, a difficult divorce, and an early bout with breast cancer. She understood how Uplift is often forged from dire circumstances that force us to attune to the angelic realm.

For this reason, the best reporting on Uplift comes from people in the trenches – like my friend Anahata Iradah who has been stranded in Adelaide, Australia, for more than two years. I gave her a call:

Anahata Iradah

Bruce: "Hi Anahata, how is it going?"

Anahata: "Thank you, Bruce, yes I am really well. I taught month five of my training in South Australia this past weekend."

Bruce: "Fantastic. Can you share why you're in Australia?"

Anahata: "To do the story justice, first some background. For the last 30 years, I have been teaching the Dances of Universal Peace."

Bruce: "Anahata, before you start, let me also add a short history. The Dances of Universal Peace originated in San Francisco in the 1960s by Samuel Lewis, an heir to the Levi Strauss and Rothschild banking families. Sufi Sam, as he was affectionately known, rejected the business world at a young age to pursue a life of spirituality. In 1923, he met Hazrat Inayat Khan, one of the great figures of Western spirituality. In the 1960s, Samuel Lewis received a vision of the Dances of Universal Peace which combined Dervish, Mantric, Jewish, Christian, and folk dances. He taught these dances for the remainder of his life playing a significant role in the spiritual awakening in America."

Samuel Lewis

Anahata: "Thank you for presenting the history. I traveled and taught the Dances of Universal Peace for many years when I joined forces with a partner who was involved in Tibetan Buddhism. Together we were invited to teach sacred dance to the Tibetan women, nuns, and lay people. She focused on the dance, and I composed the music. We traveled around the world, teaching and

composing dances and music, including at Tibetan monas-
teries at the invitation of his holiness, the Dalai Lama. Part
of the year, we lived in Maui and then would fly to India,
Nepal, Russia, and other places to teach."

Bruce: "It sounds like a rich and exotic life."

Anahata: "In a certain sense, it was a glamorous life."

Bruce: "So what happened?"

Anahata: "For one thing, thirteen years ago, my partner and
I broke up. The world we created fell apart. I spent two years
traveling and teaching alone — trying to figure out what to
do while all my possessions remained in Maui. Eventually,
my partner said, 'You've just got to move out. I don't want
your things here. You need to go.' I was on a solo tour, and
my last stop was in this tiny town in Georgia – Hogansville,
population 3,000. The couple hosting me said, 'If you've got
nowhere to go, bring your stuff here.' And so I did."

Bruce: "What a shock – jet-setting around the world and
then getting deposited in Hogansville."

Anahata: "I lost a lot of teaching and faced a big financial
loss. I took this as an opportunity to reconnect with the
earth. So, I started a garden. As I gardened, I realized to have
good soil, you need chickens. And that's how it began. I got
the chickens to feed the garden, and I became obsessed with
them. I built up my flock very quickly."

Bruce: "When we met, we knew you as the chicken lady."

Anahata: "Let's say I became very knowledgeable about
chickens. I had at least 120 in my backyard in town. One day
I heard a knock on the door. The new animal control officer
gave me a week to move them. I begged for more time, so
she gave me three weeks, and I put them on a farm. Then she

got fired. In my mind, she only existed to deliver the ominous knock."

Bruce: "The future coming in — aka The Giant Wooden Hammer — it must have been stressful."

Anahata: "It wasn't an easy situation because twice a day, I had to drive to the farm, thirteen miles each way. I reached a point where, once again, I didn't know what to do next in my life or how to get out of my circumstances."

Bruce: "How did you end up in Australia?"

Anahata: "I was still teaching, but much more limited. Every two years, I traveled to Australia to teach for three weeks. My organizers would choose a theme, and I would build workshops that combined music, dance, spiritual teaching, and meditation."

Bruce: "This was early 2020. Was coronavirus on your radar?"

Anahata: "One of my friends is an epidemiologist for the CDC. She travels to Rwanda, Senegal, and around the world fighting disease. I asked her what to do. It was February 2020 when she said to me, 'You must go; you must go now because there are only two or three cases in America. If you go now, you can travel there and back before COVID sets in America. But if you don't go now, you may never get to go.' So she pushed me out of the door."

Bruce: "That's what friends are for."

Anahata: "I landed in Queensland, Australia, did two nights of teaching, and not a peep about COVID. Suddenly, Tom Hanks and his wife were diagnosed in Queensland. The news said they must have brought it from America. They were isolated and put in a hospital."

Bruce: "They tested positive on March 11, 2020 — "The official day that COVID swallowed everything."

Anahata: "My next stop was Tasmania — what the locals call Tassie. One of my students was the CEO of Tassie Health, so we got daily updates from her during our workshop — but we still had full attendance. Nobody stayed away."

Bruce: "I remember that moment. We were still between two worlds — normalcy and our COVID future coming in."

Anahata: "The CEO phoned her office every day to give us an update. I remember her reassuring us, 'I don't think this is anything to worry about, but we just need to stay aware.'"

Bruce: "We were so young in 2020, still whistling past the graveyard."

Anahata: "We started taking extra precautions with hand washing, but nothing more. Then I flew to Sydney, where about half the normal number showed up. I felt concerned, so I called ahead to my next stop in Adelaide. My host said they had twenty-three booked, but one or two might cancel. In actuality, we went from twenty-three to six. It was the last retreat, and suddenly, people did not want to hold hands in the dances.

Bruce: "Joining hands is the essence of the Dances. So you were in Adelaide – not holding hands – and today, two years later, you're still in Adelaide."

Anahata: "Still here. During that last stop, I got an email from California telling me not to come. I was due to teach there, but they were in lockdown. I changed my ticket to fly straight back to Georgia. My travel agent called me the day before, 'Everything's fine; you're good to go.'"

Bruce: "That phrase, *everything's fine* is how the universe shows its dark sense of humor."

Anahata: "I arrived at the airport at 3:30 am for a 6:00 am flight. I looked up, and there was nothing on the board. Worse, there was no one there. I found someone from Virgin Australia who told me they had a 70 percent layoff overnight. I asked, 'Well, what do I do?' I showed them my ticket, and they said, because a travel agent had booked it, there was nothing they could do."

Bruce: "That must have been terrifying."

Anahata: "I raced back up the mountain to Adelaide Hills to talk to my travel agent. She was horrified. She went online and found one last flight leaving Australia before the national borders closed. She said, 'It's going to New Zealand, but you have to be an American citizen. And it costs $6,000 one way.' And I'm not an American citizen, so I wasn't even allowed on the plane. To this day, there are thousands and thousands of Australians stranded abroad who cannot get back into their home country because the borders are still closed!"

Bruce: "What was it like to become suddenly stranded?"

Anahata: "Years ago, I was on a flight that hit such dramatic turbulence that I did not expect to live. At that moment, my body became empty, just a blob, like an amoeba. I had that same sensation at the airport that morning. My whole world was disintegrating, and I didn't know what would happen to me. I stood there and started weeping, not because I was anxious, but because I didn't know where to turn. I didn't know what to do."

Bruce: "It wasn't just you. The whole world was shutting down."

Anahata: "My host, Amrita, wisely said, 'Let's do one thing, and then do the next thing, and see what happens.' "

Bruce: "Was it like stepping into a void?"

Anahata: "Because everything happened at the same time, I could see the whole picture. I could see what would happen in my life if I didn't get back. My animals were a full-time job, so I knew that my life, as I knew it, was not going to be the same."

Bruce: "There are few times in life when our entire world is turned inside out."

Anahata: "I literally couldn't do a single thing, and it was immediate. I could see the entire scenario unfolding before me before it actually happened."

Bruce: "Those inner lines – the expanded present moment."

Anahata: "It was like a burst of liberation. At that moment, something collapsed and opened at the same time, because I knew I wasn't going anywhere. There was also an edge of excitement because I only had one option — to surrender. My hosts, Amrita, and her husband, said, 'Well, you're going to stay here. You're going to stay with us until we figure it all out.'"

Bruce: "What about your life and responsibilities in Georgia?"

Anahata: "I have a close, but tricky, relationship with my ex-partner in Hogansville. She came through for me to help figure things out. Eventually, we decided to rent out my house. She ended up giving away all my furniture and probably heaps of my possessions. She sent me photos of my space newly painted but also *completely empty*! It was like, oh my God. You don't realize how much of your identity is in your possessions when you don't have them anymore.

Every room with everything gone, just empty spaces. It was unbelievable."

Bruce: "Suddenly, you're a stranger in a strange land, and your backstory erased. What did the government do?"

Anahata: "Even in a pandemic with a lockdown and with the borders closed, you still have to be legal. I only had a 30-day visa. A friend of a friend was an immigration attorney who helped me extend it to nine months — but I needed to show that I could support myself. The Dances of Universal Peace group here and friends raised a stipend for me so I could pay for an Airbnb and food."

Bruce: " So, Amrita was right — 'Do do one thing, then the next, and see what happens.'"

Anahata: "Yes. I started to live my life in Adelaide as if it was the only life I'd ever known."

Bruce: "I call that Stop-Start-Change."

Anahata: "I found a farmers market where a bunch of farmers and musicians came together. I went to the Saturday morning market, and they invited me to come to their Thursday night singing group. This became my network. I started to make friends easily — more so than during my ten years in Hogansville."

Bruce: "You were fortunate to get nine months of breathing room, but can't immigration take years? What was your plan?"

Anahata: "I called Kevin, my immigration attorney, and asked, 'What's next?' Right from the start, the government told me, we don't care if the borders are closed; you still have to be legal, *and* we're not giving out visas. So I was trapped in a Catch 22. Kevin thought about it and said one visa might work — a Special Program visa. He asked me if I knew anyone who could sponsor me."

Bruce: "What kind of special program?"

Anahata: "The visa lets you stay in Australia for between 12 months and two years to take part in an approved special program. This can include cultural enrichment. Kevin said it would take $3200 (that became $6,000), reams of paperwork, and six months to set up. I had to borrow the money from a generous friend. We requested for the program to run fifteen months."

Bruce: "Kevin seems very clever."

Anahata: "He is. But unfortunately, after he submitted it, the government turned it down. Kevin noticed that they hadn't printed the grounds cited for rejection in their guidelines. So, he used this opening to ask if we could reapply. One of my students in the Dances had experience arranging visas. She helped us completely revamp the application like a university-level course with a detailed curriculum, students receiving credit, and me giving tutorials. It was backed by letters of support from doctors, lawyers, CEOs, and professors. It was huge — hundreds of pages!"

Bruce: "Wow, so much support! It's one thing to submit a curriculum; didn't you need paying students?"

Anahata: "Here comes the turning point in the story."

Bruce: "I sense the Enneagram."

Anahata: "Before Kevin and I applied for the visa, a friend and I walked to the farmers market one Saturday morning like we always did. My friend mentioned that the church bazaar had just started up after being shut down for COVID. She suggested, 'Why don't we walk that way 'round instead of going straight to the market?"

Bruce: "I love this. A turning point where you actually made a turn.

Anahata: "I said, yes. Let's do it. We changed the route and headed to the bazaar."

Bruce: "I need to interject, but I'm feeling the Octave. When I was a kid, we read these Superman comics where reality turned inside out. The Man of Steel suddenly found himself on a fictional planet called 'Bizarro World.' It was an alternate universe where everything ran opposite to your expectations. I feel we're about to enter the Bazaar-o World. That's a pun."

Anahata: "That moment is etched in my memory. We walked into the bazaar; tables and booths were everywhere. Straight ahead, hanging on a clothes rack, a brilliantly colored apron caught my eye. It was an amazing piece with superb craftsmanship. I said to my friend, 'Look at that; isn't that beautiful?' What caught my eye was more than the craft. The astonishing piece of artwork on the apron – in Tibetan colors – was of a CHICKEN!"

The infamous apron

Bruce: "Cue the triumphant music: Stranded in a global lockdown – a chicken comes to the rescue!"

Anahata: "More than the chicken, I felt absolutely comfortable in the presence of the woman running the booth. I must have looked upset because she asked if anything was wrong. I explained that I had to leave my beloved chickens behind in the States. Her name was Liz. She asked, 'Why are you here?' I said I teach the Dances of Universal Peace. She was instantly curious and wanted to know more.

I said something like, it's ecumenical dancing where we take phrases from various spiritual traditions and walk in the footsteps of those traditions. We try to empathize and understand the spirit of each religion. And then she said, 'WE WANT IT!'"

Bruce: "Wow, you just put it out there – and she wanted it! What kind of church was this?"

Anahata: "It was an Anglican Church."

Bruce: "Those wild, crazy Anglicans."

Anahata: "It gets crazier. Liz called over to the next booth, 'Father Thomas, come over here!' Liz had me describe the Dances to Father Thomas. As it turned out, Father Thomas was from Kerala in southern India. I started describing projects I was working on in Kerala and Nepal. Liz jumped in and asked, 'How many do you need?' And I said, sixteen. And then she said, 'I'll let you know within two hours.'"

Bruce: "Wait… this all went down while you were admiring the chicken apron?"

Anahata: "Yes. Within two hours, she texted, "We've got thirty-five coming on Friday. Will that work?"

Bruce: "I want to pause here and feel the angels. There's a passage from John O'Donahue that begins, *'All through your life, your soul takes care of you.'*[5] We step into a crisis but sense that it's a set-up. We discover that our angels are guiding our soul project, guiding us through all manner of openings and calamity, coaxing us to grow and shed our skins."

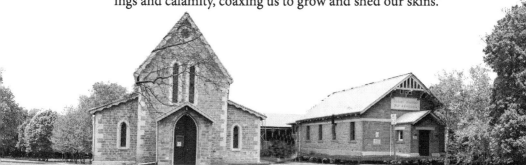

Anahata: "Very much so."

Bruce: "I've always felt that one's ability to trust comes from knowing you're loved – knowing that there are people who have your back. This begins as a child. And now you had Liz and Father Thomas."

Anahata: "I felt so at home with Liz that I got teary-eyed."

Bruce: "That's beautiful."

Anahata: "I forget to trust like everybody else and then realize that things are unfolding. At times, the whole thing freaked me out. How am I going to make this all work? And then it became absolutely evident that there is nothing I could do to make it work other than give my best. Things are going to be what they're going to be."

Bruce: "I want to move to the important part of our conversation. This is a book about Uplift. I use snatches of stories overlaid with ancient knowledge to paint a picture of the invisible world that guides the surface of life. I use angels to invite the reader to find this invisible way through attunement to the subtle world."

Anahata: "I'm not somebody that talks in terms of angels. There are more than enough people in this world who do."

Bruce: (laughs) "I don't either, but the word *angel* offers a wonderful shorthand to describe the subtle realm, the grace that enters to offer Uplift. You were in an impossible situation. How did you navigate your way through? And don't use the word *angel!*"

Anahata: "I've been forced to live on an edge at all times here — where I have to remain vigilant. I have been living at the mercy of other people who control my destiny to some extent. So, my vigilance is in every department – in my relationships, finances, and making sure that my classes are tip-top. With my Special Program visa, people had to sign up for fifteen months. That is a huge commitment in COVID times, so I am on my toes all the time to offer something meaningful. I don't have anything secure. I don't have a house. I don't have possessions. I am forced to pay attention all the time."

Bruce: "I can see that you are on your toes – but there is this other side. People have been remarkably generous."

Anahata: "I have a story that speaks to this. When I was very young, maybe thirteen or fourteen, I would visit old people while heading home from school – always a different senior citizen. I would just sit with them and talk to them. Sometimes I might help them with shopping, but mainly I would be a companion for an hour, and then I went home. It occurs to me now how innocent I was. Nobody asked me to do it, and I didn't ask for any payback – no payment at all. It came from a place that was part of me. It was not cultivated. Sometimes, I feel that a lot of the goodwill I am receiving now is not just because of who I am or what I give. I feel that we build karmic bank accounts, and at certain points, we can draw from them."

Bruce: "I'm still waiting to make my withdrawals. "

Anahata: "We don't pay in to take out. There is this sense of being taken care of. I have done things from a place of innocence for a lot of my life, and now, from a place of innocence, I am receiving."

Bruce: "Drawing from the karmic bank account is one part, but you described a reciprocal generosity that takes place in real-time — where you remain on your toes."

Anahata: "I feel we are always reading each other. We know when to come forward and when to pull back. To give an example, last December, a couple invited me to stay at their beach house in Tassie for two months. I knew it would be pushing it, but after my stay was up, I asked to extend it for two more months, and they agreed. At the end of two months, it was time to start my Tassie course. I didn't even hint at asking that favor again, so I found another place to stay. All of a sudden, they announced, 'Anahata, let's make this your home whenever you're here to teach.' We're always reading each other — coming forward, moving back; it's like a dance."

Bruce: "Let's take this to the next level to see where your soul project is taking you. How do you understand why this happened?"

Anahata: "Quite honestly, I was in a place in Hogansville that was so awful, I just didn't know what to do. I didn't know how to get myself out of it. The universe didn't want me to suffer anymore, but I couldn't work my way out. I was picked up, minus my animals, and planted in Australia."

Bruce: "Could you be laying the groundwork for the next chapter of your life — Anahata 2.0? It would be very cool if the universe were planning your next grand chapter."

Anahata: "If I'm lucky, and if I have planted the right seeds, this course could be used over and over again. It's an amazing template. It embraces musicianship, the dances, spiritual traditions, and meditation. An enormous amount of preparation has gone into it. Can I add one last thing about Uplift?"

Bruce: "Please."

Anahata: "I have a student in Tassie who is in and out of a mental institution. She is really a sweetheart, and I love her very dearly. She was the first person to sign up for the course, and she paid for it in advance. When she came out of the hospital, recently, she seemed a bit rocky. So, I said, 'If 50 percent of your spiritual practice involves difficult, penetrative work, the other 50 percent should offer joy and uplift. If it doesn't, there's something wrong with the path.'"

Bruce: "It's not just sackcloth and ashes. We wish for freedom."

Anahata: "Exactly. I said this to her because she was stuck. And I felt my job was to bring her joy, to bring joy to her practice. Joy follows the work of penetrating. I gave her some meditation techniques, and she said, 'They don't teach that in the hospital.' And I asked, 'What do they teach?' And she said, 'They talk about going through golden doorways.' I said, 'That's nice, but that's guided imagery. Your job is to feel exactly what's happening to you and let that transform you.'"

Bruce: "Let's close on that. I use lots of imagery – paddling through waves, becoming a tube, *katabasis*, funky stairs, the Lulu step, two trains, and the Octve/Enneagram. The point of these images is *to feel exactly what's happening to you and let that transform you.* Thank you, Anahata. I can't wait to see how your grand adventure unfolds."

Anahata: "Thank you. Let's always keep in touch."

Endnotes

1   https://www.space.com/antarctic-ice-shelf-collapse-as-earth-warms

2   Hesse, Hermann. Demian. Harper Perennial Modern Classics, 1715.

3   Berg, Yehuda, Angel Intelligence: How Your Consciousness Determines
     Which Angels Come into Your Life:

4   https://www.nytimes.com/2012/11/12/arts/susan-jeffers-psychologist-
     and-self-help-author-dies-at-74.html

5   *Anam Cara: A Book of Celtic Wisdom:* John O'Donohue: 9780060929435:
     Amazon.Com: Books

Epilogue
WHY NOT NOW?

"Automation means if you're milking a cow, you get a tool
that will milk it for you. But to augment the milking of a cow,
you invent the telephone. The telephone not only changes
how you milk, but the rest of the way you work as well."
~ Doug Engelbart

IF YOU'VE BEEN SAILING, you know the sense of freedom when the wind flows over the curve of the sail. If the angle to the wind is too high, the sail will luff, and if too low, the boat will stall. When the sail's elliptical shape is perfectly balanced to the air stream, it generates lift to power the boat effortlessly through the waves. This is Uplift.

Airplane wings work the same way. Air flowing over the curve of the wing creates an upward pressure to lift a 100-ton plane off the ground — except on Aeroflot.

In 1981, I boarded an Aeroflot Tupolev Tu-134 heading from Kyiv to Leningrad. Two things stood out: First, only foreigners received tickets on scheduled flights. As a result, desperate crowds waited for hours, maybe days, to catch a flight. As I climbed the stairs, I turned around to look over the fence where a throng of peasants desperately waited with their bags of cured meats and stinky cheese. Rather than feeling privileged, my hard currency robbed the Russian people of passage in their own land. Second, when I reached the top, I looked at the wing to see row upon row of exposed rivets on the metal skin.

I wondered, what kind of wing looks like clunky boilerplate? Apparently, a Soviet wing. We taxied out to the two-mile runway and then, with a feeble groan from the engines, used all 10,000 feet to clear the treetops. I peered out the window and wondered again: Are those bird nests on the branches below?

Praying for Uplift on an Aeroflot flight is a strange way to start the epilogue, so let me explain. As I clenched my fists, those rivets kept speaking to me: "It's all about *drag.*"

I think about drag a lot. During the 2008 Presidential campaign, I couldn't shake the image of Mitt Romney's Irish Setter, Seamus, strapped to the roof of his family's Caprice wagon. "He loves it; it's his favorite," Romney insisted. But the idea of Seamus in his rooftop carrier for a 12-hour ride may have cost Romney the election. Romney fought against the criticism, "My dog likes fresh air." But the idea of Seamus serving as a 70-mph wind foil was too much for the nation.

I discovered the esoteric side of drag in 1978 when my fellow Rumi lovers transformed a well-worn middle school into a sacred space for the Whirling Dervishes. While others cleaned and ironed, I hauled in gear, assembled bleachers, hung stage lighting, ran the rehearsals, operated sound, directed the performance, and broke it all down for a 16-hour day. I was too tired to eat solid food at the end, but all resistance fell away in the process. As the countdown clock wore against my body, I kept a mantra going, *"The present moment doesn't get tired."* Rain, sleet, snow, or exhaustion, the present moment never loses *presence.* It carries no drag.

Performance without effort, thought, or resistance is called *being in the zone* — an idea developed by Mihaly Csikszentmihalyi, an American-Hungarian psychologist who became fascinated by artists who got lost in their work. I prefer the term *turning inside out* — where effort becomes effortless. When you drop mental ballast and act freely without emotional drag, a limitless wind fills your sails.

Gurdjieff called this "tapping the Great Accumulator" — the big battery that powers the cosmos. The Great Accumulator runs on a perpetual charge, unlike the flea charge that powers humans between naps. Gurdjieff described an energy source outside ourselves:

> There are some people in the world, but they are very rare, who are connected to a Great Reservoir or Accumulator of this energy. This Reservoir has no limits. Those who can draw upon it can be a means of helping others. Suppose that a man needs a hundred units of this energy for his own transformation, but he only has ten units and cannot make more for himself. He is helpless. But with the help of someone who can draw upon the Great Accumulator, he can borrow ninety more. Then his work can be effective.... Those who have this quality belong to a special part of the highest caste of humanity (As told to J.G. Bennett). [1]

In 1856, ten years before Gurdjieff was born, the German physicist Rudolf Clausius concluded that the entropy of the universe tends toward disorder. The scientific quest into perpetual motion formed the backdrop for Gurdjieff's quest into continuous renewal. Gurdjieff saw how biological life depleted like a failing battery that starts at birth and ends at death. Without a soul, Gurdjieff chided, man will "die like a dog."

Since the time of Gurdjieff, a steady stream of visionaries have attempted to explain universal energy, including *Mesmerism*, *orgone* energy, the *Odic* force, and the *élan vital*. Let's not forget *Chi* and *prana*.

According to Dr. Martin Picard, head of the Mitochondrial Psycho-Biology Laboratory at Columbia University:

> "The main distinguishing characteristic between a cadaver and a living, thinking, feeling individual is the flow of energy through the body. The cells are the same, but without the energy flow, it's just an inert blob." [2]

Picard's laboratory studies the connection between the mind and the mitochondria – the cellular source for human energy:

> "My working hypothesis is that mitochondria do a lot of the
> sensing and perceiving and integrating of signals. That they are
> the cellular antenna, or little brains that receive, process, and
> integrate information."

Could mitochondria function like little satellite dishes aimed at the Great Accumulator? What's more, Picard performed a study on over ninety women who reported their mood levels daily for a week and then submitted them to mitochondrial tests. The study suggested that mood has a direct effect on our mitochondira. In other words, Uplift!

It's tricky to know whether our mitochondria operate on your flea-watt batteries or plug into the mains. Continuous renewal is the giveaway. If you've ever joined a yoga class dead tired and found yourself rejuvenated at the end, you have a taste of continuous renewal. It's counterintuitive that a hard workout would give you energy. But exercise flushes the lines so the energy can move through — just like our Reshad school mantra. But, like poor Seamus strapped to the roof, the "I thought" creates drag. In this way, we trudge through life with an Irish Setter strapped to our back.

When my chunk of "I thought" fell to the bottom of the lake, Bhagwan counseled, "Let go of the struggle and just be yourself." I talked to him afterward. He explained how all troubles stem from the resistance of the mind:

> **Bhagwan:** If you meditate and inquire into yourself and
> come into silence, you'll eventually discover that there is
> no "I." If there's no I, how can I do? It's an illusion. If the I
> is an illusion, then the thought you can do must also be an
> illusion. There's nothing you can do. It's all written. It's all
> happening.

> **Bruce:** It's a powerful illusion.

> **Bhagwan:** Yes, and the cause of a lot of problems.

Bruce: So, I have my problems. I face the problem, surmount the problem, and feel good. Soon I have a new problem and feel bad. Are you saying that we are given this melodrama, this up and down, not to become more skilled at navigating life, but to see through the illusion?

Bhagwan: The thought that you can *do* is an illusion because the "I" is an illusion. The I, through the mind, creates the illusion of the world and the illusion that you have choices to make in the world. This is the root cause of all misery.

Bruce: Yet life without doing seems passive.

Bhagwan: It's not a lethargic state or a state of resignation. It's a state of alertness. In clarity, you can do much more at a faster speed. The resistance of the mind is not there. Things move very smoothly in a flow.

Bruce: So, when you say that the entire universe is synchronous, is this the flow?

Bhagwan: Everything is of a certain order, but you're not in tune with the order if you're in the mind. You're not enjoying the state. But, if you're in a state of clarity, you can feel the synchronicity of everything. You can feel exactly in each moment that this is how it's supposed to happen.

Bruce: What about when the world is in turmoil — is this also synchronous?"

Bhagwan: Aren't the planets and galaxies synchronous? If the whole universe is moving in a synchronous manner, why wouldn't our earth and the actions of the people in our little world also be synchronous? You don't realize the synchronicity because you have the feeling that you can do.

Bruce: Okay, Bhagwan, let's drill down on the question of *doing*. After my mescaline experience, I was driving down the mountain in my VW bus, watching every action and decision, yet being unattached to any of it. The driving happened on its own accord. I attributed it to the mescaline, but now it raises questions. If we can drive the bus without being identified, something in us must know what to do.

Bhagwan: This silence or this pure consciousness has intelligence. It is intelligent. It's what gives the mind intelligence. It is the source of the intelligence of the mind. If the mind has the intelligence to drive a bus, this pure consciousness would have even more intelligence because it is the source of intelligence. Consciousness is intelligent.

Bruce: Is knowing where to go, what to do, when to do, not coming from the mind?

Bhagwan: Consciousness won't know what to do, but consciousness functions through the mind without identification. Consciousness uses the mind and acts through the mind. The mind knows the maps and the routes and knows where to go. In consciousness, the mind is now a tool that can be used without identifying. Hitherto you identified as the bus driver and thought you were driving the bus. In clarity, there is an awareness that drives the bus, that uses the mind to find the route, but there is no identification with the mind. You are using the mind.

Bruce: So, at that point, who is driving the bus?

Bhagwan: Who is driving the bus? The bus is just being driven! Who is moving the planets? Who is making the sun rise and set? A lot is going on without you doing it — without the driver doing it. A lot within your body is going on. The circulation, the breathing, the digestion, cell repairs, growth, destruction in your body is going on.
Who is doing it?

Bruce: If I have great plans and great dreams, where do they fit in with all this orchestration?

Bhagwan: You can have great dreams and plans without identification. Yet, there's nothing you can do. But a lot of activity can happen through you. You understand the situation, and the action happens. Clear cut, precise, a perfect action producing no reaction.

Bruce: What does that mean, a perfect action produces no reaction?

Bhagwan: When you act from the mind, there's always a reaction because every thought or feeling has its opposite. There will always be a reaction to any action that you "do." You have to bear the consequence of the reaction because it's yours. It's called karma. A perfect action produces no karma. There's no residue.

Bruce: Karma is the residue from imperfect action?

Bhagwan: Yes, the residue and the consequences.

Bruce: So, an action may generate drag, build a charge, and create ripples?

Bhagwan: Yes. It carries on and on. The effects come back to you — the effect of karma. This goes on and on your whole life. When you die, you still have the karma you built up. You still need to bear the consequences of your actions. When you die, they're not over. They're carried on to your next life if you can believe in that.

Bruce: When you observe people as they age, they appear to be carrying the weight of their world, the weight of their lives. I used to observe this in airports. Is that the residual karma?

Bhagwan: Yes, the more karma you carry, the more burden you carry. And with more burden, you're susceptible to diseases, aging, and death. Not only death but rebirth. Rebirth is like a punishment. You have to go through the whole process again. You have to go through it again by getting born again.

Bruce: I see myself as a creative person. Creative people act from inspiration. I might be meditating and think, "Oh, I should do this. I should try that." When these inspiring ideas arise, are they from the mind, or do they reflect the creative force seeking to manifest?

Bhagwan: Inspiration is not of the mind. Inspiration comes from a deeper place. If you can remain in the place of inspiration and work from there and not from your mind, that would produce a different quality of creation.

Bruce: When we talk about thinking, could it be that what's coming through our thoughts is actually communication from a deeper place?

Bhagwan: The challenge is not to lose that deeper place and get lost in your thoughts. Silence is the creative space. You want your creative actions to come from that place.

Bruce: So when we talk about creativity, we're describing spontaneity arising from this deeper place.

Bhagwan: From that deeper place, you're in harmony with the whole story, and you're enjoying the whole story, even if there's trauma and misfortune and all that. It's not affecting you because you see the whole.

Bruce: Maybe this is the place to bring up my story of woe. When I lost my business, I discovered that every misfortune carries the seed of fortune. The two seem inseparable.

Bhagwan: Let me tell you a story. A client of mine moved from India to Dubai to start a business importing electronics. The business was successful at first, but then after a few years, it completely failed. He was forced to go back home to India and start over. I told him, "Look, in misfortune, there's always something fortunate in it. Even if you can't see it now, you'll see it later. Be in trust." He went back to India, and his business started booming again. He realized that in Dubai, he had been wasting his time. It was a place without a soul, without culture, just a desert with buildings. But, he couldn't decide to go back to India on his own. He had to fail first. Destiny had to push and take him out of Dubai, and bring misfortune to him so that he could proceed to India and find fortune.

Bruce: I think about my dad who moved to California to fail — and how we all flourished. So what made the difference? How did your client find the path of fortune again?

Bhagwan: It wasn't easy for him to get unstuck from the situation. When you're identified, it's hard to get unstuck. The mind can't get you unstuck; the mind is what put you there. But when you access your Self, this releases you from identification. The business problem may still be there, but you're not identified with it, so things start flowing. A new situation, a new option comes, and things get resolved. It may not be in the way you think. Whether or not you're able to pay your bills ceases to be the problem. Something else may happen, in which case that problem becomes irrelevant.

Bruce: And this is what it means to let go and be yourself.

Bhagwan: Yes. When you let go, there's flow. Things start moving. In clarity, there's creativity, there's flow, there's abundance. Whether it's new opportunities or new situations arising, it's all taken care of. In this awareness, there's a trust.

Not a trust that things will go according to how you think, but trust in whichever way they go. That trust itself is an energy that prevents you from going into the situation that is causing the suffering.

Bruce: Thank you, Bhagwan.

Jung also experienced letting go in this manner. He explained:

"The art of letting things happen, action through inaction, became for me the key that opens the door to the way. We must be able to let things happen in the psyche. For us, this is an art of which most people know nothing. Consciousness is forever interfering, helping, correcting, and negating, never leaving the psychic process to grow in peace."[3]

My conversation with Bhagwan took place was seven years ago. Since then, a lot of ice has melted to bring me warily to a place of trust. Lest you forget, I was of the Pepsi Generation, Youth Generation, Baby Boomers, Woodstock Nation, Hippies, New Agers, Peaceniks, and Flower Children. And now, I'm seventy. When you reach seventy, you've seen the game. You realize that God pretty much has one script — changing the characters and plot lines — but always the same theme: From vanity and delusion, through conflict and resolution, to redemption and freedom. We discover the freedom to let the knots in the psyche untie in their own way and time.

Like a glider pilot, you can spiral up or spiral down. Since this is a book about Uplift, I'm doing my best to shake off the cobwebs of aging to get more lift — not out of misplaced vanity, but to reduce drag.

Jeanne Louise Calment, the longest-living human being, reportedly 122 years (1875 – 1997), explained near the end of her life:

Calment at age 70 in 1945

"Being young is a state of mind; it doesn't depend on one's body. I'm actually still a young girl; it's just that I haven't looked so good for the past 70 years."

Unlike Jeanne Louise, I don't plan on living to 122. I haven't followed her longevity secret (smoking from age 21 to 117), but I feel myself growing ever younger by reducing drag and turning inside out. Hour-by-hour and minute-by-minute, the pressure of time surges through me like a vital current seeking a creative life. My urgency is not to leave my mark but to stay centered in a resilience where I feel the most free.

Research may prove this out. A recent study exploring aging took all human biologic markers and converted the dataset into a single metric, DOSI — the Dynamic Organism State Indicator. (If you pull out the *Urban Dictionary, Dosi* is also slang for Orthodox Jew, a strain of potent marijuana, and an aggressive humanoid civilization on Star Trek.)

The study, with its sexy title, *"Longitudinal analysis of blood markers reveals progressive loss of resilience and predicts human lifespan,"* noted how our DOSI equilibration rate and hence our human resilience are gradually lost over time:

> No dramatic improvement of the maximum lifespan and hence strong life extension is possible by preventing or curing diseases **without interception of the aging process, the root cause of the underlying loss of resilience**.

Fixing flat tires won't keep a clunker running forever, either — but maintaining the engine will. The researchers went on to say that there is nothing in nature preventing us from intervening in the aging process:

> **We do not foresee any laws of nature prohibiting such an intervention.** Therefore, further development of the aging model presented in this work may be a step toward experimental demonstration of a dramatic life-extending therapy.[4]

Drum-roll! That dramatic life-extending therapy is Uplift. By reducing drag and breaking through the waves of resistance, the body and mind cease to be a burden.

That septuagenarian doing a handstand on the back cover is me. One of my teachers once admonished, "We don't do cool yoga poses just to post on Instagram." (How about book covers?) I should be embarrassed, but the yoga pose comes with a tale. Several years ago, I accidentally attended a crazy-stunt-yoga class — the kind of class where bendy girls flaunt the power of their bodies as weapons of mass distraction. Mandy, my teacher, demonstrated the peak pose: *Crow into Three-Point Headstand into Side Crow.* Feeling utterly out of place, I made a big show to collapse into a tangle of limbs. The pose was impossible.

"I give up," I announced.

Mandy looked me in the eye, "Don't give up. You can do this." She shared a few pointers, which I tried and tried, until a few months later, after countless tangles of limbs, bingo, Mandy's stunt became part of my repertoire and a source of deep insight into working my "edge."

The handstand story is different. So much of yoga draws from muscle memory plus mind-over-matter. When I first tried a handstand, my inflexibility limited me to a few feeble hops. After five years of hopping, I began to notice how my mind sabotaged each attempt. A subtle message short-circuited my kicking leg, *"Don't do this, Bruce. You'll hurt yourself. Humans should not go upside down."* As my kicking leg went up, I subconsciously hit the brakes. It took several years to rewire my nervous system.

My friend, Julie, discovered those same brakes with her Parkinson's diagnosis. In a profound realization, Julie discovered how Parkinson's is not an incurable illness; it's an electrical disorder. I described Julie's early-onset seven years ago in the epilogue of my book, *Fortune*:

> On a sad note, our dear friend, Julie, discovered that she has early-onset Parkinson's disease. "When I found out I had Parkinson's, I felt strangely buoyant about it," Julie confided during a walk. The leaden swing in her arm gave it away. Julie's instinct was to reboot her life completely.

Over the following months and years, Julie began an intense journey to unravel the affliction that befell her. She tried boxing, qi-gong, vigorous walking, a keto diet, and a slew of supplements to shift her symptoms. She also had to balance the medications against their side effects.

In the process, Julie learned how the electrical patterns of Parkinson's are consistent with the trauma responses she felt during childhood. "It's like the self-induced shutdown of the nervous system when a mouse caught by a cat freezes," Julie explained. For a person with a Parkinson's diagnosis, the nervous system continues to pause — even after the trauma has long ended.[5]

Julie's desire for a life reboot brought her to the quantum meditation of Joe Dispenza. "I saw how all these old mental patterns were affecting my physical chemistry. I refuse to be defined by the concept of this disease." Julie sent me this quote:

> "To break the habit of being yourself, say good-bye to cause and effect and embrace the quantum model of reality." Joe Dispenza[6]

Then, there's Sarah. Seven years ago, she appeared in the epilogue of my book, *Fortune*. At the time, I described Sarah's quest to find a partner:

> As is our tradition, Sarah put her New Year's resolutions into our fireplace at midnight and bumped into Joe at a dance a month later. Sarah and Joe had a sexually fulfilling, yet emotionally difficult, fifteen-year relationship — even buying a house together. Sarah loved Joe — that is until his eyes began to seek out other women at the dance events they enjoyed together.
>
> The dance events led to tantra events and then to something called a "play party." When Joe announced that he wanted a "polyamorous" relationship, Sarah put her foot down. Despite her valiant efforts to salvage the relationship, Joe left her. The pain was overwhelming. Sarah went through all five of Kübler-Ross's stages of grief — especially full-blown anger.
>
> I tell the story because Sarah is in her late 60s. She was hit hard with the sinking sense that she may never have another lover in her life. As she remarked, "The pubic hairs are getting gray."

After Joe left her, Sarah embarked on a six-year dating whirl that could cast an Almodóvar film. There was the penniless *bon vivant* who lived in the back of his shop with his paraplegic son, and the snowboarding biker who revealed that he was a committed bachelor, and the 70-year-old yogi who only sought eye-candy babes, and the expensive match from a matchmaker who turned out to be a full-blown Trumper, and the hyper-paranoid mountain man with a loaded gun in every room.

"I finally let go of the search and recognized that I could be content and thrive as a single woman," Sarah confided.

After embracing her single life at age 74, COVID-19 landed with a vengeance and pushed Sarah to the edge.

"Before COVID, I had been content to live alone," Sarah shared. "I could go out to lunch with a friend, go to the theater, or get a massage. Suddenly, all of those avenues shut down. I wasn't in my friends' pods, and they weren't in mine. I read some research on how loneliness contributed to inflammation – and now my body was inflamed. Previously, my social life offered ways to fulfill my need for intimacy, dissipate my heartache, and ignore my loneliness. The one thing it didn't do was force me to act on my feelings and make a change.

"One night, while sitting alone in my hot tub, my loneliness reached a peak. I declared, 'I refuse to live alone and unloved to my dying days.'"

A hidden gear must have kicked in because Sarah quickly met David, a successful psychologist. With so many shared interests, something clicked between them. A few weeks after their meeting, David confided his sense of urgency. After three failed marriages, David felt it wasn't too late to experience total commitment in love, even at age seventy-five. "WHY NOT NOW?" David beseeched.

Karen and I cheered when Sarah shared this story: "Why not now? WHY NOT Stop-Start-Change NOW!!!"

David showered Sarah with gifts, dinners out, touching compliments, and mimosas in the hot tub. They took sunrise walks with coffee and snuggled around the fire. They also shared books, wrote poems to each other, and revealed their most intimate feelings. Topping it off, David took Sarah on a ten-day romance-filled trip to Paris. *ooh-la-la!*

Sarah was not thinking about the Enneagram nine months into the romance when she received an email from David out of the blue:

"I think it might be best to postpone your trip here this week."

And without explanation, David stopped accepting calls and ended the relationship. Yes, she was *ghosted*.

I tiptoed around Sarah's emotional devastation, but I reminded her that there are seven stages of love, and each one requires a lovers' leap of its own. I was heartened when Sarah took the admonition from Kooks Only Surf.com to heart: *"Face the Wave Head-On."*

After a couple of days of fetal grief under the pillows, Sarah unleashed her creative spirit – writing a flurry of poems and prose to dig out from the ditch into which she had been dumped. In one poem, Sarah wrote:

> You spoke so beautifully.
> My heartsong amplified with these words:
>
>> *"A Great Love!*
>> *Why not now?*
>> *An I Thou Relationship,*
>> *Balanced on the razor's edge.*
>> *Here there is Christ.*
>> *Very few have what we have.*
>> *IF NOT NOW, WHEN?"*
>
> A dream?
> A vision?
> An ideal?
> A possibility?
>
> Yes, it is a possibility!
> As we grow in knowledge and empathy for each other,
> As we attend to each other,
> A sacred dance of *I Thou* emerges.
> It could be a deep and strong love
> That weathers whatever comes our way.
> Very few have what we *could* have had:
> A great love.

So, "why not now?" From wisdom painfully acquired, Sarah knew to stay with her feelings and face the experience head-on.

But then the implausible: One month after getting ghosted (and in the spirit of outside shocks), a widower contacted Sarah out of the blue. His life had criss-crossed hers at least a dozen times over the last fifty years.

Karen whispered to me: "He's head-over-heels in love with her!"

Kismet? Flushing the lines? The third slice of pie? Let's call it Uplift!

Oh, if you're wondering about Anahata, after two years, she's working the magic to become a permanent resident of Australia! Fingers crossed.

Then there's Karen. This book began sixteen months ago deep into the pandemic. As we rode the hospital elevator, beak-to-beak, the chip-voice lady reminded us to embrace Uplift:

Going up...

If you want to know how Karen's every-20-day infusion of HER3-targeting U3-1402 has been working out, you're asking the wrong question. Yes, the scans show the lymph thingy shrinking from 17.5x21.4 mm to 5.5x11.1 mm in a year. This indicates some measure of drug efficacy, but I have changed my cancer measuring tape — and you should, too.

Seven years ago, when Karen emerged triumphant from her brain tumor, I christened my beloved wife "Karen 2.0." This affectionate nickname honored the total life reboot and software upgrade needed for cancer recovery. With this current round, I've been waiting twelve months for evidence of Karen 3.0 — the upgrade where "SI" (Spiritual Intelligence) runs the program without user intervention.

Last week, Karen faced a tricky situation with her boss, Theodora. I was on the couch, doom-scrolling on Twitter, while I listened to the audible half of their phone conversation.

My ears perked when I heard Karen push back with an oddly casual bluntness, "Theodora when you say that, I feel attacked."

Whoa! I thought – pretty salty language with your boss.

After the call, I asked her, "What was that about?"

"Theodora accused me of getting triangulated." Karen shot back, flaunting her newfound empowerment. "It was weird. I usually couch my words very carefully — like walking on eggshells. My response was spontaneous and totally appropriate in the moment."

Karen, do you know what this means?"

"Huh?"

"We're abandoning *buoyancy* as our magic word. It's now, *FOK!* acronym for *Force of Karen!*"

FOK! gives light to Bhagwan's insight: "It's all about the will to live." *FOK!* is the force of personal agency.

Dr. Gabor Maté, an author-physician who retired from his practice to work in a street-front clinic to treat addicts and victims of trauma, described the power of agency:

> Sometimes [spontaneous healings] have to do with diet, exercise, or supplements – or with meditation, spiritual work, and yoga. But what's common to them all is that the individual takes agency for what happens, because what trauma does is rob you of agency.
>
> One understands that my illness is not simply some random misfortune, but actually a manifestation of my life and the trauma that happened in a social context – which robbed me of agency. But now, in my healing, I need to regain that agency.
>
> I need to be the one in charge. I need to follow my gut feelings. I need to take over my life, reclaim it... this is the nature of illness, and the nature of healing and agency.[7]

So, *FOK!* Why not now?

Karen's childhood trauma shaped her life, accommodating bullies, gaslighters, gurus, bosses, parents, and parental figures — all in an unhealthy manner. Seven years ago, when Dr. Chandler removed the tumor from her brain, Karen reported that a big chunk of lifelong anxiety and trauma came out with it. Hmm, I wondered at the time. Maybe cancerous tissue is not just a mass of rogue cells.

That was 2.0.

Yesterday, Karen's boss pressed Karen to double her workload to help the boss's colleague at a neighboring hospital. Without explanation, shame, or doubt, Karen declined. Her boss didn't press her either.

FOK! It's 3.0!

The power of agency and Uplift don't come in a swoosh. They come by releasing ballast at the precise junctures offered by life. You don't need to recognize these junctures as a Mi-Fa or a Si-Do. The universe will prompt you: "Why not now?"

Bhagwan' offered insight into this creative power during our Skype meditation today:

> Do you see the larger picture of yourself? Not imagining it, not visualizing it. But actually being the larger picture. Is your being the larger picture? An infinite being.
>
> So, why all this complication? Is it great fun? Is it drama? In Sanskrit, we call the theater of the universe *layla* — the play of creative energy that manifests mysteriously.
>
> Why does it happen? Is it a playfulness? Is it beautiful? Is it out of love? Can you witness the whole phenomenon? Silence is the unmanifest — a creative energy with infinite intelligence, infinite power, and infinite love — a creative energy that manifests.
>
> When do the problems begin? They begin when you start identifying yourself as a form. Is that the start of all problems? All people think they are separate forms. This inevitably creates conflicts born out of comparison and competitiveness, and confusion.
>
> Today, the world is experiencing great problems. There is no way out. These problems recur endlessly for thousands of years.
>
> So, is this a cruel joke? Why should we be tormented this way?
>
> It is because the Infinite Being loves to be discovered. The Infinite creates these problems so that you find yourself by freeing yourself from identification — to discover your infinite state and being.
>
> Can you see this whole phenomenon? It is a most wonderful movie. Millions of characters, playing their parts perfectly. A movie directed perfectly where everything happens as written in the script.

Are you enjoying the movie? This is only possible when you realize that it's a movie, only when you can witness the mind. Only then will you realize that it is a movie. Only then can you enjoy it as a most magnificent movie.

But if you are not the witness and are identified with body and mind, even if you call it a movie, you can't enjoy it. It's the most horrible movie. A movie full of torment, torture, suffering, heartbreak, and despair.

Why get entangled in this? Why not witness it?

Only silence can witness it. Only in silence can you see it as a movie. In silence, you can see that it's a movie. A perfect movie. Nothing has to be changed. With the most perfectly written script and you as one of the actors, you can play your role perfectly, with awareness, and enjoy your role.

This is the wonderful secret in you — waiting to be discovered and longing to be discovered — just as you long to discover it.

If the prescriptions in this book sound complicated, they aren't. Ice melts without effort, and knots untie on their own. What's more, the Octave unfolds like music, the Enneagram integrates your life, and the future comes into the present on its own schedule.

Conversely, cancer patients often lose creative agency, sailboats stall head-to-wind, and gliders are forced to land. So where's the Uplift? What is the source of hope?

J.G. Bennett teased the secret – how Uplift offers objective hope:

> "Hope does not consist in the realization of potential but in the *augmentation* of potential. This is objective hope."[8]

Raising a note by a half step in music is called *augmentation*. It's as if a chord or interval gets so set in its ways that it needs some Uplift to shake things up with a + sign. On a piano, your pinkie reaches for the next higher note to augment a chord. In life, we lift out of old patterns by offering forgiveness, dropping grudges, releasing baggage, letting go, reaching out, opening up, pushing through edges, starting fresh, taking ownership, and building a great love. Like an augmented chord, it's tense and it's messy.

The Bible speaks of creation as a once-off. In continuous renewal, the creative force is omnipresent and ever-unfolding (making it up and augmenting as it goes along). We live a creative life when this force is unimpeded *(FOK!)*. Augmenting your life process means embracing Hazard and moving through the tension in the intervals.

Ursula K. Le Guin understood what it means to augment your world:

> All of us have to learn how to invent our lives, make them up,
> imagine them. We need to be taught these skills; we need guides
> to show us how. If we don't, our lives get made up for us by other
> people.[9]

Let us remember, one more time, that great *augmenter*, Doug Engelbart, head of the aptly named "Augmented Human Intellect Research Center" at the Stanford Research Institute. He and his team dropped acid to augment human intelligence and imagine the Information Age.

What can you imagine? An industrial design career in high school? Healing a broken marriage at forty-two? Reversing a terminal diagnosis in your sixties? Becoming an author at age seventy? Reimagining love at seventy-four? Or envisioning a sustainable future for our planet?

The hardest lesson of all is to accept that we live in a benevolent universe. For this reason, the half-step of augmentation – the Uplift – lives with the angels.

We've been given this capacity for Uplift, so let's make some music. Why not now?

Endnotes

1   Bennett, J. G. *Witness: The Story of a Search*. 4th edition, 2017

2   https://www.newyorker.com/magazine/2021/11/08/energy-and-how-to-get-it

3   Carl Jung, "Commentary on the Secret of the Golden Flower," in *Psychology and the East.*

4   Pyrkov, et al (2021). "Longitudinal analysis of blood markers reveals progressive loss of resilience. Nature Communications"

5   To read more about the electrical nature of Parkinson's, visit Parkinson's Recovery Project, https://pdrecovery.org/

6   Joe Dispenza, *Breaking The Habit of Being Yourself*

7   Dr. Gabor Maté with Thomas Hübl, Collective Trauma Summit 2021

8   Bennett, J. G. *Hazard: The Risk of Realization.*

9   Ursula K. Le Guin, *The Wave in the Mind: Talks and Essays on the Writer, the Reader and the Imagination*

Mory and Bruce, 1973 | Bruce and Suleyman Dede,1976
Karen and Reshad, 1981 | Bhagwan and Bruce, 2018

Acknowledgments

I want to thank my wife, Karen, whose heartfelt courage forms the foundation of this book. More than being a good sport by putting her life in the spotlight, Karen understands as a chaplain educator, that we learn from each other. Even when hidden in humility, like Karen, we blaze a trail that others can follow.

I also want to thank Dr. Bhagwan Awatramani, my meditation teacher. Over the course of nearly 30 years, Bhagwan has catalyzed my inner transformation to write from direct experience.

I wish to thank the pivotal teacher for my Sufi upbringing, Reshad Feild. Reshad never used an easel or handout to teach the Octave. The Octave moved through him and our work as living energy – an energy we learned to harness, transform, and put to good use.

The book's foundational knowledge traces back to my prime sources, J.G. Bennett and G.I. Gurdjieff. I never met Bennett personally, but his direct students have become important friends in my life.

Other teachers to acknowledge include Mory Berman, Bhante Dharmawara, E.J. Gold, Ram Dass, Robert Bly, and Suleyman Dede. On the flip side, having pivoted $30,000 out of my young married life, Italian film producer Giovanni Mazza also qualifies as a pivotal teacher.

I would also like to acknowledge friends, family, and fellow travelers who are mentioned or quoted: Anahata Iradah, Mandy Roberts, Joseph Rosenshein, Jane Super, Donna Bell, Oran Feild, Julie Andrews, Nick Saxton, Penny Webster, Chrissi Lemire, Tommy the Painter, Mimi, Val & Jim, Sarah H., Rob Weiner, Rich Frishman, my mom, dad, and my sons Jacob and Nathaniel, Dr. Tran, and the staff at Emory Clinical Trials.

Thanks to Elliot Mintz and Sara Davidson for permission to use their Ram Dass interviews.

And thank you, dear reader, for persevering with the firehose of ideas I shoved into one book. My plan, at age 70, was to stick it all in because how many more can I write? But, knowing me, I will swear off writing for a week, get inspired by the chip-voice lady, and then onward and upward, following the Uplift!

Photos

Photos used for illustrative and thematic design are from the Shutterstock and Adobe Stock Photo libraries. Other photos include:

Introduction – The Giant Wooden Hammer

1 – Percussionist: Foreground: © Monika Rittershaus , Background: Shutterstock

Chapter 1 – A Dramatic Universe

14-17 – Woodstock – Woodstock Whisperer, CC BY-SA 4.0 via Wikimedia Commons

20 – Doug Engelbart: SRI Creative Commons

23 – Campus riots:: University of Illinois Alumni Association

24 – Nguyen Cao Kỳ: United Press International

27 – J.G. Bennett: ©J.G. Bennett Foundation

27 – Gurdjieff: Public Domain

29 – Ralph Edwards – This is Your Life: Public Domain NBC

35 – Karen and Miko – © Bruce Miller

Chapter 2 – Katabasis

38 – Voorhies Castle: ©stevel504, Flickr

39 – 16 mm camera: Stock photo

40 – Window Water Baby Moving, © Stan Brakhage, Distributed by Canyon Cinema

41 – Ed Miller: http://www.romeroy4u.com/Sherwood.html

43 – Car Wash Burbank Public Library, Burbank in Focus Office

44 – Odysseus: By Herbert James Draper - The Bridgeman Art Library, Public Domain

50 – Ram Dass: ©Chokidar Imageevent.com

54 – Reshad Field: ©Bruce Miller

Chapter 3 – The Energy Must Go Through

56 – Music Scene: ©Bruce Miller

59 – Mory Berman: ©Bruce Miller

61, 62, 64 – Institute for Conscious Life: © Bruce Miller

65 – Bhante Dharmawara: ©https://bhantevdharmawara.org/

72 – Indiana Jones and the Last Crusade: © Lucasfilm Ltd

74 – Donna Bell: ©Bruce Miller

77 – Oran and Reshad Feild: ©Bruce Miller

Chapter 4 – I Am the Octave

78 – Whirling Dervishes: ©Bruce Miller

80 – Silverlake Duplex: ©Bruce Miller

81 – Suleyman Dede: ©Bruce Miller

82 – Atatürk: Public Domain

83 – Vivekananda: Public Domain

84 – Steve Jobs: Steve Jobs - ©Matthew Yohe, Creative Commons

93 – "When Harry Met Sally" poster: ©Castle Rock Entertainment · Nelson Entertainment

94 – Jackson Pollock: ©Hans Namuth

96 – Reshad Field montage: ©Bruce Miller

98 – Ocoee: ©Whitewater Express

Chapter 5 – Different Worlds

102 – Bruce and Karen – ©Bruce Miller

109 – Joe Btfspik: ©Capp Enterprises

110 – Madame de Salzmann: https://gurdjieffbooks.wordpress.com/

111 – Gurdjieff: Public Domain

114 – Groundhog: Columbia Pictures

About the Author

After studying filmmaking and screenwriting at UCLA, Bruce Miller has spent his career as a brand strategist, media producer, writer, and marketing partner in an Atlanta brand development agency.

In the 1970s, Bruce's spiritual search led him to English author, performer, and teacher, Reshad Feild, the journey described in Uplift. Bruce and Reshad, with others, started The Institute for Conscious Life, the Mevlana Foundation, and later, Chalice Guild. In these schools, Bruce helped bring the work of Jalaluddin Rumi to America, the story recounted in Bruce's second book, *Rumi Comes to America.*

Bruce also collaborated on *Steps to Freedom, Discourses on the Essential Knowledge of the Heart* based on talks given by Reshad Feild.

Bruce has led residential seminars on the knowledge of the Octave and Enneagram, ideas brought forth by P.D. Ouspensky and G.I. Gurdjieff, and the Law of Hazard, an understanding of risk and uncertainty from the work of J.G. Bennett.

Bruce's first book, FORTUNE, *Our Deep Dive into the Mysteries of Love, Healing, and Success* explored the karmic mystery of why stuff happens.

Bruce has also written business books. *Brand Story™ – How to Position Your Shoestring Start-Up Like a National Brand*, draws on his decades-long professional career.

Bruce is an avid sailor, yoga enthusiast, and teaches the turn of the Whirling Dervishes. His wife Karen is an ordained minister and chaplain educator. Connect with Bruce at www.ithou.com

Made in the USA
Columbia, SC
21 March 2022

57946957R00154